Back Through the Veil II:

The Ancestral Histories of Several African-American Families and How They Survived from Their Arrivals in Central Louisiana to the Middle of the 20th Century

"A family is like a forest, when you are outside it is dense, when you are inside you see that each tree has its place." ~ African Proverb

Donald G. Prier, PhD

Back Through the Veil II:

The Ancestral Histories of Several African-American Families and How They Survived from Their Arrivals in Central Louisiana to the Middle of the 20th Century

Copyright © 2017, Donald G. Prier dba Beulah's Memories

CreateSpace

Nonfiction / Reference / Publishing

First Edition

ISBN-13: 978-1977567482

ISBN-10: 1977567487

EAN-13:

Dedication

This work is dedicated to the following people who, either individually or collectively, have made my life to be much better than I ever expected:

- To my father, **Oliver Peter Prier**, who, despite his death so early in my life, still provided me with a clear understanding of the value of education. He learned to read and write in the small, church-based school that was housed in the Old Jerusalem Baptiste Church west of Mansura. With these skills, he was able to teach his children how to manage their lives based on knowledge, reason, personal commitment and honesty.

- Following my father's death, I found myself growing up in a world that required the involvement of a strong father figure to guide a young black man to adulthood in a world that was filled with distractions and temptations. Fortunately, before I knew it, I found myself involved in the local baseball organizations, run by several black men who provided me with guidance and role models that helped me be as good as I ever might have been. As a result of those relationships, I always felt the need to make them proud of me and what I did. Any successes I have had was a result of that feeling. To these men, **Joseph "Peechu Do" Francisco, Jesse Jacob** and **Modella Augustine**, I will always be grateful.

- My mother, **Beulah Walter Prier**, was the solid rock on which we all built our lives. She provided the strength to keep our family both financially and emotionally stable following the death of my father. More importantly, however, although she lacked formal education, she insisted that we be competitive in school as in life. She always challenged us to give it a try, even though it might have been a risky endeavor. And when we were successful, she always applauded us with her favorite complement: "Prier Does That!!

- Last, but certainly not least, is my wife and best friend for over 47 years, **Mary Bernell Augustine Prier**. We both came to this marriage with no clue to what we were getting into. All we knew was that we wanted to do things different from the way we saw others living their lives. And so, from the very beginning, we lived lives that were far from conventional, first spending 4 years in the U.S. Army, then 9 years trying to raise a family while attending college and living in a lower economic level neighborhood in Baton Rouge.

In the end, we were successful! We got our degrees and great jobs, our children all have at least masters degrees and we are enjoying our retirements and grandchildren. And through it all, she has been the moral, spiritual and social leader of our family. When she is not around, as my daughter, Dorian, once said, "Everything goes from colorful to gray".

Preface

The publication of **Back Through the Veil, Book I** (Prier), in 2016, was the culmination of over 20 years of research into family genealogy and history. In the process of organizing the final version of that book, it became clear that publishing the planned combination of history and genealogy together would not work well.

First of all, the amount of history of African-Americans in the area around Mansura, Louisiana was much larger than imagined and continued to grow as time went by and more investigations were pursued. As the use of technology was applied to managing historical and genealogical documents, new information such as court and church records, family stories and pictures, and demographic information on small towns became as accessible as any computer desktop.

Secondly, as the book developed, it became more and more difficult to incorporate both the general history of Mansura, Louisiana and specific family information without creating a considerable amount of confusion. It soon became clear that the history and genealogy stories needed to be told separately, and, as a result, Book I was published with as little genealogy information as possible.

Once Book I was published, putting the genealogy information into a stand-alone book presented another challenge. Genealogy, by itself, can be cold and boring if it is presented as just a set of facts about a specific family. In fact, a whole family can be presented in a single-page family tree and is likely only interesting to members of that particular family.

In order to publish the genealogy information and still maintain the same level of interest as in Book I, **Book II** generally consists of chapters dedicated to one family each, although, some families have natural branches that grew into large families, themselves. Each family is discussed, not as a family tree, but as a set of profiles that include the basic genealogy information, stories that help describe the lives of the members of that particular family, and a few pictures that go as far back as possible to give the reader a more concrete image of what that family looked like, where they lived and how they resemble their descendants today.

Once this general format (i.e. genealogy, stories and pictures) was chosen, the next challenge was how to determine which families to include.

As can be seen in the Introduction and throughout Book II, one of the most important goals of this book is to provide a bridge from the current Mansura families back to their African ancestors.

In order to do this, a given family must exist today in significant numbers and have been present in 1870 or 1880 (Based on U.S. census records).

Using this simple criterion, the following families were chosen to be profiled in this book:

- **Augustine**

- **Batiste**
- **Berzat/Luc**
- **Blackman**
- **Celestine**
- **Demouy**
- **Dupas**
- **Francisco**
- **James**
- **McGlory**
- **Oliver**
- **Prier**
- **Sampson**

The reader needs to recognize that, even though their family name is not listed here, many of the people who are discussed are their ancestors. For example, the **McGlory** descendants include the following current names: **Augustine, Lacarte, Lucas, Pierre, Prier, Sampson, Washington** and many others.

In this writing, the presence of a given family in either the 1870 or 1880 U.S. census was used as the starting points for the African-American family histories described below. Since the last U.S. census data was made public in 1940, little information contained in this book came from a time after 1940.

Pictures, on the other hand, were added when they existed for a given family. In some cases, the lack of old pictures from a given family made it necessary to use more recent pictures on order to provide the reader with as much visual information as possible. This is important in order to add some level of reality to the written information. Hopefully, no one will be offended if their family members are or are not included.

In most cases, unless otherwise indicated, the family information described here came exclusively from the appropriate U.S. census, other public records, knowledgeable family members, and church baptism and burial records (Church). Each chapter was reviewed in detail by at least one knowledgeable family representative who provided enough expertise to assure that the material presented was as accurate as possible.

All information contained herein has been carefully screened to provide as much privacy to both families and individuals as is possible, especially for those still alive.

Finally, this work is the beginning chapter in the histories of many families. It is written with the hope that it will provide enough information and generate enough interest within each family to cause them to use the information provided here as the starting point in a continuing history of their families.

Table of Contents

Bayou des Glaises

This small, lazy stream today was an important trade route for the transportation of farm products during the Slavery Period. Many plantations lined its shores as it traveled along from Long bridge through Moreauville and past Borodino other small stops along the way.

After slavery, many former slaves acquired property along this small stream.

Today, both black and white residents have their homes and churches along its quite shores.

Introduction

In ***Back Through the Veil, Book I*** (Prier), the history of the African-Americans living in the Mansura, Louisiana area from about 1800 through the 1940s, 1950s and 1960s was discussed. This work was focused, primarily, on the overall history of the area versus specific families.

As is well known, the family is the basic unit of civilized human life. Not only does it provide an environment for the procreation and nurturing of the young, but it also is a school of learning where children acquire and develop the skills they need to survive in the world. It is also a base of operation from which young adults can venture out and return, should they waver in their flights to independence. Without families, life would be so much more chaotic and our abilities to reach our full potential would be very limited.

In this book, the profiles of 12 African-American families that were present in the Mansura area during the period from right after the Civil War to the mid-20th century are developed and discussed. These families were chosen because their sizes in the Post-Civil War period made it likely that they would (1) have members who were born in slavery and might provide us with a link to their particular slave-holding plantations or even their homelands in Africa and (2) still have members around today who might be able to provide additional information that would make this document even more vivid and accurate.

In addition to the 12 families, several additional families that grew from those original families or that developed simultaneously, are discussed, e.g. Cadoree, Celestine, Gabriel, Luc, etc.

While it is intriguing to attempt to trace a given family back to its roots in Africa, such as was done in Alex Haley's book, *Roots* (Haley), the probability of this being done successfully is extremely low.

This is true because:

- The many stages of captivity that the slaves were put through after their captivity in Africa removed all of their identities, including African names, tribes, languages, etc.;
- The horror of the "Middle Passage[1]" across the Atlantic Ocean, packed deep inside slave ships, forced the slaves to become separated from their other tribal members, further leading to destruction of their identities;
- The tortuous "Breaking" period on the Caribbean islands caused the slaves to recognize that in order to survive, they had to adapt to the new cultures being forced upon them and forget their past;
- Having several generations and tribes of slaves living anonymously, under non-African names, in the living hell that was American slavery, further completed the transition from Africans to people with no past;

---

[1] The horrible part of the slave trade where millions of African prisoners died while packed aboard the slave ships for weeks at a time.

- And, finally, overcoming the near total brainwashing that African-Americans endured over time has removed most notions of where the journey to this moment began. Most who grew up before the Civil Rights Movement of the 1950s and 1960s have vivid memories of being punished and, often, humiliated, by parents who feared that having their children know that all black people on this continent came from the African continent was stupid and dangerous.

However, tracing a given family back to the first member to be born in North America is relatively straightforward. In fact, there will be a number of cases where the earliest known members of a given family in the Mansura area has stated that their parent(s) came from Africa!

These are exciting pieces of information that can be the beginning to a path back home. Should anyone decide to set out on this journey, much work and good luck is involved. However, the rewards cannot be understated!!

Louisiana Foods with West African Origins

Corn

Yams

Okra

Gumbo (Jeffreyw)

Jambalaya (Jeffreyw)

Rice (Vadakkan)

Chapter 1: From Africa to Mansura

When the readers of this book go through the histories of the various families profiled here, they will read about several early Mansura residents who told of their parents being born in Africa. Before beginning to study the family histories in this book, a word of advice is needed: It is important for the readers, as they review the history of each family, to do their best to imagine what life was like for those family members who were living through those historical times.

For example, when you read that the father of Joseph Luc was born in Africa, try to imaging him being captured in Africa by slave traders and then being forced to endure the horrible conditions of that captivity as he was forced to march hundreds of miles over very rough terrain with little food or water.

Imagine him locked for months in the stifling and disease-ridden conditions inside the slave prisons along the African coast, often going days without food or water.

Try to visualize him packed in the bottom of the slave ship during the "**Middle Passage**"[2] across the Atlantic. Lying there, barely able to breath or move for days. Feel his desperation as he hoped for a chance to leap into the sea and drown rather continue this hell on earth.

Imagine him being "**Broken**" on one of the Caribbean island or in the sweltering swamps of Louisiana. Feel his suffering and despair as his body and mind deteriorated under the constant inhumane work conditions where the work was hard and long and the beatings and starvation never ended…unless death arrived to provide relief.

This introductory chapter is intended to provide you, the reader with the information needed to form that mental picture.

This introductory chapter is divided into the following periods:
- **Capture and Arrival in America**
- **Living in Slavery in Louisiana, including Black Slave Holders in Avoyelles Parish**
- **Freedom and the Reign of Terror**

Capture and Arrival in America

---

[2] The "Middle Passage" was the terrible sea voyage from the African coast to the Caribbean islands that took weeks to accomplish and, during which, millions of African captives died the most horrible death imaginable.

The first known African slaves to arrive on the North American continent landed in Jamestown, Virginia in 1619, where they were brought in to work the lucrative tobacco crops (Slavery in America).

During the 17th and 18th centuries, slavery grew, especially in the U.S. South, with the growth of the cotton industry following the invention of the cotton gin in 1793.

Overall, 6-7 million slaves were imported to North America after slave labor became the backbone of the U.S. economic structure.

While there continue to be considerable discussions regarding this subject, many believe that the majority of African slaves ended up in captivity as a result of being captured in battles among their African people, likely instigated by European slave traders. Others were sold into slavery due to debts or as punishment for crimes or disagreements.

Most of the slaves were captured on the western side of Africa:

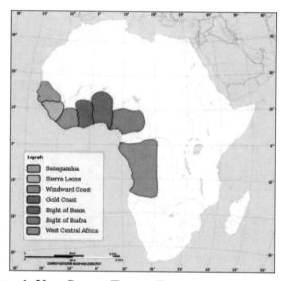

FIGURE 1. KEY SLAVE TRADE REGIONS OF AFRICA (GABA)

The French, who were the first true colonizers of the vast Louisiana lands, captured and transported most of their slaves from the ports of **Dakar**[3] and **St. Louis**[4] in the **Senegal-Gambia** area (Shown in **Figure 1**).

Today, Senegal is a largely Muslim country made up of numerous ethnic groups (e.g. 43.3% **Wolof** 23.8% **Fula**, 14.7% **Serer** and 15% Other), most of whom originated in the various geographically-separated regions shown in **Figure 2**.

---

[3] Dakar is the capital and largest city of Senegal. It is located on the Cap-Vert peninsula on the Atlantic coast and is the westernmost city in the Old World as well as on the African mainland.

[4] Saint-Louis, or Ndar as it is called in Wolof, is the capital of Senegal's Saint-Louis Region. Located in the northwest of Senegal, near the mouth of the Senegal River, and 320 km north of Senegal's capital city Dakar

FIGURE 2. CURRENT-DAY SENEGAL[5]

The people of Senegal-Gambia demonstrate traditional African features (See **Figures 3** and **4**, below), very similar to those of true African-Americans whose ethnicity has not been mixed with that of other races such as Native American or European.

FIGURE 3. WOMAN AND CHILDREN ON A STREET IN SENEGAL[6]

---

[5] By Dubaduba - CIA Worldfactory, Public Domain, https://commons.wikimedia.org/w/index.php?curid=186173

[6] By Bernard bill5 - Own work, CC BY-SA 3.0, https://commons.wikimedia.org/w/index.php?curid=12587

FIGURE 4. GETTING FISH FROM BOATS IN SENEGAL[7]

The captives, now chained together in the hands of ruthless warlords and European slave traders, were forced to travel up to 1000 miles to the coast over long and treacherous terrain. Only about half the captives survived due to beatings, starvation and disease. Those too weak to continue were either killed or left to die along the way (WGBH).

FIGURE 5. 1803 IN SENEGAL[8]

Once they arrived on the African coast, the captives were held for up to a year in underground bunkers in a series of about 60 jails or forts until the slave ships arrived. These forts served as trading posts where the Europeans traded textiles, firearms, alcohol, beads and other trinkets for human beings.

FIGURE 6. BRITISH AND DUTCH FORTS NEAR ACCRA, GHANA[9]

Once the ships arrived and the Europeans had traded their goods to the African warlords, the emptied cargo holds were then filled with human cargo. Since the trip across the Atlantic, referred as the **Middle Passage**, could take up to 4 months, as many slaves as possible were packed below deck in small spaces that were too low for standing. The assumption was that many in that initial cargo would die along the way and the more you began the trip with, the greater your chances were of having a large number of slaves to sell once the ship arrived in the Americas.

[9] By Jan Kip - ATLAS OF MUTUAL   https://commons.wikimedia.org/w/index.php?curid=33312910

The slaves were often forced to either lie side-by-side on the floor or between each other's legs to accommodate the most "cargo". This type of arrangement often required the slaves to lie in human waste and blood.

FIGURE 7. DESCRIPTION OF A SLAVE SHIP HUMAN CARGO (CARGO)

The air in the slave-filled cargo holds was usually hot and unbearable and diseases such smallpox and yellow fever were common. Often, the living remained chained to the dead until the ship's surgeon had the bodies thrown overboard. In some cases, when the slave ship came near land, desperate slaves leaped into the water, despite being chained to others, and drowned.

FIGURE 8. NEWLY CAPTURED SLAVES ABOARD THE DECK OF A SLAVE SHIP (WEEKLY)

Overall, a total of about 54,000 trips across the Atlantic Ocean occurred during the slave trade.

Between 1 and 2 million Africans died during these horrible voyages.

Most of the enslaved Africans transported to the Americas, landed in the West Indies, Central America and South America (mostly Brazil) (Frankel). Only about 5% ended up in British America.

The French ranked 3rd, behind Portugal and England, in the number of slaves transported from Africa to the Americas. They concentrated on shipping the vast majority of their slaves to the island called **Saint-Dominique** (a.k.a. **Haiti**).

By the time the Haitian Revolution occurred in 1791, the French had transported 1,165,000 slaves to the Americas with 773,000 going to Saint-Dominique. Others went to Martinique (217,200) and Guadalupe (73,000).

These French islands were major economic engines for the French, producing nearly 40% of the sugar and 60% of the coffee imported to Europe (S. Staff). To accomplish this, violence and murder of the slaves to force more labour out of them was the norm.

Once the slaves arrived on the Caribbean islands, they were either sold to slave merchants there, sold directly to plantation owners or transported to other islands or to Louisiana for resale.

The slaves were then marched hundreds of miles into the inland to clear more land for the farmers to expand their farm land or to replace those slaves who had died from the harsh treatment by the French.

FIGURE 9. OVERSEERS PUNISHING SLAVES ON A RURAL PLANTATION[10]

---

[10] Jean-Baptiste Debret [Public domain or CC BY-SA 4.0 (http://creativecommons.org/licenses/by-sa/4.0)], via Wikimedia Commons

New Orleans was the first true French settlement in Louisiana. Its location was chosen in 1718 due to its proximity to the large Mississippi river which provided access to the interior of the continent and perfect conditions for a port to transfer materials to Europe.

FIGURE 10. NEW ORLEANS IN 1726[11]

By 1721, New Orleans had become the political and commercial center of the French government in Louisiana. Its leaders actively encouraged more settlers to come and farm the land in the region.

As the new settlers arrived and began to attempt to clear and farm the land in the interior to produce indigo and sugar cane, it soon became clear that huge numbers of workers would be needed. By 1719, the French settlers began importing large numbers of enslaved Africans. Overall, by 1763, the French had imported 6000 slaves into Louisiana.

Spain acquired all of Louisiana west of the Mississippi River at the end of the **Seven-Year War** (1756-1763) (W. P. Staff). This opened up Louisiana to massive imports of slaves from Africa. By 1795, there were 19,926 slaves and 16,304 free people of color[12] in Louisiana.

Avoyelles Parish's first recorded visit by white men was by **Bienville** and his soldiers in January, 1718 (W. Staff). They recorded friendly meetings with two groups of Native Americans called the **Tamoucougoula** and the **Tunicas**.

Joseph B. Rabalais (1736 - 1788) is believed by some to be one of the first permanent white settlers in Avoyelles Parish (JosRabAncestry). His daughter, **Celeste Rabalais** (b. 1778) was the first child to be listed as baptized Catholic in St. Paul the Apostle Catholic Church records in Mansura. He owned land north and east of Mansura that extended to near **Grande Ecore** as well as at **Lake Pearl**[13].

---

[11] Ink & watercolor view by Jean-Pierre Lassus, from the collection of the Centre des archives d'outre-mer, France (DFC Louisiane 71-6A), via book "Common Routes, St. Domingue - Louisiana", Historic New Orleans Collection, 2006.
[12] Spain, despite importing far more slaves than the French, also enacted much more liberal policies regarding allowing slaves to become free. This, greatly increased the numbers of FPC's in Louisiana.
[13] He owned land in Section 52, T1North, and Range 4 East of Louisiana Meridian extending east of the Town of Mansura on Grand Ecore Bayou. He also owned 388 parcels, 10 arpents by 40 arpents on Lake Pearl.

In the 1785 Avoyelles Post Census (JosRab1785Census), Joseph B. Rabalais was listed, along with his wife, two children and 15 slaves, suggesting that he could have been one of the earliest slave holders in the Mansura area.

The 1785 Avoyelles Post Census also included Mansura area slave holders such as **Dominique Coco** (10 slaves) and **Joseph Joffrion** (6 slaves).

By 1860, right before the Civil War, the slave population in Avoyelles Parish had grown to 7,185 black people who were held in captivity by 521 Slave Holders (1860).

Living in Slavery

The area shown below in **Figure 11** illustrates the current general area around Mansura, Louisiana, that is the location of many of the people and places described in this book. As will be discussed, some of the highest concentration of former slaves occurred: (1) inside the town of Mansura; (2) just to the north of Mansura, in an area called Grande Bayou; (3) along a stretch of hilltop land that bordered a steep drop down into the swampland to the east, called "Down the Hill"; and (4) the southern end of that hilltop that was called Grande Ecore.

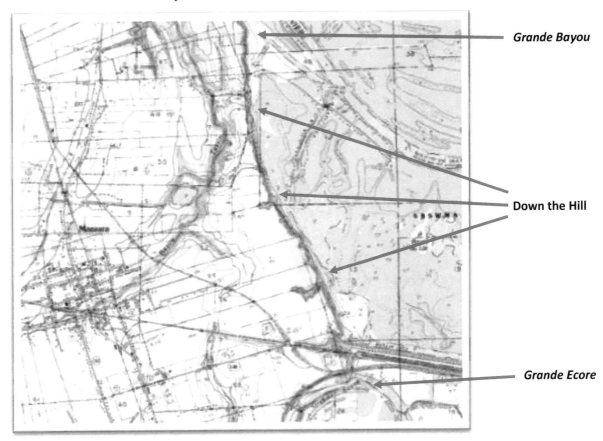

Grande Bayou

Down the Hill

Grande Ecore

FIGURE 11. MANSURA MAP - TODAY (U. S. SURVEY)

As will be discussed later, the reasons for the existence of these remote settlements of black people that began right after the Civil War are complex and many. Predominant among those were the ingrained fear of the more violent members of the white population whose hatred of Blacks was well known and often demonstrated in the form of extreme violence.

Some of the horrors of living in slavery were described in books such as ***Twelve Years a Slave*** (Northrup) and ***Back Through the Veil*** I (Prier). All of the people who are shown in the beginnings of the various family trees described in this book went through that same hell on Earth.

Yet, despite the beatings, murder, endless toil and general inhuman treatment, the desire for freedom remained on the minds of the slaves. As shown in the document below, slaves running away was a daily occurrence, even though capture could mean horrible torture or death.

FIGURE 12. THE DAILY PICAYUNE NEWSPAPER, NEW ORLEANS, 20 MARCH, 1852[14]

---

[14] By Staff of the Daily Picayune [Public domain], via Wikimedia Commons

Octavia George's Story

Although there was a good bit of details about what it was like to live in slavery NEAR Mansura in *Back Through the Veil* I, a newly acquired document describes what slavery was like IN Mansura[15]. This document is a transcript of an interview of former slave, **Octavia George**, by a member of the Oklahoma Writer's Project, a subset of the Federal Writer's Project (O'Dell).

Octavia George was described as being 86 years old at the time of the 1938 interview (George). She claimed to have been born in "Mansieur", Louisiana in "Avoir" Parish in 1852 and that she was the daughter of **Alfred** and **Clementine Joseph** . She said, "*I don't know much about my grandparents other than my mother told me my grandfather's name was Fransuai (Francois?), and that he was a one-time king in Africa.*"

From Ancestry.com (SMCALLISTER505), the following information was found about Octavia:

- Octavia Joseph was born on December 9, 1852, in Avoyelles Parish, Louisiana, the [only] child of Alfred and Clementine [Crawford] Joseph. She married **Aurelian George** and they had four children together;
- In the 1880 census (OctAur1880), Aurelian (25) and Octavia (24) were living near Grand Bayou, outside of Mansura, LA. Living with them were their son, **Hilaire** (5), and their two daughters: **Eugenie** (3) and **Agnes** (1). Also, living next door to them was the widow, **Clementine Crawford**.
- Octavia then married **Paul Toussaint** on December 10, 1889, in Avoyelles Parish, Louisiana. She died in Oklahoma City on December 18, 1939, at the age of 87.

Some of Octavia's recollections of being a slave in Mansura from her birth until freedom came in 1865, when she was 13 years old, are summarized as follows:

She lived on a large plantation owned by a slave holder whose last name was DePriest[16]. He was a Frenchman who was married and had eight or nine children. He lived in a *"Big fine house and had a fine barn".* She called him *"Master"* and his wife *"Mistress"*. She described his children as being very mean and who would fight the slave children, but the slave children were not allowed to fight their little white masters and mistresses.

Some white people lived nearby who worked on the Depriest plantation. They didn't own slaves and had to work for the rich plantation owners.

Octavia's job was to take care of the white children and to feed the black children. She sadly recalled how the black children were fed beans and cornmeal mush in boxes or troughs under the house. When the food was brought to them, they gathered around the box or trough just as cows and horses do.

She felt that the Depriests were good masters and mistresses. They allowed them to go to church with them on Sunday and to have two to three acres of land for their personal use such as growing vegetables to eat or sell. Any money they earned from the sale of vegetables was used to buy clothes and other necessities. On Sunday, they were able to eat some of those vegetables along with duck, fish or pork.

---

[15] This document was so kindly provided to me by **Ms. Margie Ferguson**, of Chicago, IL and a member of the Joshua family of Moreauville, LA.
[16] No one by that name appeared in the U.S. census for that era. However, this information is coming from the memory of an uneducated former slave. Most names of people and places from that time are distorted as a result. It could have been "Dupuy".

On Christmas and New Year's Day, the slaves were allowed to get drunk without the fear of getting whipped.

Most of the slaves lived in log cabins. Their beds were home-made with moss mattresses. Octavia said that she enjoyed going out and collecting the moss from trees on the plantation. Everyone wore cotton clothes. Shoes were made from pieces of leather cut from a cowhide.

The Depriest plantation was very large and the work was very hard. The overseer was a *"mean old fellow"* who kept a gun and rode around on a *"big fine horse"*, going from one bunch of slaves to the next.

Everyone had to be up by 5 O'clock in the morning and worked all day until dark. Once done with their day's work, they then had to do their night work such as cooking, milking cows and feeding the stock.

Slaves were punished for stealing, running off and disobeying their master's rules. Slaves did run away but the master would have them hunted using blood hounds. They were usually caught, although, in some cases, the runaway slave was able to kill the blood hound and escape.

There were no jails on the plantation. All punishment was administered by the slave holder or the overseer. Punishment usually meant being chained hands and feet and beaten while lying over a barrel or a large log. They were beaten until the blood flowed freely. If the whipping wasn't effective, the slave was either hung or burned at the stake.

When a slave died, their body was taken directly to the graveyard without a church burial. No one was allowed to sing at the gravesite.

Slaves were often sold. They were auctioned off just like cattle or horses. The *"big fine healthy slaves"* were worth the most.

When news that they were free came, the slaves ran away and hid near the Mississippi River. They had been hiding there for three days, eating roasted fish that they had caught with their bare hands, when Depriest suddenly arrived and told them that they were free to do whatever they wanted to.

They all returned to the Depriest farm where they found their former mistress crying uncontrollably at the loss of her *"ni--ers"*.

Octavia recalled how she was hurt at the news of Abraham Lincoln's death. She mourned him for three months, wearing a black arm band every day.

She commented that as far as Jeff Davis, she didn't care anything for him.

Black Slave Holders in Avoyelles Parish (Franklin and Schweninger.), (Berlin), (H. L. Gates)

It is a well-known fact that many Blacks were slave holders in Louisiana and other states during slavery, although it is a topic not too well known for Avoyelles Parish. For example, in 1830, there were 3775 black slave holders in the South who were holding 12,760 people in slavery. Of that number, over 80% of those slave holders were in Louisiana, South Carolina, Virginia, and Maryland.

A common characteristic of the Louisiana black slave holders was that they tended to be of mixed race or mulattoes. The majority of those mixed-race slave holders resided in New Orleans, a result of *placage'*, an arranged relationship between wealthy, white gentlemen and quadroons, very light-skinned women of African descent.

FIGURE 13. COLONIAL LOUISIANA, EARLY 18ᵀᴴ CENTURY (PINPIN)

That free, mixed-race population, called *gens de couleur* or Free People of Color (FPC), acquired their wealth by either being concubines or children of the white gentlemen. They, through this odd process, acquired farms, plantations, and slaves which they, then, passed on to their children.

The slaves, thus acquired, were treated no better, and sometimes much worse, by their mixed-race slave holders than the Whites. The harsh conditions under which the slaves were forced to work the rice, sugar cane and cotton fields resulted in the same type of long hours, beatings, poor housing and foods, etc. as was the case when the slave holders were white. Runaways was the same persistent issue as with the white slave holders.

It has been a common myth that most slaves of mixed-race slave holders, were relatives of theirs whom they had purchased to set free. That belief can be quickly dismissed when the racial makeup of the slave holders, who were mostly mulattoes, are compared their slaves, who were mostly black. Just as their white counterparts, the mixed-race slave holders were motivated by their desire for wealth and social and political position, not by any desire to set people free.

Outside of New Orleans, other well-documented areas with large populations of mulattoes were the Cane River[17] area in northwest Louisiana and the Attakapas[18] region in the vicinity of St. Landry Parish in south Louisiana (i.e. Frilot Cove, Bois Mallet, Grand Marais, Palmetto, Lawtell, Soileau etc.).

The origins of those groups were somewhat different from New Orleans. Here, the early occupation of those regions by the French troops during the early 18th century and the large, and out of control, slave population in Louisiana resulted in a large number of long-lasting relationships developing between those soldiers and their slave mistresses over time (Midlo-Hall).

Once their military service was over, many of the former French soldiers remained in that region and became land owners and planters. In many cases, children who resulted from the relationships between those soldiers and the female slaves, were awarded their freedom and land after their fathers died. Over time, a class of mulattos similar to that in New Orleans developed (Midlo-Hall).

In Avoyelles Parish, Louisiana, a few individual FPC's were recorded as holding slaves, either via purchase or inheritance[19]. However, no single large group of mixed-race people existed in Avoyelles who were both large land owners and slave holders and who had the critical mass to be considered a social class. Instead, a few individuals who were the products of various illicit romantic relationships were found around the parish. Although some of those mixed-race individuals managed to acquire land for farming and a few slaves, most became tradesmen, such as carpenters, brick masons, etc.

However, one individual of mixed-race descent and holding as many as 20 slaves, was noticed in several records in the Mansura-Marksville area – **Olympe Joffrion** (Jeanine-McNeil)..

Olympe Joffrion was described as the son of **Joseph Joffrion, II** (1774 – 1821), the son of one of the earliest white settlers in Avoyelles, as mentioned above. His father, **Joseph Joffrion** (1753-1829) and mother, **Marie Francoise Bouchard** (1756 – 1830), were born in Pointe Coupee and St. Landry Parishes, respectively (Jeanine-McNeil). They appear to have had three children: **Joseph II** (1774-1821), **Celestin** (1776-1857), and **Genevieve** (1779-1803).

Joseph II was said to have fathered a set of children with a woman called **Lucille Lavalais**: **Aimee** (1806 - 1869), **Lucien** (1807 - 1847), **Olympe** (1813 - ??), **Clair** (1814 – 1863), and **Marie Galate** (1815 - 1901). Lucille is believed to have been a Free Person of Color, although there are no public records to prove it[20].

The records of each of Lucille and Joseph II's children were examined to determine whether there was evidence that they were of mixed race. Only in the case of Olympe was there mention of race:

[17] The Cane River region is home to a unique culture; the Creoles. Generations of the same families of owners and workers, enslaved and tenant, lived on these lands for over 200 years. A national park tells their stories and preserves the cultural landscape of Oakland and Magnolia Plantations, two of the most intact Creole cotton plantations in the United States (Wikipedia.com).
[18] Attakapas Parish was a former parish (county) in southern Louisiana and was one of twelve parishes in the Territory of Orleans, newly defined by the United States federal government following the Louisiana Purchase. At its core was the Poste des Attakapas trading post, now St. Martinsville (Wikipedia.com).
[19] Private communication from Susane Lavalais Boykins
[20] Private communication from Susane Lavalais Boykins

- In the probate sale to dispose of the property and slaves belonging to his brother, Lucien Joffrion, Olympe was listed as "**Olympe Joffrion, F.M.C.**" (OlymJoffProbSale)
- In the 1870 U.S. Census for Avoyelles Parish, Olympe Joffrion was listed as a Mulatto (OlymJoff1870).

Olympe Joffrion married a white woman named **Emelie Peyton** on December 4, 1834 in Adams County, Mississippi. The St. Paul Catholic records show five slaves being baptized by Olympe Joffrion. Those are listed below with their dates of birth and mothers:

- **Marie**, 14 Apr 1836, **Nancy**;
- **Alfred**, 20 Sep. 1843, **Manon**;
- **Hyppolite**, 14 Nov 1844, **Marie Louise**;
- **Octave**, 2 Nov 1842, **Manon**;
- **Paulin**, 15 Nov 1844, **Caroline**.

In the 1850 U.S. Census for Avoyelles, Olympe (38) and his wife, **Celeste** (22)[21], were listed with the following children: **Merion** (14), **Felix** (5), and **Angelie** (3). Also living with them was a wood chopper named, **Jean Boilevin** (20). Everyone in that household was considered to be white.

In the 1850 U.S. Census Slave Schedule for Avoyelles Parish, Olympe was listed as holding 20 slaves in captivity (OlymJoff1850).

In the 1860 U.S. Census (OlymCel1860), Olympe (47) and Celeste (31) were listed along with the following children: **Mariam** (24) and **Felix** (13). Also living with them was **Joseph O. Joffrion** (26).

In 1870 (OlymCel1870), Olympe (57) and Celeste (42) were listed with the following people: **Alzide** (24), **Julie** (18) and an unnamed baby girl. In that census, Olympe was described as a **mulatto**.

No additional records on Olympe Joffrion were found for this study.

Thus, based on the above information, **Olympe Joffrion was certainly the largest mixed-race slave holder in the Mansura-Marksville area.**

Freedom and the Reign of Terror

You will remember from *Back Through the Veil,* (Book I) how freedom for most Blacks in the U.S. came with the signing of the **Emancipation Proclamation** in 1862, followed by the end of the Civil War and the ratification of the 13th, 14th and 15th Amendments.

However, Whites in the South immediately began to develop steps to remove that freedom. Those steps included the **Black Codes**, the **Jim Crow Laws**, and, basically, mob rule that included threats and harassment, violence, and murder committed by individual perpetrators and by mob lynching.

---

[21] Not clear what became of Emelie. However, the age gap among the children (11 years) suggests that Mariam and Felix could have had different mothers.

It was during this period that symbols of white supremacy such as flags and monuments to leaders of the Confederacy were erected.

By 1900, most of those new freedoms had vanished and "Reign of Terror" begun.

Below are two stories of such violence that occurred IN Mansura, Louisiana. These stories are provided here to give the reader a better understanding of what life was like for a typical black person living in the Mansura area during the "**Reign of Terror**" period that covered the years from 1865 through 1940. Although most of the violence had subsided by 1920, the feeling of fear and intimidation remained.

The first story has been passed down within the Augustine and McGlory families[22]. It vividly describes a particularly violent event that occurred inside the town of Mansura during the 1890's:

> *At some point between 1888 and 1890, **Gervais Magloire** and his family were forced from their home in Mansura by a group of white thugs who attacked their home during the night, forcing Gervais, along with his two oldest daughters, **Helen** and **Victoria**, to flee to Mississippi[23]. His wife, **Victorine**, and their two youngest children, **Joseph** and **Lula**, were forced to hide in the bushes for several days before they were finally found.*

> *Gervais, Helen and Victoria ended up living in Mississippi. Gervais remarried and never returned to Mansura.*

> *Eventually, Helen and Victoria returned to Mansura after living in Mississippi for several years. Interestingly, since they both had left Louisiana as small children, neither spoke their native French. Their mother, Victorine, however, spoke only French, making communication between her and her children difficult.*

The second story of violence in Mansura directed towards blacks was reported by the New Orleans Times Picayune[24] on September 11, 1892 and was titled: *The Lynching at Mansura, Louisiana, September 2, 1892* (Author).

This story shows a number of remarkable similarities to the story above and may actually be the same story, but with different names used to describe those involved. A follow-up story appeared in the Times Picayune on November 4, 1892 (Author).

> *On September 2, 1892, a Mansura black man by the name of **Sylvain**[25], who was said to be a local school teacher, was accused of stealing a hog by a group of white men. That night, a group of about 18-20 white men approached his house with the intentions of flogging him. When the mob ordered Sylvain to come out, threatening to break down his door, he refused and armed himself.*

> *The door was then broken down and, as the mob attempted to enter his house, Sylvain fired into the group, killing a person by the name of **Duco**. As the mob members ran in every direction, leaving Duco dead in the doorway, Sylvain fired another round killing a horse and wounding another member of the mob. He then made his escape.*

---

[22] From the Augustine and McGlory family oral histories as told by **Mary Bernell Augustine Prier**

[23] From family oral history, this was a group referred to by local Blacks as the "White Caps".

[24] A copy of the Mansura incident appearing in the Times Picayune was also kindly provided to this author by **Ms. Margie Ferguson**, of Chicago, IL

[25] There were a number of black men whose last name was Sylvain listed in the 1870 and 1880 U.S. census for Avoyelles Parish. It was not possible to connect any of them with this incident.

*The next day, a larger mob began searching for Sylvain. Soon, they came to a mulatto by the name of **Laurent**[26], who was laying bricks. He was quickly seized and hung for no clear reason except that they believed he may have known the whereabouts of Sylvain.*

*The mob then went to the home of **Gabriel Magloire**, a reportedly quiet and good man who was a minister and who owned the property on which he lived[27]. He was captured by the mob and questioned about the whereabouts of Sylvain. When he claimed to know nothing, he was hung until he was near death. He was then let down and allowed to recover. He was again questioned about Sylvain with the same results as before. He was hung again and, as before, brought down when he was near death and then allowed to revive.*

After being questioned once more about the whereabouts of Sylvain and telling the mob that he knew nothing, Gabriel Magloire was hung for the final time. As the mob members departed, each one fired his pistol into Gabriel' lifeless body. They then went to the priest and ordered him not to bury Gabriel Magloire.

From Ancestry, Gabriel Magloire appeared in several public records:

- Appeared as a 6-year-old slave child, whose mother was **Marie**, in the probate sale following the death of **Jean Baptiste Lemoine**. That sale was held on November 9, 1860 and is shown in Table 5 below (JBLemSale).
- In 1870, he was a 16-year-old living with his parents, **I.H.** and **Arthemese Magloire** (GabMag1870)
- He was named as a victim of an 1892 lynching in a story published in Ancestry.com by **Pierre Magloire McGlory** (msrae65).

It is not clear from the story if Sylvain was ever located. No charges were filed against him by the local grand jury.

The sheriff went out and arrested about 18 of the lynch men. However, by November, all were acquitted despite having committed those terrible crimes while completely unmasked and in open daylight.

Although the people in the two stories have different names, the reader will quickly see how it's possible for some of the details of the real event to have been changed to protect the escaping "Sylvain".

The two examples cited here are but small examples of what life was like for Mansura Blacks during slavery and the ensuing Reign of Terror. There are, likely, numerous other examples that were never recorded and are lost to history.

---

[26] A number of Laurent family members, most of whom were mulatto brick layers, were mentioned in Book 1 of ***Back to the Veil***. It is not clear from the newspaper article which Laurent was being referred to here.
[27] **Gabriel Magloire** appeared in both the 1870 and 1880 U.S. Censuses for Avoyelles Parish (GabMag1870), (GadMag1880). In 1880, he was a 25-year-old living with his wife, **Euphemie**, and 2 children, **Pierre** and **Marie**. There are no further census records regarding him.

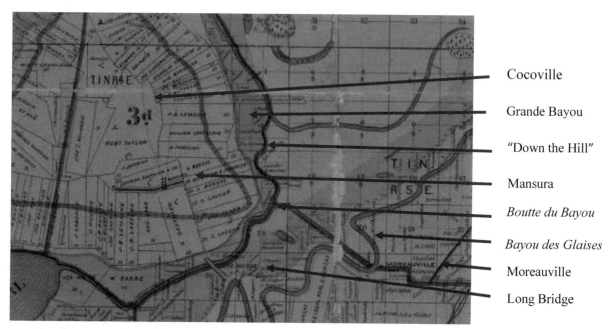

Cocoville

Grande Bayou

"Down the Hill"

Mansura

Boutte du Bayou

Bayou des Glaises

Moreauville

Long Bridge

FIGURE 14. CIVIL WAR ERA MAP SHOWING AVOYELLES LANDMARKS (S. ROBERTSON)

All of the landmarks shown on this map figured prominently in the lives of the slaves in the Mansura-Moreauville area. For example:

- **Cocoville** - the site of the early Catholic Church and cemetery and several large plantations, including ones belonging Dr. Moncla, Pierre Lemoine and Laurent Normand.
- **Grande Bayou** – Location of a high concentration of mixed-race people
- **Down the Hill** – The large black community that spanned the edge of the Mansura Bluff from Grande Bayou to Boutte des Bayou.
- **Bayou des Glaises** – Slow, winding stream where many plantations shipped goods to market. Later, many former slaves made their homes.

Chapter 2.
The Augustine Family

Samuel Augustine
Son of Avit Augustine

An Introduction to the Augustine Family

The known history of the Augustine family of Avoyelles Parish, Louisiana began around 1800 with two slaves: **Ursin** and **Jean Pierre** (See Below). These two men were brothers. Ursin was believed to have been born in Jackson, Mississippi (JsAugDeath), while there is no indication as to where Jean Pierre was born. Unfortunately, there are no records indicating who their parents were or whether or not they had other siblings.

> *An important point to be aware of: Both men tended to name their children after each other. For example, Ursin had sons named Ursin and Jean Pierre while Jean Pierre had sons named Ursin and Jean Pierre. This leads to much confusion. An attempt was made to reduce that confusion by adding suffixes to each name. For example, Ursin's two sons were named Ursin II and Jean Pierre II while Jean Pierre's sons were named Ursin Jr. and Jean Pierre, Jr*

Once the end of slavery had arrived, the members of the Augustin family moved nearer to each other, generally along the edge of the Mansura Bluff[28] in a community called "Down the Hill" (See shaded area in **Figure 14**) or along *Bayou des Glaises*, near Moreauville (JPAug1870). This can be attributed to the following factors:

- Ursin Augustin, Sr. spent his time as a slave on the Lemoine plantation which was described in an 1850 probate sale as being on the Avoyelles Prairie "dan les bas" (*In the bottoms*) (UrsAugProb). This suggests that this land was in the same location (i.e. on Old River Road or Grande Bayou) as that owned by Zenon's father, Pierre Baptiste (P.B.) Lemoine (See **Farm 49**, just north of Mansura in **Figure 14**).

- Members of Ursin's family eventually lived on or near land he had purchased that was located on *Bayou des Glaises* (See **Figure 14**) in Moreauville[29].

- Jean Pierre Augustin, Sr. also purchased and died on land located along *Bayou des Glaises*.

Ursin Augustine is unique for having lived to be around 100 years: i.e., he was born before the Louisiana Purchase and lived through the harshest slavery era, the Civil War, the arrival of freedom for the slaves, Reconstruction and, finally, died in the 20th century.

Over the years, the Augustines farmed the land from Grande Bayou to Moreauville and Long Bridge. They formed part of the backbone of the large African-American community that persisted in that area, an area still called "Down the Hill".

During the early part of the 20th century, a number of Augustine and other family members moved into the town of Mansura where they formed a share cropper community on the land owned by the Coco family, referred to by many former tenants as the "Coco Plantation. This farm, however, still reached from L'Eglise Street in Mansura all the way back to "Down the Hill".

With the arrival of farm mechanization, the manual labor requirements needed on the local farms slowly disappeared. With it went the communities located "Down the Hill" and the "Coco Plantation,". Today, many African-American families, and Whites, still make their homes along Bayou des Glaises.

Historical Highlights

Ursin Augustin, Sr. was first noted in the September 20, 1835 baptismal records of St. Paul the Apostle Catholic Church (Church) where he was shown serving as the godfather to a slave child named **Clementine** (See Below). At that time, he, and possibly, his future wife, **Constance**, were held captive on a plantation owned by **Zenon Lemoine**, a local farmer (See Below).

---

[28] The Mansura Bluff describes the edge of the plateau on which the town sits. Beyond that edge is a 20 foot drop to the marsh land below and to the east.

[29] This information was provided by witnesses in a law suit involving the children of Ursin held in the District Court for the Parish of Avoyelles, filed December 19, 1881.

Jean Pierre Augustin Sr. was believed to have been born around 1808 and grew up as a slave of **Dorcino Armand** of Moreauville, LA. After slavery was over, Jean Pierre married **Felicite'**, a former slave of **Pierre Lemoine** and they moved into a house that he purchased on Bayou des Glaises in Moreauville. He died in April, 1870 from "Dropsy of the Heart" (JBAugDeath).

Jean Pierre's death occurred before the 1870 U.S. census was completed, where former slaves might have been included for the first time. Thus, any census records of him and his family were left out. However, after his death, records of an 1881 succession regarding the legal ownership of his former property and who would care for his minor children, shed a considerable amount of light on him and his life.

In order to effectively profile Ursin Augustin, Sr., his brother, Jean Pierre Augustin, Sr. and their offspring, this chapter will be divided into two parts: **1. Ursin Augustin**, Sr. and **2. Jean Pierre Augustin, Sr.**

1. Ursin Augustin, Sr.

As will be discussed below, both Ursin Augustin, Sr. and his wife, **Constance Desire** (a.k.a. **Theresa Lemoine**) and many of their children, were held as slaves on the plantation owned by the Lemoine family of Avoyelles Parish. For that reason, it is appropriate and informative to review a bit of information regarding that family.

The Slave Holders of Ursin and Constance Augustine

Jean Baptiste Lemoine and his wife, **Catherine Simon** (JBLem), owned land immediately south of the current location of **St. Paul's Cemetery** and extending east, along the current **Old River Road**, to the **Mansura Bluff**, an area still called **Grande Bayou** or **"Down the Hill"** (See **Figure 14**).[30] He and his son, **Pierre Baptiste Lemoine** (Zenon's Father), jointly cultivated that land during the early 1800s (Sturgell).

Pierre Baptiste Lemoine was listed as holding several slaves in captivity, as well as selling some during the early 1800s (Hall). Some of his slave transactions are shown in **Appendix A**. Several conclusions can be made regarding the people he traded or held in slavery:

- His slave sales occurred between 1801 and 1815;
- While there may have been slaves already held on his plantation, at least 18 were bought and sold in these recorded transactions. Here are some facts about those people:
  o Two were born in Louisiana;
  o Five were brought in from Tennessee;
  o One was brought in from Virginia;
  o One was brought in from Jamaica;
  o Up to six were from Africa;
  o Three were of unknown origin.

---

[30] Robertson, S. B. *Map of Avoyelles Ph, La.* [New Orleans, La.: S.B. Robertson, 1879] Map. Retrieved from the Library of Congress, https://www.loc.gov/item/2012592318/. (Accessed June 05, 2017.)

- Many slaves were sold as members of a group, some of which numbered as many as 11;
- Many sales were of a slave mother and her children;
- All of the slaves listed, including those coming directly from Africa, already had been given European names.

Zenon Lemoine, a child of Pierre Baptiste Lemoine and **Lucy Bordelon**, was born on February 17, 1802. He married **Josephine Rabalais** on June 27, 1820 and died on August 2, 1850 (ZenLemLife). He grew up to become a significant local farmer and slave holder.

In the 1850 U.S. Census Slave Schedules, Zenon Lemoine was listed as holding 64 African-Americans in slavery. This included 35 males and 29 females. There were 26 children under 10 and 3 adults over 60 (ZenLemSlaves1850).

Zenon Lemoine died on August 2, 1850 and is buried in St. Paul the Apostle Cemetery in Mansura (ZenLemDeath).

Ursin Augustin Sr.'s Life

Ursin was born a slave in the Jackson, MS area around 1800 (UrsAug1900). Who his parents were, what was his exact date of birth and who his original slave holder was remains unknown.

As mentioned above, on March 7, 1837, Ursin, while a slave of **Zenon Lemoine**, appeared as the godfather to a slave child named **Clementine** who was being baptized by one of the Catholic priests in Avoyelles Parish (Church). Clementine, who was born on September 20, 1835, was the daughter of Paulin, a slave of **Martin Dufour**, a local planter.

In 1850, after the death of Zenon Lemoine, a probate sale was held to dispose of his property. Included in that sale were 76 slaves, as shown in **Appendix B**.

Ursin and his family were listed as some of the slaves sold as part of that sale (See **Table 1** Below) (ZenLemProb).

TABLE 1. SUCCESSION OF ZENON LEMOINE, 1850

Slave	M/F	Age	Purchaser	Price
Ursin	M	46	Joseph Moncla	$930
Constance and her 5 Children:	F	39	Ceran Gremillion	$1710
• Jean Pierre	M	10		
• Avit	M	7		
• Pavit	M	7		
• Andre'	M	5		
• Celestin	M	2		
Gustin	M	23	Joachim Juneau	$1140
Dorsaint	M	21	F.B. Coco	$1200
Sosthine	M	19	Hillaire Lemoine	$1090
Louisa	F	17	Jean Bte. Rabalais	$875

Jacques	M	13	Jean Pierre Lemoine	$735
Auguste	M	12	Dorsaint Armand	$500

Sadly, Ursin was sold to a local doctor, **Dr. Joseph Moncla**, whose home was located near **Cocoville**, LA, (See **Figure 14**). **Constance**, Ursin's wife, and her five minor children (**Jean Pierre, Avit, Pavit, Andre'** and **Celestin**) were sold together to **Ceran Gremillion**, a local farmer, for a total of $1710.

Ursin and Constance's six other children (**Gustin, Dorsaint, Sosthine, Louisa, Jacques and Auguste**) were sold separately to various other local farmers.

Presumably, Ursin remained held captive on the Moncla plantation until he was freed when the Civil War ended.

All were reunited once slavery was over, after 15 years of separation!

Ursin next appeared as a witness in a December, 1881 law suit described as "Ursin Augustin, fils et al. versus A.L. Boyer, et al. (See Below). Here he testified to the legitimacy of his late brother, Jean Pierre Augustin, Sr.'s ownership of a parcel of land on Bayou des Glaises.

Ursin Augustin last appeared in the 1900 U.S. Census, at which time he was living near Mansura with his daughter, **Josephine** and her husband, **Alfred Carmouche** (UrsAug1900). They were living next door to his son, **Jean Pierre Augustin II**. He indicated his age to be 100 and his place of birth as in Louisiana.

Ursin Augustin, Sr. died on October 5, 1901 (M. Bordelon). His age was listed as 111 (!).

Ursin Augustin Sr.'s Family

During his life as a slave, Ursin fathered at least 13 (!) children with at least two slave women: **Manette Sylvert** and **Constance Desire** (a.k.a. **Therese Lemoine**):

- **Manette Sylvert** only appeared in one record: In a February 16, 1872 "Act of Acknowledgement", Ursin stated that he and former slave, Manette Sylvert[31], were the parents of the slave child known as **Ursin** (UrsAugAck). That child was **Ursin Augustine II** (Ursin's son) who will be discussed later.

  [The older Ursin will now be called Ursin Augustin, Sr. to distinguish between the two.]

  No further records of Manette Sylvert were found.

---

[31] It should be noted that the transcribed records of this document claim that Ursin's child, Ursin, Jr.'s mother was named "Maucite". However close inspection of the document indicates that her name is, indeed, Manette.

- **Constance [Desire]**[32] was a slave initially held by **Zenon Lemoine** of Mansura (ConsDes1837). She appeared in the St. Paul Baptismal records as the mother of a slave child, **Andre**, who was born on July 8, 1845 and baptized on January 2, 1846 as part of a group of six slave children (See **Table 2** Below) (Church).

TABLE 2. SLAVES BAPTIZED BY ZENON LEMOINE

Slave Child	Birth Date	Mother
Andre'	8 Jul 1845	**Constance**
Antoine	27 Aug 1845	Rosa
Edmond	13 Nov 1845	Laure
Famy (Francoise)	8 Nov 1844	Marianne
Marie	13 Aug 1845	Henriette
Pierre	Unk.	Unk.

The slave woman, **Constance**, sold to **Ceran Gremillion**[33] during the slave sale shown in **Table 1**, above, was the same person shown baptizing Andre' in **Table 2**. She turned out to be Ursin's wife, **Constance Desire** (See Below).

Also, Constance's young children[34] (i.e. **Jean Pierre, Avit, Pavit, Andre'** and **Celestin**), sold along with her in **Table 1**, turned out to be Ursin's children. In addition, the older slave children (i.e. **Gustin, Dorsaint, Sosthine, Louisa, Jacques** and **Auguste**) sold to other plantations at that time, also turned out to be Constance and Ursin's children.

Ursin Sr.'s son, **Avit**, stated on his marriage license that he was the oldest son of "d'Augustin and Constance", indicating that Constance, the slave being held by Zenon Lemoine, was indeed his mother[35].

In the February 16, 1872 Act of Acknowledgement, Ursin Augustine, Sr. publicly recognized that some of the children listed in **Table 1** (i.e., **Gustin, Jacques, Auguste, Avit, Pavy, Andre, Jean Pierre, Louise,** and **Dorsin**), belonged to him and Constance (Desire) (UrsAugAck). He also acknowledged that **Ursin, II,** who was not on the Lemoine plantation, and **Josephine,** who was not born at the time of the probate sale, were his children, as well.

Constance Desire, now known as **Therese Lemoine,** married Ursin Sr. on May 6, 1867 in Avoyelles Parish[36].

---

[32] Although listed as a slave named Constance, at some point, following the end of slavery, Constance assumed the last name, "Desire" and then changed her whole name to Therese Lemoine (A. P. Office). This name change was further confirmed during the testimony regarding the law suit among the members of Ursin's family (See Jean Pierre Augustin section below). It is possible that her baptismal name was Theresa but she assumed the name Constance during her life. However, when she got married to Ursin Sr., she was compelled to use her original name, Theresa, and added the surname of her slave holder, Lemoine. She then returned to her life-long name, Constance.

[33] **Ceran Gremillion** was a local farmer in the Mansura area. In the 1850 U.S. census, he (23) was listed as being married to Azima (20) and he was a farmer worth about $1500 (CerGrem1850). He was holding two people in slavery: one 20-year old mulatto male and one 15-year old black female. By 1870, he and his wife, Azema, were living in Avoyelles Parish, Subdivision 5, with their seven children: Amanda (15), Celina (14), Azelia (12), Darius (10), Anna (8), Clara (5) and Maria (2) (CerGrem1870).

[34] **Celestin**, a two-year-old boy, also sold during the probate sale, must not have survived slavery and was not listed in Ursin's Act of Acknowledgement.

[35] Avit's marriage license, issued by St. Paul's Catholic Church

[36] U.S.GHN.LAGHN.org

Ursin Sr. (67) and Therese (65) first appeared together in the U.S. census of 1870, living near Mansura (U.S. Census Bureau). Living with them were four black males and one black female: **Sylvest** (15), **Perry** (25), **Haraine** (10), **Silas** (16), and **Josephine** (17) (See below), who could have been their children (or even grandchildren, cousins or other relatives) before marriage[37]. Unfortunately, no further records of Perry, Haraine, or Silas Augustine have been found.

Ursin and/or Constance's children appeared in later public records, as follows:

- **Sylvest Augustin** (27) and his wife, **Celestine James** (23) appeared in the 1880 census, living near Mansura (1880 U.S. Census). Living with Sylvest and Celestine were their 2 sons: **Abraham** (1) and **Landry** (3); and their daughter, **Rebecca** (6). They were living next door to **William James** and his family, suggesting that Celestine could have been William's oldest daughter (See **James Family Below**).

- **Gustin Augustin** was born in 1827, the oldest of Ursin, Sr.'s children. He was one of the older children of Ursin listed in the Zenon Lemoine probate sale shown in **Table 1**. He was named as a child of Constance and Ursin, Sr. in Ursin's Act of Acknowledgement in 1872 (UrsAugAck).

  Gustin married **Clarisse Celestin** in Avoyelles Parish, LA on July 12, 1866 (GusAugMarr).

  In the 1880 U.S. census for Avoyelles Parish, Gustin Augustin (57) and his wife, **Clara** (30) were farmers, living near Grande Bayou, north of Mansura, LA (GusAug1880). Living with them were the following children: **Stella** (12), **Ludovic** (11), **Apolinie** (7) and **Gustave** (4).

  In the 1900 U.S. census, Gustin (74) was a widow, living near Mansura, LA with his daughter, **Lovinia** (20) and his granddaughter, **Estella Brook** (2).

  It is not clear when or where Gustin or Clarisse died.

- **Dorsin Augustin** was born in 1829, presumably on the Zenon Lemoine plantation. He was sold, along with his father, Ursin Augustin, Sr. and his siblings as part of the Zenon Lemoine probate sale in 1850, shown in **Table 1**. He was purchased by **F.B. Coco**.

  His father, Ursin Augustin, Sr. claimed him as one of his children in his Act of Acknowledgement (UrsAugAck).

  Dorsin died on January 23, 1867, well before the 1870 U.S. census was taken (DorAugLife). As a result, little is known about him.

- **Sosthene Augustin** was born in 1831 on the plantation owned by Zenon Lemoine (See **Table 1** above). He was sold as part of the 1850 probate sale to **Hillaire Lemoine**, a local farmer.

  Sosthene was mentioned as being deceased in December, 1881, during the testimony of his father, Ursin Augustin, Sr., regarding the ownership of a portion of land on Bayou des Glaises[38].

---

[37] Since Ursin Sr. did not acknowledge **Sylvest**, **Perry**, **Haraine** and **Silas** in his Act of Acknowledgement, they may have been Therese's children.
[38] Op cit. Reference 23

It's not clear if he was married or had children.

- **Louisa Augustin** was born in 1833 and sold to **Jean Bte. Rabalais**, as part of the Zenon Lemoine probate sale (**Table 1**). She was claimed by Ursin Augustin, Sr. as one of his children in his Act of Acknowledgement (UrsAugAck).

  In the 1870 U.S. census, Louisa (33) was living with her brother, **Auguste** and his wife, **Elizabeth**, near Bayou des Glaises in Moreauville, LA (JacqAug1870).

  She married **Eli Johnson** on February 6, 1877 in Marksville (LouAugMarr). Eli eventually became a minister of the gospel, appearing on the marriage certificates of several local weddings (e.g. Marie Augustine to Jean Baptiste Francois, 1895; Clara Dupas to Avit Augustine, 1894).

  Louisa (60) and Eli (54) Johnson appeared in the 1900 U.S. census (LouAug190). They were living along Bayou des Glaises.

  In the 1920 U.S. census, Louisa (65) and Eli (74) were living on Front Street in Moreauville, LA[39]. They were living alone and listed as farmers (LouEliJoh1920).

  No further records of Louisa or Eli have been found.

- **Jacques Augustin** was born in 1837, based on his age (13) at the time he was sold to **Jean Pierre Lemoine** in 1850 (See **Table 1** above). He was named as a child of Constance and Ursin, Sr. in Ursin's Act of Acknowledgement in 1872 (UrsAugAck).

  Jacques married **Alida Alexander**[40], the daughter of **Olida Sylvain** and **Jean Baptiste Alexander**.

  Jacques (32) and his wife, **Alida** (27) **Augustine** appeared in the 1870 census living near Moreauville or Long Bridge (JacqAug1870). Living with them were the following children: **Lucien** (12), **Gustave** (7), **Cora** (6), and **Arsene** (1 month).

  In the 1880 census, "Jack" (48) and "Aleda" (42) were living near Marksville, LA (JacqAug1880). Living with them were their children: **Gustave** (21), **Cora** (15), **Arsene** (12), **Mary** (8), and **Elizabeth** (4).

  Alida (64), now called **Eulalie**, appeared in the 1900 U.S. census, living near Mansura, LA, with her daughter, **Elizabeth Ravare Francisco** and Elizabeth's husband, **Pierre** (AliAug1900). Also present was their son, **Joseph Curtis Francisco**.

  Aleda died in Marksville, LA on January 7, 1921. There are no further records on Jacques.

  Records of their children are as follows:

  o **Lucien Augustine** married **Charlotte Titus** on March 24, 1882 (LucCharMarr). They had the following children: **Hosie, Saul, Jack (Jacob), Homer, Clemile, Estella, Honore, Gracie, Carrie, Elestra, Florence,** and **Celina**.

---

[39] As in most cases, former slaves rarely knew what their actual ages were since few understood the passage of time as measured using a calendar.
[40] Alida was listed in the public records as a Jean Baptiste. However, this was demonstrated to be incorrect by Susane Boykins.

o **Gustave Augustin** (1859 – 1955) married **Fannie Patton** on January 13, 1885 (GusAugMarr). No children are indicated.

o **Mary Augustin** (1877 - ??) married **Shelby Francisco** in 1895 (MarieAug1895). They had three children: **Marie G., Anna** and **Francisco.**

o **Elizabeth Augustin** (1876 – 1964) married **Pierre Francisco** on January 26, 1898 (ElizAugMarr). They had one child, **Joseph Curtis Francisco.**

   She married **Hippolite "Polite" Ravare** on January 23, 1902 (ElizAugMarr2). They had seven children: **Louis, Henry, Toyate, Gertrude, Selina, Areda,** and **Sammy.**

o **Louis Augustin** (1877 - ??). It is not clear what became of him.

It is not clear what became of **Cora** and **Arsene** Augustin.

- **Auguste Augustin** was born in 1838 on the plantation owned by Zenon Lemoine of Mansura. He was sold to a local plantation owner named **Dorsaint Armand** in the probate sale shown in **Table 1** above. He was claimed by Ursin Augustin, Sr. as one of his children in Ursin's Act of Acknowledgement (UrsAugAck).

Auguste married **Elizabeth (Betsy) Drummer** on March 20, 1870 (AvitClaraMarr).

Residing with Auguste (29) and Elizabeth (19), in 1870, were **Louisa** (33) and **Ursin Augustin** III (16), as well as 2 children: **Melanie** (9) and **Odien** (4) (JacqAug1870). Louisa was likely Auguste's sister and the same person sold to **Jean Bte. Rabalais** in the 1850 slave probate sale (**Table 1**).

Auguste and Elizabeth gave birth to their daughter, **Mary Jane**, on November 28, 1878 (Dufour).

In the 1880 U.S. Census, although only first initials were used, along with last names, gender, ages and relationships, the following assumptions can be made regarding Auguste and Betsy's family:

o "A" = Auguste (39),
o "E" = Elizabeth, a.k.a. Betsy (28),
o "A" = Adolph (10),
o "L" = ____, (8),
o "J" = ___ (4) and
o "M" = Mary Jane (1) (AdAug1880).

More study is needed here to identify "L" and "J".

Auguste (70) and Betsy (45) appeared in the 1900 census (I. U. Census), living near Cottonport with no children. They indicated that Betsy had given birth to 5 children and all 5 are alive in 1900. Not listed with them was their daughter, **Mary Jane**, who had married **William D. Blackman** in 1898 (AvitClaraMarr) and had moved to Grande Ecore, near Mansura, Louisiana.

In the 1910 census, Auguste (70) and Betsy (60), were living near Cottonport along with their 30-year-old son, **Adolph**, and their 17-year-old granddaughter, **Viola Williams** (U. C. Bureau).

Betsy (70) appeared in the 1920 U.S. census, living with her daughter, **Mary Jane** (41), and Mary Jane's husband, **William Blackman** (45) (I. U. Bureau). They were living near Grande Ecore, outside of

Mansura. Also, residing with them were William and Mary Jane's 2 sons, **Pilger** (19) and **Cleophas** (16), and their daughter, **Betsy** (4). There are no further definitive records of Louisa, Ursin (III), Melanie, or Odien.

- **Jean Pierre Augustin, II**[41] was born about 1840 on the plantation owned by Zenon Lemoine of Mansura. He was sold, along with his mother, Constance, to a local planter, **Ceran Gremillion**, in the probate sale shown in **Table 1**[42].

In the Ursin Sr's Act of Acknowledgement, he claimed Jean Pierre II as one of his children (UrsAugAck).

Jean Pierre II (30) and his wife, **Pauline Landorf** (18) appeared in the 1870 U.S. census (JPAug1870). They were living between his father, Ursin, Sr. and his brother, Andre' near Moreauville, LA. Living with them were the following children: **Jean Pierre III** (2), **Aurelie** (5) and **Sosthine** (1).

Interestingly, Pauline Landorf seemed to be present in the Pierre Normand inventory shown in **Table 5**. Her father, **Paulin**, and her mother, **Marie**, were listed along with her and her siblings, **Paulin**, **Meline** and **Marceline**[43].

In the 1880 U.S. census, a family was listed using only their first initials, last names and ages[44]. From this information, it can be assumed that:
- "J" = Jean (33),
- "P" = Pauline (20),
- "A" = Aurelie (15),
- "S" = Sosthine (11),
- Joseph Augustin (7) and
- A=**Unknown Name** (4).

If these assumptions are correct, then Jean Pierre III, who would have been 12, was no longer present.

Jean Pierre II appeared in the 1900 U.S. census as a 59-year-old widower living in Mansura, LA. Living with him were his son, **Horace** (17), his daughters: **Maria** (14) and **Adela** (12) and his grandson, **Cesair** (9) (I. U. Census), all born after the 1880 census, above. They were living next door to his sister, Josephine, and her husband, Alfred Carmouche. His father, Ursin Sr. was also living with Josephine and Alfred.

Jean Pierre Augustin, II died in Mansura, LA on May 30, 1923 at the age of 76 (JPAugJrDeath).

It's not clear what became of his wife, Pauline, although she must have died prior to the 1900 census, since he was listed as a widower then.

The Children of Jean Pierre Augustin, II were as follows:

- **Jean Pierre III** (b. 1868) – Unknown Fate.

- **Aurelie** (b. 1865) – Unknown Fate

---

[41] Jean Pierre Augustin, born ca. 1840, is listed here as "II" to distinguish him from his uncle, Jean Pierre Augustin, Sr., who was born around 1808 and his cousin, Jean Pierre Augustin, Jr.,

[42] There are some questions about his actual age in the sale. He was listed as 10 but later records indicate that he should have been only 3 at the time.

[43] Information provided courtesy of Susane Boykins.

[44] While the age differences between Jean and Pauline are the same as in 1870, the exact ages don't add up.

- o **Sosthine** (b. 1869) – He (29) appeared in 1900 U.S. census, living with his wife, **Josephine** (28) near Mansura. They had been married 11 years and had had 7 children with 6 still alive. Living with them were the following children: **Paul** (10), **Preston** (9), **Pauline** (7), **Arnaud** (5), **Leon** (2), and **Marie** (2/12).

- o **Joseph** (b. 1873) – He (24) appeared in 1900 U.S. census (JosAug1900), living with his wife, **Mary C. Thomas** (20), near Bayou des Glaises. They had been married three years and had had two children, both alive: **Clifton** (2) and **Amanda** (1).

- o **Horace** (b. 1883) – Appeared in the 1900 U.S. census as a 17-year-old young man, living with his father, Jean Pierre Augustin II (1. U. Census).

  In the 1910 U.S. census, he appeared as a 24-year-old man who had been married to **Mary** [Unknown Last Name] for 2 years (HorAug1910). They had two children: **Lovarai** (B/F, 1) and **Octavia** (11/2).

  In the 1920 U.S. census, Horace (35) and his wife, **Marie** (27) were living east of Mansura, LA (HorAug1920). Living with them were their children: **Vevate** (11), **Octavia** (9), **Edward** (6), **Mitchell** (5) and **Jenine** (2 1/12). Also living with them were Horace's uncle and aunt: **Charley** (80) and **Malena Thomas** (80).

  Horace died on April 10, 1928 at the age of 48.

  It is not clear where or when Marie died.

- o **Maria** (b. 1886) – Fate Unknown

- o **Adela** (b. 1888) – Fate Unknown

- **Pavy Augustin** was born in 1843, a twin with Avit Augustine. He was sold, along with his mother, Constance and four siblings, in 1850 to **Ceran Gremillion**. He was named as a child of Constance and Ursin, Sr. in the Act of Acknowledgement in 1872 (UrsAugAck).

  Pavy was briefly mentioned as one of the parties to a law suit regarding who was entitled to the 10 acres of land originally purchased by Ursin Augustine[45]. Here it was suggested that he had children but none are named specifically.

  No further public records of Pavy Augustine were found.

- **Avit Augustin**, was a slave child, born in 1843, on the plantation owned by Zenon Lemoine. He was a twin with Pavy[46]. When he was seven years old, he was sold, along with his mother, Constance and his four siblings, to **Ceran Gremillion** (See **Table 1**).

---

[45] Op cit. Reference 23
[46] There are no records of what became of Pavy Augustine although he was mentioned briefly in the law suit over Ursin's property mentioned in footnote 27 above.

Although family history claimed that he had seven wives[47], there are only records showing Avit married five times:

o   Avit appears to have married **Lily Drummer** at some point but there are no records of the actual marriage. Only a Social Security application makes such a claim (AvitLilySS). In that application, she claims to be the mother of Avit's son, **Modella Augustine**.

o   Avit Married **Ludy (Lida) Johnson**, the younger daughter of **Miles** and **Eliza Johnson**, on May 10, 1866 (AvitLadyMarr). The ceremony was performed by Th. Aug. Rebours, the local Catholic priest. Witnesses were: **A.B. Coco**, **Philogene Coco** and **Landry Bordelon**.

   In the 1870 census, Avit (24) and Lida (21) appeared with one son, **Miles** (3), and seemed to be living near Long Bridge, LA (JacqAug1870).

   Avit and Ludy appear in the 1880 census with the following children: **Modella** (8), **Loval** (5), **Samuel** (3), **Oliver** (1) and **Jack** (10) (1880 U.S. Census).   It is not clear if Jack was the same person as Miles, who appeared in the 1870 census.

o   Avit married a widow, **Clara Dupas,** on January 18, 1893 (AvitClaraMarr). The wedding was performed by Minister of the Gospel, **Eli Johnson**. Witnesses were: **Adolph D. Augustine; Marsalan Augustine** and **Frank Marsalan**.

o   Avit appeared in the 1900 census as a widowed 60-year-old. Living with him were 3 sons: **Modella** (23), **Giles** (18) and **Loval** (16) and 1 daughter, **Clara** (10).

o   Avit married **Susan Allison** on December 13, 1905 (AvitSusanMarr). The Catholic wedding was performed by **Father J.E. Chauvin**. Witnesses were: **L.B. Lavalais, Celestin Prevot** and **Abel Francisco**.

o   Avit married **Jane Lavalais** on October 10, 1923 (AvitJaneMarr). The service was performed by **Reverand Wiliam L. Blackman**. Witnesses were: **Ernestine Blackman** and **Pilger Blackman**.

Avit died in Moreauville, LA on April 22, 1935 at the age of 95.

Avit's confirmed children were:

o   **Jack** (b. 1870) - No other information found.
o   **Modella** (b. 1872) – Married **Louise James,**
o   **Giles** (b. 1872) – Married **Emma Titus**
o   **Loval** (b. 1875) – No other informatin found.
o   **Samuel** (b. 1877) – Married **Sedonia Sampson**
o   **Oliver** (b. 1879) – Married **Marie Antoinette Berzat**
o   **Clara** (b. 1890) – Died as a teenager.

- **Andre Augustin** was born on July 8, 1845 and baptized by his mother, Constance, as shown in **Table 2**. He was listed as a 5-year-old who was sold, along with his mother, Constance, and her other children, as part of the Lemoine probate sale discussed above, to Ceran Gremillion (**See Table 1**).

---

[47] Augustine family history

Andre' married **Marie Louise "Louisa"** [Unknown Last Name] on April 21, 1870.

Andre' (27) and Louisa (22) appeared in the 1870 U.S. Census for Avoyelles Parish (AndrAug1870). Shown residing with them was their 1-year old son, **Dervin**, and 2 farm laborers: **Lucille (40)** and **Ophelia (24)**, as well as a 7-year old boy, **Aaron**. Their house was located next door to his brother, Jean Pierre II, and 2 houses away from his father, Ursin Augustin, Sr.

Andre' was named as one of Ursin Augustin Sr.'s living children in the 1871 property succession discussed above (See Footnote 23).

The 1880 U.S. census appears to show a family living on Bayou des Glaises that could be Andre's (AndAug1880). It, unfortunately, only listed the people surveyed by last names and first initials:

o   "A" = Andre'(39),
o   "L" = Louisa (28),
o   "A" =**??** (M/10),
o   "L" =**??** (M/8),
o   "J" =**??** (M/4), and
o   "U" =**??** (F/1).

It is not clear when Andre' died.

Louisa (62) next appeared as a widow living near Moreauville, LA in the 1910 U.S. Census for Avoyelles Parish (LouAug1910). Living with her were the following: Her son, **Dorsin Augustin** (41) and his wife, **Offelia** (30), her three Augustin granddaughters: (**Alma E.H.** (5), **Emly V.E.** (3) **and Ethyl E.C.**) and another granddaughter, **Lily V. Scott** (12).

There are no further records of Andre', Louisa, Dervin, Lucille, Ophelia, or Aaron.

- **Celestin Augustin** was born in 1848 and was a 2-year-old boy at the time of the Zenon Lemoine probate sale. He was sold along with his mother to Ceran Gremillion.

No further records of Celestin Augustin were found.

- **Josephine Augustin,** who was born in 1860, did not appear in the Zenon Lemoine succession since she was not born at the time (1880 U.S. Census). She was claimed as Ursin Augustin Sr's child in his Act of Acknowledgement.

She (20) and her husband, **Alfred Carmouche** (26), appeared in the 1880 census (1880 U.S. Census). They appeared to be living near Grande Ecore, outside of Mansura, LA. They were living next door to her brother, **Jean Pierre Augustin II,** and his family.

In the 1900 census, Josephine and Alfred were living in the town of Mansura, LA (I. U. Census). Living with them were: their single sons, **Marius** (21) and **Joseph Carmouche** (17), their niece, **Marcea Etrecia** (8) and Josephine's father, **Ursin Augustine, Sr.** (100). They had been married for 29 years and had 4 living children. Not shown was their son, **Paul Carmouche**, who had married **Izaline Brandte** on December 7, 1897 (AvitClaraMarr).

In the 1910 census, Josephine (59) and Alfred (60) were living alone in Long Bridge or Mansura, LA (U. C. Bureau). Josephine died on January 10, 1934 in Mansura at the age of 82. Alfred died on February 12, 1943 in Mansura at the age of 89.

- **Ursin II** is named in Ursin Augustin, Sr.'s Act of Acknowledgement, as his child with **Manette Sylvert** (UrsAugAck). Unfortunately, there are no further records of Manette either during or after slavery.

   Since Ursin II was not a child of Constance Desire and Ursin, Sr., he must not have been on the same plantation (Zenon Lemoine) as they were. **Further study is needed to determine who his parents were and what became of him.**

   The St. Paul records show a marriage between Ursin Augustin and **Fannie Harris** in a Catholic ceremony on August 22, 1867 in Avoyelles Parish, LA (UrsJrMarr). The evidence proving that this was Ursin II is not conclusive[48].

   No further records of them were found.

Ursin Augustine Sr. died on October 5, 1901 and is buried in St. Paul's Catholic Church Cemetery, Mansura (M. Bordelon, Ursin Augustine, Sr.). His descendants include most of the African-American families in and around Mansura.

****

I.   Jean Pierre Augustin Sr.

Ursin Augustin, Sr. and Jean Pierre Augustin, Sr. were brothers. It is not clear when or on which plantation they were held together or who their parents were. Since they each ended up on different plantations as adults, one or both of them had to have been sold during their early life.

Much less information about Jean Pierre Sr. is available than on Ursin Sr. For example, Jean Pierre Sr. was known to have been a slave on the plantation owned by **Dorcino Armand** at the end of the Civil War (JPAugCourt). However, it is not clear whether or not he was held on any other plantations, such as the Pierre Normand plantation, where his wife, **Felicite'** was being held.

However, based on bits and pieces of information, it is possible to put together a framework to describe both their lives to some degree.

---

[48] There are, unfortunately, several records of Ursins during the period from 1866 to 1870. Some are conflicting.

Still, much additional work is needed to further determine who his family was, both during and after slavery, which plantation was he held on, was he really Ursin's brother, who were there parents, etc.

The Slave Holders of Jean Pierre, Sr. and Felicite'

As in the case of Ursin Augustin Sr., it is important and informative to review who the people holding Jean Pierre Sr., his wife, Felicite' and their families in captivity were. These are reviewed below:

- ## Dorcino Armand

    Jean Pierre Augustin Sr. was held as a slave on a plantation owned by **Dorcino Armand** at the end of the Civil War. There are no clear records of Jean Pierre Sr., prior to then.

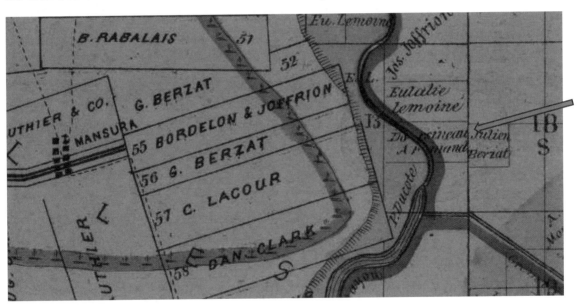

FIGURE 15. MAP SHOWING LOCATION OF DORCINO ARMAND PLANTATION (S. B. ROBERTSON)

Dorcineau "Dorcin" Armand II was born on February 15, 1827 in Louisiana (DorArm1850). His parents were **Dorcineau Armand I** (1807-1860) and **Eulalie Dufour** (1813-1860) (DorArmII). He married **Emeline "Meline" Lemoine** on February 16, 1847 in Avoyelles (DorArmMarr).

Dorsin Armand is listed as having served in the Confederate Army as a private with the 1st Field Battery, Louisiana Artillery (DorArmWar).

In the 1860 U.S. census for Avoyelles Parish, LA, **Dorcain** (33) and Meline (32) Armand were listed along with the following children: **Leonard** (11), **Josephine** (9), **Ebrard** (5), **Alfred** (3) and **Angelina** (7 Months). They were farmers, living on 80 acres of land that was just north of Boutte du Bayou, about two miles east of Mansura, LA (DorArmLand). Their real estate was valued at $30,000.

They were listed as holding 29 slaves in captivity in 1860 (DorArmSlaves). Those slaves ranged in ages from 1 to 60 and consisted of 15 males and 14 females. This included 14 children ages 10 and below. The slaves were housed in 6 "Slave Houses".

Meline Armand died in 1870, in Avoyelles Parish, LA (DorArmII).

Dorsineau Armand II died on October 20, 1893 in Bordelonville, LA (DorArmII).

- ## The Normands

Felicite', Jean Pierre Augustin, Sr.'s wife, was held captive on the **Pierre Normand** Plantation, located on Bayou des Glaisess near Moreauville, LA, where she remained until after the Civil War (See **Figure 1**).

FIGURE 16. MAP SHOWING ONE OF PIERRE NORMAND'S PLANTATIONS (S. B. ROBERTSON)

As described in detail in *Back Through the Veil* (Prier), the Normand family of Avoyelles Parish were a prominent local family whose wealth and social position was based on the use of slave labor. The original Avoyelles Parish Normands were **Jean Pierre Normand** and his wife, **Marguerite Vicnair**, who arrived during the late 1700s. They eventually had five children (bettyebridges81):

- o **Francoise** (1767-1848);
- o **Justine** (1769-1855);
- o **Pierre** (1774-1846);
- o **Laurent** (1780-1842);
- o **Jean Baptiste** (1791-1803).

Pierre Normand married **Irene Marie Joffrion**. They had three children, including **Pierre Belizaire Normand**, and held at least ten slaves.

44

Pierre Belizaire Normand (a.k.a. **Pierre Normand, Jr.**) was born in Avoyelles Parish on March 3, 1799. He married **Lucille Lemoine** on June 28, 1825. They had five children:

o **Pierre III**;
o **Claire**;
o **Clarisse**;
o **Clara**;
o **Alcide**

By 1830, Pierre Normand, Jr. and his wife were holding 40 slaves on their farm north of Moreauville. They later purchased additional land between Boutte de Bayou and Bayou des Glaises, near Moreauville.

The St. Paul Baptismal Records lists six slaves being baptized by Pierre Normand, Jr. (See **Table 3**). Two of those, **Jean** and **Ursin,** were mothered by Jean Pierre Augustin Sr.'s future wife, **Felicite'**:

TABLE 3. PIERRE NORMAND SLAVE BAPTISMS (A. R. DUCOTE)

Child Name	Date of Birth	Father	Mother	Godfather	Godmother
Jean	8/11/1832	Not Listed	**Felicite'**	Octave	Seraphine
Roselle	11/15/1832	Not Listed	Emelie	Williston	Marie
Jean	June, 1833	Francois	Unk.	Sylvain	Salie
Paulin	8/3/1837	Not Listed	Marie	Joseph Lafond	Lucille Lemoine
Ursin	1/16/1838	Not Listed	**Felicite'**	Paulin	Marie
Marinette	3/16/1838	Not Listed	Azelie	Williston	Marie

In an 1847 record of the Pierre Norman family, 22 slaves were listed along with their ages and value (M. Normand). These are shown in Table 4 below:

TABLE 4. PIERRE NORMAND PROPERTY INVENTORY

Slave Name	M/F	Age	$$
Frederick	M	55	800
Melie (Wife)	F	55	200
Tim	M	22	700
Rosette	F	14	400
Paulin	M	33	600
Marie	F	24	1100
Paulin	M	9	
Meline	F	5	
Marceline	F	3	
Pauline	F	18 Months	
Willis	M	38	600
Aselie (Wife)	F	32	
Marienette	F	9	
Bazile	M	7	
Clementine	F	3	
Severine	F	1	
Silvan	M	17	600
Felicite'	F	44	700
Urlin [Ursin]	M	9	

Celestine	F	16	500
Jean Pierre	M	15	450
Eliza	F	38	500
Joe	M	35	550
Simon	M	40	600

Included in that slave inventory were Felicite' and her two children, **Jean Pierre Jr.** (15) and **Ursin Jr.** (9).

Felicite's child, Ursin Jr., apparently remained there in slavery until after the war (See below) (JPAugCourt).

Her other son, Jean Pierre Jr., must have died while still being held in slavery.

The Lives of Jean Pierre Sr. and Felicite' Augustin

Jean Pierre Augustin Sr. – Jean Pierre Sr. was born about 1808 (JPAugDeath). He was held as a slave on the Dorcino Armand plantation until slavery ended at the conclusion of the Civil War.

His information was not included in the 1870 census, that was the first one that collected information on all free people in the U.S., including former slaves. As a result, we know little about his early life.

Most of the information regarding Jean Pierre Augustin Sr.'s life was provided in testimony given in the 1881 Avoyelles Parish trial, *"Ursin Augustin, fils et al. versus A.L. Boyer."* (JPAugCourt)

Felicite' Augustin – Felicite', based on her age in **Table 4**, was born around 1803. As indicated in **Table 3** and **Table 4**, she gave birth to and baptized two children, Jean Pierre II (b. 1832) and Ursin Jr. (b. 1838).

The testimony in the above-mentioned property dispute confirmed that Jean Pierre Augustin Sr. and Felicite' had two children: **Jean Pierre, Jr.**, who died in 1861, and **Ursin Jr.**, who was still alive in 1881.

Jean Pierre Augustin Sr. and Felicite' were married on August 15, 1866, the year following the end of slavery (JPAugMarr). An important entry in that record is that **Felicite' was referred to as the widow of Joseph[49]**.

Felicite' Augustin died sometimes during the year 1872 and was buried at Sacred Heart Catholic Church in Moreauville, LA (FelAugDeath).

---

[49] No records have been found indicating who Joseph might have been.

The Property Dispute - That suit involved Ursin Augustin Jr., Jean Pierre Augustin Sr.'s son, and some of his siblings, in a dispute regarding who was the true owner of the land on which Jean Pierre Augustin Sr. had lived and died after slavery was over.

Some of those providing written testimony were: Ursin Augustin Sr., Ursin Augustin Jr., and Pierre P. and Alcide H. Normand (Pierre Belizaire Normand's sons).

Here are some of the key points from that testimony:

- Jean Pierre Augustin Sr. was a former slave of Dorcino Armand;
- He was also known as: "Jean Augustin", "Jean Gustin" and "Old Gustin";
- He was married to Felicite', a woman who was formerly a slave of Pierre Belizaire Normand;
- He was the person who purchased a parcel of land on Bayou des Glaises from **J.M.M.B. Lacour**. That land was located behind **Mary Gremillion**.
- His son, Ursin Augustin Jr., was living with Jean Pierre Augustin Sr., at the time of Jean Pierre Sr.'s death. He continued to live on that land for "a few years" and then moved away.
- Jean Pierre Augustin Sr. died on the land in dispute in 1870.

Additional Information on Jean Pierre Augustin Sr. was discovered in court records completed following his death. Here, he was described by a woman named **Rosette Frederick** and by Ursin Augustin Jr., as having been married to Rosette at some point and that they had two minor children, **Marcelin** and **Harry**, at the time of his death (JPASucc). In sworn court documents, Rosette and Ursin Augustin Jr. swore to act as undertutors to those two minor children.

Some additional study located Marcelin and Harry living north of Mansura with a family headed by **Robert** (35) and **Rosette** (40) **Rogers** in 1870 (HenAug1870). That family included the following children: **Augustin Augustin** (16), **Frederick Augustin** (14), **Marcelin** Augustin (12), **Henry**[50] **Augustin** (11) and **Marie Augustin** (6). The regular age spread among the children strongly suggested that they must be siblings. They were living next door to a family headed by **James Frederick** (45), who could have been Rosette [Frederick's] brother.

Rosette Roger's age here (40) is a reasonable match for the age that the slave child, Rosette, in **Table 4** would be in 1870 (37), indicating that **they are likely the same person**.

Also, Rosette would have been 24 when the oldest of those children, **Augustin**, was born. This made it **possible for her to be the mother of all of the children** living with her and her husband, Robert Rogers in 1870.

Since we already know that Rosette and Jean Pierre Sr. were the parents of Marcelin and Harry, it seems reasonable that **they were the parents of Augustin and Frederick**, as well. Marie remains a mystery.

The Other Children of Jean Pierre Augustin Sr.

---

[50] Further study demonstrated that Harry and Henry Augustin were the same person (RosRog1870).

The later records of those children living with Robert and Rosette Rogers reveal the following information:

- **Marcelin Augustin** – Marcelin Augustin (55) and his wife, **Alice Pierre** (48), appeared in the 1910 U.S. census for Avoyelles Parish, Ward 8 (Moreauville/Plaucheville), along with their seven children (MarcAug1910): **Rose** (18), **Maggie** (16), **Esebel** (15), **Adolph** (12), **Lena** (11), **Evylina** (8), **Alice** (5), and **Enice Williams**. Also residing them were **Enice** William's children: **Mary Anne** (8), **Booker T** (6), **Cleveland** (5), **Ada** (4), "**W. Krikes**" (2) and a 1-month-old, unnamed baby girl.

  In 1920, Marcelin (65) and Alice (59) were still living in Ward 8 (MarAug1920). Living with them were their four daughters: **Isabel** (24), **Evalina** (18), **Alice** (15) and **Lina** (21), who was married. Also present were Lina's four children: **Mary Mathers** (19), **Booker T Mathers** (16), **Charened Mathers** (15, **Ada Mathers** (12) and **Colvilber Mathers** (10).

- **Harry/Henry Augustin** – In the 1880 U.S. census, Robert (32) and Rosette (48) Rogers were living just north of Mansura (HenAug1880). Living with them were his stepson, **Harry Augustin**[51] (19), and his stepdaughter, **Mary Jacobs** (14).

  Henry Augustin (39) and his wife, Lucille (39) appeared in the 1900 U.S. Census for Avoyelles (HenAug1900). They were living along Bayou des Glaises between Moreauville and Bordelonville. Living with them were the following children: **Marie** (13), **Joseph** (13), **Pierre** (12), **Rose** (9), **Otis** (6), **Wade** (4), **Winnie** (3) and **Lola** (2).

  Henry Augustin became the father of most of the Augustines residing in Moreauville and Borodino.

- **Augustin Augustin** – It is not clear what became of Augustin Augustin.

- **Frederick Augustin** – In the 1900 U.S. census, Frederick Augustin (43) and his wife, **Melina** (40) were farmers, living either near or inside the town of Mansura, LA (FredAug1900). Living with them were his cousin, **Octavie Landor** (20) and a servant, **Louis Williams** (15).

Jean Pierre Sr. died in April, 1870 from "Dropsy of the heart" (JPAugDeath). This was, unfortunately, without having his information included in any U.S. census records, especially the 1870 which was the first one that contained specific information about former slaves. Ursin Sr., on the other hand, lived into the 20th century and is recorded in the 1900 census.

[51] Note the name change from Henry to Harry!!

Current Status

The Augustine family of Avoyelles Parish is one of the largest African-American families in the area and has remained so since its members first appeared well before the U.S. Civil War.

Over the years, the name, "Augustin" (Pronounced **Oh Geese Tan**) was changed to Augustine (Pronounced **Aug us teen**) by adding the "e".

Through intermarrying with numerous other families, the Augustine family tree is now broad and has branches in many other locations, both outside of Avoyelles Parish and outside the state of Louisiana.

The Augustines can generally be described as 1) Hardworking people, who don't mind doing what it takes to get the job done; 2) Humble and fun-loving, with religious affiliation an important aspect of their lives and 3) Outdoorsmen, where every generation makes sure that their children learn the basic hunting and fishing skills needed to survive off the land.

While the Augustines had always been basic farmers, more recently, they have branched out into other areas including construction, education, manufacturing, transportation, and the U.S. military.

What began as a group of generally uneducated slave farmers has grown into a family that can claim many productive citizens with numerous college graduates, several with advanced degrees.

Augustine Family Pictures

Children of Modella & Eloise Augustine

Alvin Augustine

Edna Augustine Sampson
(100th Birthday)

Bayou Noir, Near Mansura, LA

One of the many lakes, bayous and rivers that exist in the near vicinity of Mansura. A wide variety of fish and other animals can be found in these.

Chapter 3.
The Batiste Family

Clarice Gaspard Jean Batiste(ClarJBte)

An Introduction to the Batiste Family

Like many of the other, African-American names, the Batiste name has gone through several changes over the past century and a half, beginning as "Jeanbaptiste" and transitioning to "Jeanbattis", "Jean Baptiste", "John Baptiste", "Jean Bte", "Baptiste" and, finally, "Batiste".

During the days of the slave trade, several slaves were recorded in Louisiana with the name, Jean Baptiste (Hall). For example, a four-year-old boy was purchased by Jean Rabalais, Sr. of Avoyelles Parish, along with his mother in 1814 for $825. Unfortunately, there is no information available to connect those people with the Jeanbaptiste or Batiste family of today.

Generally speaking, no recorded history could be found to connect the Batiste family to slavery in Avoyelles Parish.

In any case, the Jean Baptiste family that will be studied in this work began in Mansura, Louisiana with the marriage of Joseph Jean Baptiste in 1878. This marriage date is late by comparison to many of the other families (i.e. during the 5-10 years following the Civil War). Also. Their children were born from 1876 to 1907, much later than other families in this book. A consequence of this is that, while up to four generations of the other families are profiled here, only three generations of the Jean Baptiste/Batiste family can be completed without running into privacy issues[52].

Many of the early Jean Baptiste family members remained in the Mansura area but at least two of Joseph and Clarice's children made their homes in the Hickory Hill area, west of Marksville. Eventually, family members moved to all parts of the country and traveled the world.

Historical Highlights

The Lives of Joseph and Clarice Jean Baptiste

A few bits of information that might be connected to the history of the Batiste family have accumulated over the years. These items will be reviewed below.

Joseph Jean Baptiste

- The earliest confirmed people with the **Jeanbaptiste** surname in the Avoyelles Parish area were **Joseph Jeanbaptiste** and his wife, **Clarisse Gaspard**.

- **Joseph *Emile* Jean Baptist** was born in Avoyelles Parish, LA around 1845 (Brown). Some family members attempted to show that he was of Native-American descent[53].

- He is believed to be the child of **Joseph Hypolite Jean Baptiste** (1829-1917) and **Marguerite** [Last Name Unknown] (1830-1878) (lanie1956). No public or church records have been found to verify this, however.

- A Union soldier named Joseph Jean Baptiste from Louisiana served as a private in Company B, 6th Regiment, of the Louisiana Infantry (Colored) during the Civil War (JosJBteWar). Again, there are no records to verify that this is Joseph Jean Baptiste from Mansura, LA.

Clarisse Gaspard

- Little recorded information exists on who Clarisse Gaspard was and where she came from.
- She was remembered by her granddaughter, **Sarah Batiste Prevot**, as a mulatto who had hair down her back[54].

---

[52] DISCLAIMER: A critical constriction used in presenting information in this work is to avoid profiling individuals who might still be alive or whose information might be considered private or personal by some.
[53] Based on family information provided by Arnold Prevot.
[54] From eye witness account provided to Arnold Prevot by his mother, Sarah Batiste Prevot, Clarice's granddaughter.

- Clarice's mother, **Isabel Stephens**, is believed to have had a child by a white man, possibly a slave holder[55].

The Lives of Joseph and Clarisse Jean Baptiste

Joseph Jean Baptiste married **Clarice Gaspard**[56] on December, 14, 1878 in Avoyelles Parish, LA (JosClarMarr). They eventually became the parents of at least 15 (!) children. This resulted in a very large number of descendants who likely married into or were associated with, nearly every other black family in Avoyelles Parish.

Joseph Jean Bte. (35) and **Clarice** (17), appeared in the 1880 U.S. census for Mansura, LA (JoJBte1880) . Living with them were their son, **Joseph Jr.** (4), and their daughter, **Marie** (10 months). Joseph was described as Black while Clarice was described as a Mulatto. Also, living with them were his divorced mother-in-law, **Isabel Stephens** (34) and his two brothers-in-law: **Simeon Stephens** (21) and **Joseph Stephens** (13). Both Joseph and Clarice indicated that their parents were born in Louisiana[57].

In the1900 U.S. Census for Avoyelles Parish, Joseph **John Bte** (55) and his wife, Clarisse (38), appeared as farmers, living in, or near, the town of Mansura, LA (JosClar1900). Living with Joseph and Clarisse was their daughter, **Maria** (16), and their eight sons: **Martinus** (18), **Edward** (15), **Clebert** (13), **Hernendez** (9), **Hamilton** (7), **Jules** (4), **Julice** (2) and **Theophile** (2).

In the 1910 U.S. Census, Joseph (65) and Clarisse (45) **Jeanbattis** were living in the town of Mansura, LA (JosClar1910). Living with them were their three daughters: **Victoria** (7), **Reginia** (5) and **Isabela** (1) and their seven sons: **Louis** (a.k.a. **Hernandez**)[58] (20), **Hamilton** (18), **Jules** (15), **Julius** (12), **Theophile** (10), **Plaurent** (8) and **Ambroise** (3). Their sons, **Joseph, Jr., Martinus, Edward** and **Clebert** and their daughter, **Maria Jean**, were now married and living elsewhere (See below).

Joseph Jean Baptiste died on September 12, 1911 in Mansura, LA at the age of 67 (JosJBteDeath).

Clarisse Gaspard Batiste died in Mansura, LA on November 6, 1940 at the age of 78 (ClarBatDeath).

The Children of Joseph and Clarice Jean Baptiste

Joseph and Clarice Jean Baptiste appear to have had the following 15 children over their 33 years of marriage. The profiles of each of their children are shown below, in the order of their births:

---

[55] Based on personal research conducted by Arnold Prevot.
[56] There is very little recorded information on Clarisse Gaspard.
[57] It's not clear why Clarice was a Gaspard while her mother and siblings were Stephens.
[58] When their ages are compared from 1900 to 1910, Hernandez and Louis appear to be the same person.

- **Charles Joseph, Jr.** was born in Avoyelles Parish on June 24, 1876. He appeared in the 1880 U.S. census for Avoyelles Parish as a 4-year-old child living with his parents (JoJBte1880).

He married **Marie Jacobs** in Avoyelles Parish on December 1, 1898 (JosMarJBte).

In the 1910 census, **Joseph Jeanbattis** (36) and his wife, **Maria** (28) were farmers who had been married 10 years (1900) and had had 4 children, all still living (JosMar19010). Living with them were the following children: **Preston** (9), **Eola** (5), **Elcie** (4) and **Alice** (2).

In the 1920 census, Joseph (45) and Marie (44) were living in Ward 3 of Avoyelles Parish, east of Mansura (JosMarJr1920). Living with them were the following children: **Preston** (19), **Eola** (14), **Elsa** (13), **Mabel** (8), **Carrie** (7) and **Celina** (3)[59].

In the 1930 U.S. census, Joseph (55) and Marie (50) were living in the northern part of Ward 3, north of Mansura (Likely Grande Bayou) (JosMar1930). Living with them were their five daughters: **Elsie** (22), **Mabel** (18), **Carrie** (14), **Celine** (13) and **Mary** (7). Also present was their two-year-old grandchild, **Rollin Francisco** (2).

It is not clear when or where Joseph and Maria Jean Baptiste died.

The children of Joseph and Maria were as follows:

- **Preston Joseph** (b. 1900)[60]
- **Eola** (b. 1906),
- **Elsie** (b. 1907),
- **Mabel** (b. 1912),
- **Carrie** (b. 1913)
- **Celine** (b. 1917) and
- **Mary** (b. 1923)

- **Martinus,** a.k.a. **Martin,** was born in Avoyelles Parish, LA in 1882 (JosClar1900). He married **Eunice Oliver** in 1903. He registered for the WWI draft, indicating that he was a married farmer living in Mansura LA (MarBatDraft).

In 1920, **Martin Jean Baptist** (43) was living with his wife, **Eunice** (37), in Grande Bayou, on the northeast side of Mansura, LA (MarEun1920). Living with them were the following children: **Mathew** (14), **Octavia** (10), **Lena** (8), **Winston** (6), **Irma** (4), **Alice** (2) and **Dennis** (9 months).

In 1930, Martin J (50) and Eunice (45) Baptiste were living near Grand Bayou (MarEun1930). They had been married 27 years. Living with them were the following children: **Lena** (20), **Joseph** (17), **Annie** (14), **Dennis** (10), **Paul** (8) and **Josephine** (4).

Martin Jean Baptiste died on December 21, 1961 in Mansura, LA (MatBapDeath).

---

[59] Not clear what became of Alice.
[60] **Preston Joseph Batiste** (1900 – 1982), married **Pauline Mayeux** (1903 - 1984) (PresBat). They became the ancestors of many of the Baptistes in the Marksville and Hickory Hill, LA area.

The children of Martin and Eunice were as follows:

- o **Mathew** (b. 1906),
- o **Octavia** (b. 1910),
- o **Lena** (b. 1912),
- o **Winston/Joseph**[61] (b. 1914),
- o **Annie/Irma**[62] (b. 1916),
- o **Alice** (b.1918),
- o **Dennis** (b. 1920),
- o **Paul** (b. 1922) and
- o **Josephine** (b. 1926)

- **Edward** was born about 1883 in Mansura LA (JosClar1900). He married **Alice Jacob** from Marksville, LA.

  He registered for the World War I draft on September 12,1918, where he indicated that he was a married farmer and that his home was in Marksville, LA (EdBatDraft).

  In the 1920 U.S. Census, Edward (37) and **Alicia** (35) were living on Hickory Hill Road, west of Marksville, LA (EdAli1920). They owned their land and both could read and write. Living with them was a 3.5-year-old orphan. They don't appear to have had children of their own.

  Alice Batiste died on July 25, 1984 in Marksville, LA and is buried in St. Richards Cemetery in Hickory Hill, LA (AliBatDeath).

  Edward Batiste died on July 4, 1974 and is buried in St. Paul the Apostle Cemetery in Mansura (J. Bordelon).

- **Maria** was born in Avoyelles Parish, LA in 1884 (JosClar1900). She married **Ferrier St. Romain** around 1903 (MarFerStR1930).

  In 1910, Ferrier (25) and Marie (24) were farmers living next to her brother, Joseph Jeanbattis, near Mansura, LA (MarFer1910). Living with them were the following children: **Boston** (4), **Etta** (3), **Mary** (2) and **Clarence** (0).

  In 1920, Ferrier (33) and Maria (31) were farmers living on the west side of Mansura, LA (MarFer1920). Living with them were the following children: **Eta** (10), **Corine** (10), **Clarence** (14), **Leonor** (9), **Matilda** (7), **Rosina** (2), **Majesca** (3), **Levonia** (5) and **Clara** (1).

---

[61] These seem to be the same person, based on their ages. Further study is needed.
[62] These seem to be the same person, based on their ages. Further study is needed.

In 1930, Ferrier (47) and Maria (45) had the following children living with them: **Mathilde** (20), **Leonard** (18), **Majesca** (16), **Rosena** (14), **Lovenia** (11), **Clarise** (10), **Laura** (7) and **Dorothy** (5) (MarFer1930).

Maria Jean Baptiste died on November 16, 1937 and is buried in St. Paul the Apostle Cemetery in Mansura, LA.

Ferrier St. Romain died on November 5, 1970 and is buried in St. Paul the Apostle Cemetery in Mansura, LA.

The children of Ferrier and Maria St. Romain were as follows:

o **Boston** (b. 1906),
o **Etta** (b. 1907),
o **Mary** (b. 1908),
o **Clarence** (b. 1910),
o **Leonard** (b. 1912),
o **Mathilda** (b. 1913),
o **Rosina** (b. 1916),
o **Majesca** (b. 1917),
o **Lovenia** (b.1919),
o **Clarise** (b. 1920),
o **Laura** (b. 1923) and
o **Dorothy** (1925)

- **Clebert** was born in Mansura, LA in March, 1887 (Topalicia). He appeared in the 1900 U.S. census, along with his parents, Joseph and Clarisse Jean Baptiste (JosClar1900). He married **Rosa Lavalais** in Avoyelles Parish, the daughter of **Fulgence Lavalais** and **Fannie Coco** (Topalicia).

In the 1920 U.S. census, Clebert (35) and Rosa (25) were living near the Mansura-Hessmer highway (ClebRos1920). Living with them were the following children: **Vinson** (7), **Ruffus** (4), **Milborn** (3) and **Leonard** (10 months). Also, living with them was Clebert's brother, **Jules** (21).

Rosa L. Batiste died in Avoyelles Parish on January 28, 1934 (RosaBatDeath).

In the 1940 U.S. census, Clebert (53) was a single parent[63], living on the Cottonport Highway, inside the town of Mansura, LA (ClebBat1940). Living with him were the following children: **Vinson** (27), **Rufus** (25), **Milburn** (23), **Fulgencio** (21), **Leroy** (19), **Ester** (17), **Narin** (15), **Curtis** (13) and **Clebert, Jr** (7).

Clebert Batiste died in Mansura, LA on January 28, 1948 (ClebBatdeath).

Clebert and Rosa's children were as follows"

o **Vinson** (b. 1913),

[63] Rosa had passed away in 1934

- o **Rufus** (b/ 1915),
- o **Milburn** (b. 1917),
- o **Leonard/Fulgencio**[64] (b. 1919),
- o **Leroy** (b. 1921),
- o **Ester** (b. 1923),
- o **Narin** (b. 1925),
- o **Curtis** (b. 1927) and
- o **Clebert, Jr.** (b. 1933).

- **Hernendez** was born in April, 1891 and appeared in the 1900 U.S. Census for Avoyelles Parish as a 9-year-old, living with his parents, Joseph and Clarisse Jean Baptiste (JosClar1900).

  As indicated in the footnotes, Hernandez seems to be the same person as **Louis**, who was listed in the 1910 U.S. census, as a 20-year-old. That is the same age that Hernandez would have been in 1910. There were no further records of Hernandez.

  In the 1920 U.S. census, **Louis Batiste** (27) and his wife, **Clara Jacob** (25), were listed as living near Marksville (LouBat1920). Living with them were their daughter, **Bertha** (3) and their son, **Bascom** (1).

  In the 1930 U.S. census, Louis (38) and Clara (37) were living north of Mansura, LA (LouBat1930). Living with them were the following children: **Bertha** (13), **Bascom** (11), **Louisa** (10), **Albert** (7) and **Louis** (3).

  In the 1940 U.S. census, Clara (46) was listed as a widow living outside of Marksville, LA (ClarBat1940). Living with her were **Bascom** (21), **Albert** (17), **Alton** (13) and **Bertha** (22).

- **Hamilton**, a.k.a. "Tag", was born in Mansura, LA in February, 1893. He appeared as a 7-year-boy, living with his parents in the 1900 U.S. Census for Avoyelles Parish (JosClar1900).

  In the 1910 census, **Hamilton Jean Baptiste** was listed as an 18-year-old single man, living at home with his parents (HamBat1910). He indicated that he could read and write.

  At some point, Hamilton married **Mary Ida Prier**[65]. She passed away at an early date.

  When he registered for the World War I draft, he indicated that he was married, with a wife and two children to support (HamBatWWI).

  In the 1930 U.S. census, Hamilton was a widower, living in the town of Mansura (HamBat1930). Living with him were his five sons: **Roderic** (10), **Bascom** (8), **Cleveland** (6), **Wilson** (4), and **Sims** (2); and his three daughters: **Elma** (14), **Volcie** (12) and **Irene** (3).

---

[64] Seem to be the same person, based on age.
[65] From Oliver Prier family stories.

In 1940, Hamilton (47) had remarried to **Gertrude Barbin** (47) (HamBatSSI) and was living with his mother, **Clarisse Batiste** (89) on the Cottonport Road in Mansura (HamBat1940). Living with them were the following children: **Lodrick** (20), **Lester** (19), **Cleveland** (18), **Wilson** (16), **Irene** (13), **Sims** (12), **Edward** (6), **Paul** (4), **Arthur** (3) and **Table** (1).

Hamilton Batiste died on June 3, 1969 and is buried in St. Paul the Apostle Cemetery in Mansura, LA (HamBatDeath).

Gertrude Barbin Batiste died on June 3, 1972 and is buried in St. Paul the Apostle Cemetery in Mansura, LA (GertBatDeath).

The children of Hamilton and Mary Ida Batiste were as follows:

o **Elma** (b. 1916),
o **Volcie** (b. 1918),
o **Lodrick** (b. 1920),
o **Bascom** (b. 1922),
o **Cleveland** (b. 1924),
o **Wilson** (b. 1926),
o **Irene** (b. 1827) and
o **Sims** (b. 1928).

The children of Hamilton and Gertrude Batiste were as follows:

o **Edward** (b. 1934),
o **Paul** (b. 1936),
o **Arthur** (b.1937) and
o **Table** (b. 1939).

- **Jules** was born in August, 1896 in Mansura, Louisiana. He appeared as a 4-year-boy, living with his parents in the 1900 U.S. Census for Avoyelles Parish (JosClar1900).

  In the 1910 census, Jules Jean Baptiste was listed as a 15-year-old single man, living at home with his parents (HamBat1910). He indicated that he could read but could not write.

  In the 1920 census Jules was listed as a 21-year-old single farmer, living with his brother, Clebert Batiste (ClebRos1920).

  Jules married **Lena Lavalais** in 1921 (JulLenBapMarr).

  In the 1930 census, Jules (34) and Lena (25) were living in Mansura, LA on the Cottonport Road (JulLena1930). Living with them were the following children: **Lillian** (9), **Fannie** (7), **Mercedes** (5), **Dorothy M** (4), **Margaret** (3) and **Thomas** (0).

  In the 1940 census, Jules (45) and Lena (39) were living in Mansura, LA on the Cottonport Highway (JulLen1940). Living with them were the following children: **Fannie** (17), **Mercedes**, (15), **Dorothy** (13), **Margarita** (12), **Thomas** (10), **Marie** (8), **Rose Anne** (6), **Jules Jr.** (4) and **Clyde** (11months).

In the 1954 U.S. City Directory, Jules and Lena Batiste were listed as residing on 9th Street in Alexandria (JulLena1954).

It is not clear where or when Jules or Lena passed away.

The children of Jules and Lena Batiste were as follows:

o **Lillian** (b. 1921),
o **Fannie** (b. 1923),
o **Mercedes** (b. 1925),
o **Dorothy** (b. 1927),
o **Margarita** (b.1928),
o **Thomas** (b. 1930),
o **Marie** (b. 1932),
o **Rose Anne** (b. 1934),
o **Jules Jr.** (b. 1936) and
o **Clyde** (b. 1939).

• **Julice** a.k.a. **Julius** or **Jess,** was born in Mansura in 1898 (JosClar1900). He appeared as a 2-year-boy, living with his parents in the 1900 U.S. Census for Avoyelles Parish (JosClar1900).

In the 1910 census, Julius Jean Baptiste was listed as a 12-year-old single boy, living at home with his parents (HamBat1910). He indicated that he could read and write.

In the 1930 census, Julius Batiste (33) and his wife, **Pauline** [Last Name Unknown] (32) were living in Mansura, LA on the Cottonport Road (JulPauBat1930). Living with them were the following children: **Hilda M** (10), **Paul B** (8), **Inez** (6), **John R** (4), and **Margaret** (1).

In the 1940 census Julius, now called "**Jess**", (43) and Pauline (43), were living in Mansura, LA on the Cottonport Road (JulPaulBat1940). They were living between the homes of Julius' brothers: Clebert and Jules. Living with them were the following children: **Hilda Mae** (20), **Paul** (18), **Inez** (15), **John** (14), **Marguerite** (12), **Victoria** (9), **Sarah Mae** (6) and **Gerald** (2).

Pauline Batiste died on July 23, 1950 in Mansura, LA (PaulBatDeath).

It's not clear where or when "Jesse" Batiste passed away.

The children of Jess and Pauline Batiste were as follows:

o **Hilda Mae** (b. 1920),
o **Paul** (b. 1922),
o **Inez** (b. 1925),
o **John** (b. 1926),
o **Marguerite** (b.1928),
o **Victoria** (1931),

- ○ **Sarah Mae** (b.1934) and
- ○ **Gerald** (b.1938).

- **Theophile** was born in Mansura, LA in 1898. He appeared as a 2-year-old boy in the 1900 U.S. census, along with his parents, Joseph and Clarisse Jean Baptiste (JosClar1900).

  In the 1910 census, Theophile Jeanbattis was listed as a 10-year-old boy, living at home with his parents (HamBat1910). He appeared to be in school at that time.

  On his World War 1 draft registration, he was listed as a single farmer, with his mother as his next-of-kin (TheoBatWW1).

  In the 1920 census, Theophile **Batiste** was described as a 19-year-old mulatto man, farming with his mother and siblings in Mansura, LA (TheoBat1920).

  Theophile married **Carrie Mayeux** of Marksville in 1924 (TheoCarrMarr).

  In the 1930 census, Theophile (30) was listed, along with his wife, Carrie (24), as farmers living west of Marksville, LA (TheoCarBat1930). Living with them were two children: **Leonard** (5) and **Buvens** (3).

  In 1940, Theophile (39) and Carrie (34) were farmers, living west of Marksville, LA (TheoCarr1940). Living with them were the following children: **Leonard** (14), **Byron** (13), **Irvin** (9), **Alan** (6), **Hilary** (4) and **Losie** (1).

  Theophile Batiste died in 1950 and is buried in Holy Ghost Cemetery in Marksville, LA (TheoBatDeath).

  Carrie Batiste died on December 19, 1982 and is buried in Holy Ghost cemetery in Marksville, LA (CarBatDeath).

  The children of Theophile and Carrie Batiste were as follows:

  - ○ **Leonard** (b. 1926),
  - ○ **Byron** (b. 1927),
  - ○ **Irvin** (b. 1931),
  - ○ **Alan** (b. 1934),
  - ○ **Hilary** (b. 1936),
  - ○ **Losie** (b. 1939),
  - ○ **Theresa Ann** (b. 1945),
  - ○ **Barbara** (b. 1947).

- **Plaurent,** a.k.a. "**Condo**", was born in Mansura, LA in 1902. In the 1910 census, He was listed as an 8-year-old boy, living at home with his parents (HamBat1910).

Over time, he appeared to believe that his name was **Florence** (Not **Plaurent**) and changed it to "**Clarence**" to avoid having it sound like a girl's name[66]. To most folks, he was "**Mr. Condo**".

In the 1930 U.S. census for Avoyelles, Clarence (28) and his wife, **Carrie Ann Thomas**[67] (27), appeared as farmers living in Mansura, LA (ClarBatCar1930). They indicated that they had been married 10 years (1920). Living with them were the following children: **Paul** (11), **Raphael** (9), **Stella** (7), **Sybil** (4) **Alice** (2) and **Nora** (1).

Clarence F. Batiste died on December 24, 1972[68].

Carrie Batiste died on March 2, 1982 and is buried in St. Paul Cemetery on Mansura, LA (CarBatDeath).

The children of Condo and Carrie Batiste were as follows:

o **Paul** (b. 1919),
o **Raphael** (b. 1921),
o **Stella** (b. 1923),
o **Sybil** (b. 1926)
o **Alice** (b. 1928)
o **Nora** (b. 1929), and
o **Sarah** (b. 1930).

- **Victoria** was born about 1903 in Mansura, LA and first appeared in the 1910 U.S. census as a 7-year-old girl, along with her parents and siblings (HamBat1910).

In the 1920 census, she was listed as a 16-year-old girl, still living with her parents in Mansura (TheoBat1920).

She married **Prudent Guillory** in about 1918 (VicBatSSN)

In the 1930 U.S. census, Victoria (28) and her husband, Prudent Guillory were shown as living in Ward 4, west of Mansura, in the vicinity of Hessmer (VicJBTe1930). Living with Victoria and Prudent in 1930 were the following children: **Felix** (10), **Mary** (7), **Elizabeth** (5) and **Theresa** (3).

There are no further records of Victoria Jeanbattis Guillory.

The children of Prudent and Victoria Guillory were as follows:

o **Felix** (b. 1920),
o **Mary** (b. 1923),
o **Elizabeth** (b. 1925) and
o **Theresa** (b. 1927).

[66] Batiste Family Story
[67] Carrie Ann's last name provided by Arnold Prevot
[68] Clarences' death date provided by Arnold Prevot

- **Reginia** was born in Mansura, LA in 1905 and appeared in the 1910 U.S. census, along with her parents, Joseph and Clarisse Jeanbattis, and siblings (HamBat1910).

  In the 1920 U.S. census, she was a 15-year-old girl, still living in Mansura with her parents and siblings (TheoBat1920).

  In the 1930 U.S. census, Regina (26) was married to **Joseph Paulin Sampson** (30) and living north of Mansura on the Large Road (RegBat1930). They appear to have gotten married around 1919. Living with them were the following children: **Agnes** (8), **Zeline** (6), **Ambroise** (4), **Arthur H** (3), **Peter** (1) and **Victoria** (0).

  In the 1940 U.S. census, Regina (36) and Joseph (40) were still living on Large Road in Mansura, LA (RegBat1940). Living with them were the following children: **Agnes** (18), **Selina** (16), **Ambrose** (14), **Arthur** (13), **Peter** (11), **Mary Emma** (9), **Marie** (7), **Madgelain** (3) and **Joseph** (1).

  Regina Batiste Sampson died on November 28, 1984 and is buried in St. Paul's cemetery in Mansura, LA (RegBatSamDeath).

  Joseph Paulin Sampson died on April 7, 1985 and is buried in St. Paul's cemetery in Mansura, LA (JosPauSampdeath).

  The children of Joseph and Reginia Sampson were as follows:

  - **Agnes** (b. 1922),
  - **Selina** (b. 1924),
  - **Ambrose** (b. 1926),
  - **Arthur** (b. 1927),
  - **Peter** (b. 1929),
  - **Mary Emma** (b. 1931),
  - **Marie** (b. 1933),
  - **Madgelain** (b. 1937) and
  - **Joseph** (b. 1939).

- **Ambroise** was born in Mansura, LA in 1907. In the 1910 census, Ambroise Jeanbattis was listed as a 3-year-old boy, living at home with his parents (HamBat1910).

  In the 1920 census, Ambrose Batiste was a 13-year-old boy, living with his parents in Mansura (TheoBat1920).

  In the 1930, Ambrose Baptiste (23) and his wife, **Inez** [Last Name Unknown] (23), were living in New Orleans (AmbInezBap1930).

In the 1940, Ambrose (34) and Inez (32) Baptiste were living on Duffosat Street in New Orleans (AmbInez1940).

In 1956, Ambrose and Inez Batiste still lived on Duffosat Street in New Orleans, LA (AmbInez1956). He was listed as a mail clerk for Freeport Sulfur. They had no children.

There are no further records of Ambrose and Inez Batiste.

- **Isabella** was born in Avoyelles Parish in 1909 and appeared as a 1-year-old girl in the 1910 U.S. census with her parents and siblings (HamBat1910).

In the 1920 U.S. census, Isabella, now called **Elizabeth**, (10) appeared with her parents and siblings (TheoBat1920).

No further records of her were found.

Current Status

The Batiste family of Avoyelles Parish, is one of the largest African-American families in the area. Interestingly, despite their large size today, their records do not go nearly as far back into slavery as those of others.

The Batistes have always been a family of hard working farmers, many owning their own land (i.e., versus sharecropping). More recently, members of the Batiste family can be found pursuing successful careers in diverse areas such as education, medical, law enforcement and the military.

The Batiste family began in Mansura, Louisiana and spread throughout the parish. Eventually, members traveled to other parishes such as Rapides and East Baton Rouge; and states such as Oklahoma, Florida and Texas.

Batiste Family Pictures

Clarence & Carrie Batiste

Down the Hill
From the Old River Road Side [Today]

For nearly 100 years, the top of that hill was lined with small, wood-frames houses where former slaves and their families lived. Those houses ringed the large farms that lay behind them and stretched as far as the main street in Mansura.

Access to the houses required a make-shift stairstep that consisted of posts, driven into the ground, side-by-side. A board was then nailed on top of each pair of posts, creating a step. A set of these steps was built from the bottom level to the top of the hill.

Chapter 4:
The Luc and Berzat Families

Luke and Agnes Berzat

An Introduction to the Luc and Berzat Families

Several African-American families in the Mansura area include the Lucs and Berzats as their ancestors. The name "Luc" disappeared during the first half of the 20th century. However, the Berzat name remains and has spread to other parishes and states, as well[69].

---

[69] There were other groups of Berzats living in the Cocoville and Mansura area during the mid-late 1800s. Most of those were listed as mulattoes who were Free People of Color during slavery (GabBerz1870), (JulBerz1850). Their relationship to the current Berzat family is unclear (Berz1870). Some will be briefly discussed in the chapter on the Demouy family.

The Berzat and Luc families are presented together here due to the early marriage of **Josephine Luc** and **Jean Baptiste Berzat** in 1869. Any remaining Lucs were absorbed into other families. A majority of both the Berzats and Luc descendants are the products of that marriage.

----

1. The Luc Family

Historical Highlights

Josephine Luc's father, **Joseph Luc**, was born in Louisiana in about 1816 and his father was a slave brought from Africa (JosLuc1900). His early wife and Josephine's mother, **Victoire**, was also a slave in the Mansura, LA area, although little is known about her.

There are only recorded bits of information that might be linked to Joseph Luc in slavery:

- At the death of **Justine Normand** of Cocoville in 1865, a probate sale was held on June 4, 1865 to dispose of her property (JosLucSale1). Included in that sale were four slaves: **Eulalie** (50), **Joseph** (46), **Daniel** (14) and **George** (15). This Joseph was sold to **George Berlin**, a local slave holder who held 20 slaves in 1860 (GeoBer1860). This Joseph would have been born around **1819**, based on his age at the time of the sale, a date that was also close to that of Joseph Luc's stated birth date, in **1816**.

  This are the only recorded example of a slave named Joseph who fell into the same age group as Joseph Luc. It is quite possible that this Joseph would later become Joseph Luc. Unfortunately, there is no further recorded evidence linking him to this or any other plantation. **Further work is needed here.**

- The most important information regarding Joseph Luc and his life during slavery comes from oral history that was provided by his daughter, **Josephine Luc** (See Below). Josephine was fortunate enough to have lived from the 1840s, during slavery, until the 1940's when she was over 100 years old. This resulted in her interacting with many people during her life to whom she told her life story.

  Some of the key pieces of information provided by Josephine about her family are as follows:
  - She clearly remembered that her mother was a slave named **Victoire**;
  - Victoire made sure that Josephine knew that her father was a slave named **Joseph**;
  - Although Joseph was on different plantations, Victoire made sure that Josephine always knew where he was;
  - Once slavery was over, Josephine was reunited with her father and joined him in adding the last name, Luc.

Using Josephine's information as a starting point, it became possible to search for more information regarding her mother, Victoire. Since the Berzats were known for their dedication to the Catholic Church, it seemed reasonable to search the baptismal records of St. Paul the Apostle Catholic Church in Mansura for Victoire (A. R. Ducote).

As it turned out, the church baptismal records contain many instances of the name "Victoire" in various roles including Child, Mother or Godmother. **Table 5** includes only those cases where "Victoire" was the **mother** having her child being baptized.

TABLE 5. CHILDREN BAPTIZED WITH VICTOIRE AS THEIR MOTHER

No.	Slave Baptized	Mother	Birthday	Slave Holder	Godfather	Godmother
1	Ulalie	**Victoire**	3/26/1839	Augustin Mayeux	Norbet, Slave of Augustin Mayeux	Marie, Slave of Pierre Normand, Jr.
2	Octave	**Victoire**	Oct., 1838	Lucien Joffrion	Francois, Slave of Wd. Antoine Bordelon	Melie, Slave of Lucien Joffrion
3	Marie Arseire (??)	**Victoire**	8/20/1844	Lucien Joffrion	Unknown	Unknown
4	**Josephine**	**Victoire**	5/9/1837	Marceline Dufour	Achille (Slave)	Manette (Slave)
5	Jean Baptiste	**Victoire**	6/8/1836	Wd. Pierre Bordelon	George Baron	Delphine Lacour
6	Charles	**Victoire**	10/24/1831	Lucien Joffrion	Basile, Slave of Lucien Joffrion	Elizabeth, Slave of Lucien Joffrion
7	Bastien	**Victoire**	5/19/1836	Unknown	Jacques, Slave of Felix Marcotte	Rosette, Slave of Felix Marcotte
8	Azelie	**Victoire**	9/7/1844	Augustin Mayeux	Unknown	Unknown
9	Adelina	**Victoire**	3/20/1832	Lucien Joffrion	Jean Baptiste (slave)	Josephine (slave)

As can be seen on **Line 4** of **Table 5**, there is only one case where a newborn slave named Josephine had a mother named Victoire. In that case, the slave mother was being held captive by **Marceline Dufour**, a local planter and slave holder. The godparents, **Achille** and **Manette** had no listed slave holders.

The baby's birth date was listed as 5/9/1837. Josephine Luc Berzat indicated to the 1870 census takers that her birth year was about 1840 (JBBerzat1870). Since few slaves had any means to keep track of the passage of time, that three-year difference in birth years is not unusual and the two numbers can be considered to be the same.

Thus, it is very likely that Josephine, the child of Victoire in the birth records, is, in fact, Josephine Luc Berzat.

Joseph Luc's Family

Since Joseph Luc was about 50 years old when slavery ended, there are no records showing him with a wife and a family of young children. However, in order to gather together anyone who might be his children, it appeared reasonable to identify those people using the unusual last name, **Luc**, and assume they might be his relatives.

As it turned out, several people appeared in the various records in Avoyelles Parish with the last name, Luc. Since Joseph Luc was the oldest of them, it is reasonable to investigate the possibility that they might be related to him, possibly his children.

Based on a comparison of his age to these others in the Mansura area with the same last names, Luc or Luke, Joseph's family is proposed to be as shown in **Table 6**:

TABLE 6. "PROPOSED" JOSEPH LUC SLAVE FAMILY

Relation to Joseph	Identity	Birth	Reference
Father	Unknown African	Unknown Time or Place	(JosLuc1900).
Mother	Unknown African	Unknown Time or Place	(JosLuc1900).
Joseph Luc	Self	1816	(JosLuc1900).
Slave Spouse	**Victoire** (Slave)	Unknown Time or Place	Family History[70]
Child	Josephine Luc	1840	(JBBerzat1870),
Child	Francois Luc	1845	(FranLuk1900),
Child	Jean Baptiste Luc	1847	(Luc 1870 - Takers)
Child	Marguerite Luc	1855	(Luc 1870 - Takers)

Joseph's parents were listed as born in Africa but with no recorded name in the 1900 census (JosLuc1900).

Victoire is assumed to be his only slave wife, although that was rarely the case for many slave men.

The "Luc Children" shown in **Table 6** (i.e. Josephine Luc, Francois Luc, Jean Baptiste Luc and Marguerite Luc) can be profiled from later recorded information, as shown below:

- **Josephine Luc** was born about 1840 in Louisiana (JBBerzat1870). She was the daughter of **Joseph Luc** and a slave woman, **Victoire** (See Above). As indicated above, she was held, along with her mother, Victoire, on a plantation owned by Marceline Dufour.

  The dramatic story of Josephine Luc's escape from the plantation at the end of slavery was told in *Back to the Veil* (Prier):

  > In that story[71], the slaves were alerted that slavery was over by the ringing of the bells and much shouting and celebration. As Josephine attempted to run past the slave holder's house with her 4-year-old daughter, **Victorine**, the slave holder's wife attempted to stop them and ordered her to return to do her duty, which was to comb the slave holder's wife's hair. Josephine refused and, instead, raised the back of her dress and told the woman to "Kiss!". She then fled with the rest of the slaves.

- **Francois Luc** was born around 1845 in Louisiana. No records have been found indicating which slave plantation he might have been held on[72].

  Francois' age (i.e. born in 1845), compared to Joseph Luc (i.e. born in 1816), suggests that he could be Joseph's son (See Above).

---

[70] Josephine Luc lived into the 1940's. Her son, Luke Berzat, and her daughter, Victorine, both lived into the 1960's and 1970's. They communicated their stories with people who remain alive today.
[71] Story provided by Mary Bernell Augustine Prier from her family history
[72] Francois was one of the more common slave names who were baptized at St. Paul's, making it difficult to identify a specific person.

Francois was shown in the 1900 census as a 55-year-old single man, living in the town of Mansura and working as a servant to Jean Chauvin (FranLuc1900). At that time, his name was spelled "**Luke**". There are no records of his marriage or children.

No additional public records on Francois Luc were found in this study.

----

o **Jean Baptiste Luc** was born about 1847 in Louisiana (Luc 1870 - Takers). No additional records were found indicating which plantation he might have been held on.

Just as in the case of Francois, above, his age difference from Joseph Luc makes it possible for him to be Joseph's son.

Jean Baptiste Luc appeared as a 23-year-old man in the 1870 U.S. census as a part of Joseph Luc's family.

He married **Irma Dupas** in Avoyelles Parish on February 15, 1872 (JeanBteIrmaDupMarr).

In 1880, Jean Bte (31) and Irma (26) were living near Cocoville, LA along with their three children: **Rosina** (7), **Francois** (5) and **Jean Baptiste** (1).

Jean Baptiste Luc died on August 6, 1885 and is buried in St. Paul the Apostle Catholic Cemetery in Mansura (StPaulBurIV).

Rosina Luc died on March 27, 1904 at the age of 25. She is buried in St. Paul the Apostle Catholic Cemetery in Mansura (StPaulBurV).

No further records of Irma, Francois or Jean Baptiste Luke have been found.

----

o **Marguerite Luc** was born around 1855 in Louisiana (Luc 1870 - Takers). She appeared in the 1870 U.S. census as a 15-year-old girl living in the home of Joseph and Sylvania Luc.

No further records of her were located.

Joseph's Post-Slavery Life

No records were found to indicate what became of Victoire once slavery was over.

Joseph Luc married **Sylvanie Adams** in 1866 and first appeared in public records as a 55-year-old man married to 44-year-old Sylvanie in the 1870 census (Luc 1870 - Takers). Living with them were **Jean Baptiste Luc** (23) and **Marguerite Luc** (14), probably his children, as well as **Melie Adams**

(33) and **Arthemise Adams** (15) possibly her siblings. A 24-year-old, **Eloie Neck**, was also residing with them.

In the 1880 census, Joseph and Sylvanie were living 4 houses away from Joseph's son, Jean Baptiste Luc, and his family in the vicinity of Moreauville (Luc 1880 - Census Takers). Living with them was Sylvanie's 45-year-old sister, **Severine Adams**.

In the 1900 census, Joseph (85) and Sylvanie (68) Luke were living next door to Avit Augustine near Grande Ecore, outside of Mansura (JosLuc1900). Living with them were 3 grandchildren: **Cleophine Luke** (19), **Joseph Laurent** (18) and **Joseph P. Clay** (12). Sylvanie indicated that she had given birth to two children and one was still alive. **In that census, Joseph indicated that his father was born in Africa.**

****

2. The Berzat Family

Historical Highlights

It is important for the readers to know that there were three groups of Berzats in Avoyelles Parish at various times:

- **White Berzats** such as **Edvin** and **Julia Berzat** (EdvBerz1860) who appeared in the 1860 U.S. Census for Avoyelles Parish with their children: **Marie**, **Julien** and **Paulin**.
- **Mulatto Berzats (or Berza)** such as **Julien** and **Edvise Berzat,** who were Free People of Color and appeared in the 1850 U.S. Census for Avoyelles Parish with their children: **Gabriel**, **Julies**, **Theophile**, **Justinien**, **Juliette** and **Mary Jeanne** (JulBerz1850). Some of these were also ancestors to the Demouy family of Mansura (See Later).
- **Black Berzats** – There appear to have been more than one group of black Berzats or Bazarts in Avoyelles Parish around 1900. For example, a group of families who spelled their names, Bazart, were living in Ward 1, located in the Northwestern portion of Avoyelles parish (bazarts1900). Those families were headed by the following:

  - **Joseph Bazart** (34). Living with him was his brother, **Harvey Bazart** (23) and his female cousin, **Aurrellia Bazart** (34);

  - **Sarah Bazart** (56). Living with her was her daughter, **Annett Bazart** (19) and three sons: **William** (30), **Samuel** (17) and **Joseph** (7).

While there currently are a few families in the Mansura area with the last name, Bazart or Bazert, it is not clear whether or not they are related to the families listed above. **Additional study is needed here.**

In the Mansura area, the group that began with the marriage of Jean Baptiste Berzat and Josephine Luc (and their parents) will be discussed in this book. The other groups are outside the scope of this work.

Jean Baptiste Berzat

Jean Baptiste Berzat was born in 1815 in Avoyelles Parish, Louisiana (MissMercy). He was the son of **Julien M. Berzat**, FMC (1791 – 1855) and **Edvise Joffrion**, FWC (1806 – 1860) (See Above).

Jean Baptiste Berzat served in the Union Army's United States Colored Infantry under the alias, John Grimes during the Civil War (JBBerzat).

Jean Baptiste and Josephine's Life

Jean Baptiste Berzat and **Josephine Luc** were married by a Catholic priest on December 5, 1869 (JBTE_JosMarriage). As part of their marriage, they declared four children to be their own: **Victorine** (8), **Victor** (6), **Jean Baptiste** (2), and **Mary Delphine** (Infant).

In the 1870 U.S. census, Josephine appeared as a 30-year-old woman married to Jean Baptiste Berzat, a 55-year-old black male (JBBerzat1870). They were living just west of *Boutte du Bayou*, about 2 miles from Mansura (Robertson). They had four children living with them: **Victorine** (9), **Victor** (7), **Berzat,** (3) and **Delphine** (1). Also living with them was an 18-year-old black male, **Louis** [**Berzat**], who turned out to be Jean Baptiste's oldest child[73].

Josephine and Jean Baptiste appeared in the 1880 census (JBBerzat1880), living about 6 miles west of Mansura[74], near the current city of Hessmer (Robertson). Living with them were the following children: **Victorine** (17), **Victor** (15), **Berzat** (12), **Delphine** (10), **Josephine** (7), **Heloise** (6), **Luc** (a.k.a. "**Luke**" (3)), and **Antarnette** (5 months).

Josephine was last listed in the 1940 U.S. census, living in Mansura, LA with her son, **Luke Berzat** and his family (JosBerz1940). She was listed as being 103 years old.

Josephine died on October 30, 1941 and is buried in St, Paul the Apostle Catholic Cemetery in Mansura (JosBerDeath).

Jean Baptiste and Josephine Berzat's Children

---

[73]From Family History provided by Leanna Augustine Sampson.
[74] Based on proximity to Zenon Laborde's farm in 1880 census and on Library of Congress Map of Avoyelles Parish, 1879.

As indicated above, Jean Baptiste Berzat and Josephine Luc were the parents of eight children: **Victorine, Victor, Berzat, Delphine, Josephine, Heloise, Luc** (a.k.a. **"Luke"**), and **Antarnette**. Each of these will be profiled below:

- **Victorine Berzat** was born in 1861 (VicBerzMag1870). She married **Gervais Arnat Magloire** on May 19, 1881 (JosLucJBBerzMarriage).

  Gervais Arnat Magloire was born in Avoyelles Parish, Louisiana in about 1841, the son of **Joseph Magloire** and **Celestine Gabriel** (JoMagMarr) (See **McGlory Chapter**).

  Gervais and Victorine had the following children: **Helen** (Born:1881), **Victoria Beulah** (Born:1884), **Joseph Armond** (Born:1886) and **Lula** (a.k.a. **Ola**, Born:1888).

  Below is a continuation of an interesting, although tragic, story regarding Gervais and Victorine that was in the Introduction to this book. This story began during the late 19th century and continued well into the 20th century[75]:

  > *During the early 1890's, Gervais and Victorine were farmers, living in Mansura with their four children on property that they owned. One night, their home was attacked by a group of white thugs wearing hoods. Their family was chased from their home and forced to hide in the cotton fields to avoid being beaten or killed.*

  > *Gervais managed to escape with his two older girls, Helen and Victoria, and ended up in **Rodney, Jefferson County, Mississippi**. Victorine and her two children, Joseph and Lula, hid in the cotton field for several days before she was eventually found by her brother, Luke Berzat and taken to his home.*

  > *In 1900 (JosMcG1900Census), Gervais was listed in Jefferson County, Mississippi as **Joseph McGlery** (39) and married to **Mary Smith** (30)[76]. They shared a home with his two children: **Ellen** (18) and **Victera** (16); Mary's two children: **Estella** (12) and **Joseph Smith** (10); and their two children: **Rebecca** (6) and **Ernestine McGlery** (5).*

  > *In 1910, **Joseph Magloria**, now a widower, still resided in Rodney, Mississippi (JosMag1910). Residing with him were his three daughters: Ellen (27), Ernestine (12) and Rebecca Magloria (14); his son, **A.V. Magloria** (13) and his nephew, **Walter Selistine** (18).*

  > *A family history story told of how Joseph's son, A.V. (?) left for work one day and never returned[77]. No one ever knew if he had been attacked or had simply run away.*

  > *Victoria, now called **Beulah** (Or "Tee Tant Toy") and a widow, had returned to Mansura and was living with her brother, Armand (22), her mother, Victorine (50), and her sister, Ola (16) (VicMag1910).*

  > *Helen returned to Mansura sometime after 1910. She married **Poland Guillory** in 1917 (HelPolGuil1920). She died on July 2, 1967 in Mansura.*

---

[75] This story was repeated by the descendants of both Gervais Magloire and Victorine Berzat. The reader will likely notice the striking similarities between this story and that of Sylvain, described in the introduction to this book. These stories appear to be the same one, however, described from two different perspectives: the white writers for the Times Picayune and the families of the victims. The different names cited, Sylvain versus Gervais, could have occurred due to writer's errors or purposely done by the families of Gervais Magloire to protect him.

[76] The two Smith children could be from an earlier marriage, suggesting that her name at the time she married Joseph was **Smith**.

[77] Family history provided by Mary Bernell Augustine Prier.

Victoria (Tee Tant Toy) married **Eddie Hollis** *and lived in Mansura near the corner of the "Large Lane" and L'Eglise Street until her death on June 27, 1964* (VicHolDeath).

Lula (a.k.a. Ola) married **Willie Walter** *and remained in Mansura until her death on March 15, 1969.*

Gervais never returned to Louisiana.

- **Victor Berzat** was born in Louisiana in about 1863 (JBBerzat1870). He married **Mary Barker** on November 29, 1888 in Avoyelles Parish, Louisiana (VicBerMarMarriage).

Victor died on November 28, 1891 at the age of 28 and was buried in St. Paul the Apostle Catholic Cemetery in Mansura (StPaulBurV).

No further public records were found of Victor or Mary Berzat and whether or not they had children.

- **Berzat** was born in Avoyelles Parish, Louisiana in about 1868 (JBBerzat1870).

In the 1870 U.S. Census, Jean Bte and Josephine had a 3-year old son listed as "**Berzat**" whose age was between Victor (7) and Delphine (1). In the 1880 census, they are listed with a 12-year-old son named "**Jean Batiste**" whose age is between Victor (15) and Delphine (10). Although this appears to be good evidence that Berzat and Jean Baptiste are the same person, family history refutes this. The belief is that Berzat grew up and moved to Donaldsonville, Louisiana. **Further study is needed here.**

No further records were found on either Berzat Berzat or Jean Baptiste Berzat.

- **Delphine Berzat** was born in 1869 in Mansura (JBBerzat1870). She last appeared in public records while still living with her parents in 1880 (JBBerz1880). No additional records of her were found.

- **Josephine Berzat** who was named after her mother, was born in 1873 in Mansura (JBBerz1880). She died on August 28, 1891 in Mansura at the age of 19 (StPaulBurV). No records of her being married or having children were found.

- **Heloise**, a.k.a. **Eloise, Berzat** was born in Mansura, Louisiana in 1874 (JBBerz1880). She married **Joseph V. Barker** in 1895 and became the mother of six girls: **Celise, Ozite, Zoe, Annielou, Eva** and **Niefae Barker** (OlivAug1910).

In 1900, Joseph (30) and "Louisa" (22) were living near Mansura, Louisiana with three children: Celise (3), Ozide (2) and Zoe (3/12) (JoeHel1900).

In 1910, Joseph (37) and Eloise (34) were still living in Mansura and had the following six children: Celise (14), Ozite (12), Zoe (9), Annielou (6), Eva (5) and Niefae (3) (JoeHel1910).

It is not clear what became of Heloise. However. Joseph Barker married **Agnes Bailey** in Ellis Texas on November 27, 1927 (JosAgnMarr).

In 1930 (JosAg1930), Joe (63) and Agnes (32) were living in Ellis, Texas with the following children: Her two Bailey children, **Velma** (8) and **N. B.** (6) and his four Barker children, **Celie** (1.5), **Price** (1month), **Carrie** (14) and **Eva** (18). Also, living there was his niece, **Sarah Jones**.

Joseph V.T. Barker died in Precinct 3, Ellis, TX on May 10, 1930 (JosBarDeath).

- **Luc "Luke" Berzat** was born in Mansura about 1877 (JBBerz1880). In 1900, he was a 23-year old, single head of household, living inside the town of Mansura. Boarding with him were four farm laborers: **Milly Knight** (B/F, 64, Boarder); **Josephine Knight** (B/F, 18, Boarder); **Mack Winfield** (B/M, 40, Boarder) and **Josephine Herron** (B/F, 25, Boarder).

Luke married **Agnes Barker,** the daughter of **Alfred** and **Artemise Barker**, in 1904. In 1910, they were farmers living in the vicinity of Grande Ecore, near Mansura (LukAgBer1910). Living with them were their four-year old twins, **Lefron** and **Joy**, their son, **Paul** (1) and Luke's mother, **Josephine [Berzat]** (70).

Eventually, Luke and Agnes' family included the following children:

- o **Lefron**, (b. 1907),
- o **Dolfrey**, (b. 1909),
- o **Paul**, (b. 1910),
- o **Johnson**, (b. 1911),
- o **Lucas**, (b. 1915),
- o **Pearl**, (b. 1918),
- o **Ambroise**, (b.1921),
- o **Anthony**, (b. 1922),
- o **Gerome**, (b. 1923) and
- o **Agne**s, (b. 1927).

All of their children could read and write and were involved in the community, including the church and local sports. Dolfrey Berzat is remembered as "**Professor Berzat**", one of the teachers at the Mansura Colored Convent School during the 1930s[78].

Agnes Berzat, a.k.a. "*Taunt Ah Got*" was well remembered for her selling concessions during the local baseball games[79]. There are two beliefs regarding how she acquired her nickname: (1) That it was the French pronunciation of Agnes or (2) She got the nickname, "Ah Got" by calling out during the game: "Ah got candy", "Ah got popcorn", etc.

Luke, a.k.a. "*Nonk Luc*" was a fixture as a member of Our Lady of Prompt Succor's ushers. He died on October 12, 1961 and is buried in St. Paul the Apostle Catholic Cemetery (LukBerzDeath).

Agnes Berzat died in Mansura LA on December 7, 1971 and is buried in Saint Paul the Apostle Catholic Cemetery in Mansura, LA (AgBerzDeath).

---

[78] Leanna Sampson
[79] Story told to Mary Bernell Augustine Prier by her mother, Laura Augustine.

D.G. Prier

- **Marie Antarnette Berzat** [80] was born in 1884 in Mansura, Louisiana (JBBerzat1880). She married **Oliver "Kit" Augustine** in 1906 (OlivAug1910).

  In 1910, Oliver (31) and Mary (26) were farmers, living near Mansura, LA (MarBer1910). Living with them were their two children: **LeRoy** (3) and **McGoldrick** (2 months).

  In 1920, Oliver (42) and Marie (36) were farmers, living just east of Mansura, LA (MarBer1920). Living with them were the following children: Leroy (12), Mack (10), **Alverda** (8), **Zeline** (5) and **Isabella** (1).

  By 1930, Oliver (53) and Mary (46) were farmers, living east of Mansura, LA on Rabalais Lane (MarBer1930). Living with them were the following: Mcglory (21), Zeline (15), Isobel (11), **Alvin** (9) and **Leanna** (7). Oliver's brother, **Giles Agustine** and his wife, **Emma**, lived next door. Their son, LeRoy and his wife, Irene, lived a few houses away.

  Mary Antarnette Augustine died on February 17, 1967 and is buried in St. Paul the Apostle Catholic Cemetery in Mansura, LA.

  Oliver Augustine died in 1981 and is buried in St. Paul the Apostle Catholic Cemetery in Mansura, LA.

  Oliver and Mary children were as follows:

  o **Leroy** (b. 1908),
  o **McGlory** (b. 1910),
  o **Alverda** (b. 1912),
  o **Zeline** (b. 1915)
  o **Isabella** (b. 1919) and
  o **Leanna** (b. 1923).

Current Status

Over the past few decades, the name, "Luc" has generally vanished from the Mansura, LA area.

The early members of the Berzat family were active leaders in many aspects of the Mansura community, playing roles such as farmers, athletes, educators and religious leaders.

The Berzat name is largely gone from the area. Some members who still bear that name have generally taken up residence in other parishes or states.

And yet, many families in the Mansura area can claim the Lucs and Berzats as ancestors including the Augustines, Sampsons, Blackmans, Murrays and others.

---

[80] In some of the other records, Antarnette was called either Marie or Mary. This suggests that her name may have been **Marie Antarnette**.

Berzat Family Pictures

Victoria Berzat

Dolfrey Berzat and Family

Long Bride, a small community that lay at the bottom of the Mansura bluff, found itself at the bottom of a large lake during the flood of 1927.

In this picture, boats can be seen in the distance transporting refugees to land and the waiting rescue vehicles lined up there.

Thanks to Charles Riddle for Use of Tarver Flood Pictures

Chapter 5.
The Blackman Family

Rev. William L. Blackman

An Introduction to the Blackman family

The Blackman family took root in Avoyelles Parish later than other families due to Nathan Blackman's late arrival there. Nevertheless, they quickly became one of the premier black families of Mansura during the nineteenth and twentieth centuries due to their early leadership within the black community. They provided faith, knowledge and pride via their activity in religion, education, civil rights and land ownership.

Historical Highlights

Nathan Blackman was born in **North Carolina** in May, 1850 (NBlkmn1900). He married **Anna Carter** on February 23, 1871 in Avoyelles parish (NatBlaMarriage). She was born in **North Carolina** in 1854. Both indicated that their parents were born in **North Carolina**.

Nathan (50) and his wife, **Mary A.** (46), appeared in the 1900 census for Avoyelles Parish, living near Moreauville (NBlkmn1900). They were listed as farmers who had been married for 29 years[81]. Mary said that she had given birth to 12 children and 8 remained alive.

---

[81] Because 29 years from 1900 is 1871, the year that Nathan and Anna were married, it is very likely that Anna Carter and Mary A. Blackman are the same person.

Their children living with them included 2 sons: **Thomas** (20) and **Benjamin** (12); their daughter, **Ida** (9); also, their married daughter, **May** (22), her husband, **James Randall**, and their 2 children: **Pinkey** (2) and **Edna** (4 months).

In 1910, Nathan Blackman appeared as a 65-year-old man, living with his son, **Henry Blackman** (38) and Henry's wife, **Emma** (34) (NBlkmn1910).

No public records of Nathan or Anna's deaths were found for this study.

Nathan and Anna Blackman's Children:

James Henry Blackman

Henry was born in 1872. He (28) and his wife, **Emma Robertson** (26) appeared in the 1900 census for Avoyelles Parish (HenBlkmn1900). He was listed as "**J.H. Blackman**" and they were described as farmers living in the Grande Ecore area, east of Mansura. They had been married for 8 years (HenEmmMarr). They had 2 daughters: **Lou Anna** (7) and **Darris** (1); and 3 sons: **Shedrick** (4), **Kirby** (3), and **John** (2). Also residing with them was a 64-year-old boarder named **Henry Clay**.

In 1910, Henry and Emma had 4 sons listed: **Shattric** (15), **Kirby** (14), **Darius** (11), and **Pury** (4 months) (NBlkmn1910). They were farmers and had been married for 19 years. Emma indicated that she had had 6 children and 5 survived. Both parents could read and write. Henry's father, Nathan Blackman, was living with them.

Henry (47) and Emma (40) appeared in the 1920 census for Avoyelles Parish (HenBlkmn1920). They were listed as living on the Long Bridge Road, east of Mansura. Living with them was a girl, **Dorris** (21) and a boy, **Pury** (10). Henry indicated that his father (Nathan) was born in **North Carolina**.

In 1930, Henry and Emma were shown living on a farm near Boutte du Bayou on what was called "Rabalais Land" by the census taker (HenBlkmn1930). Living with them was their son, Pury (20), and his wife, **Alverda** (18). Once more, Henry indicated that his father, Nathan, was born in North Carolina. Living next door to them were **Oliver** and **Mary Augustine** and Henry's nephew, **Pilger**, and his wife, **Beatrice**.

Pury Blackman married **Alverta Augustine**. He became a very well-known and respected carpenter and builder in the area.

William Blackman, a.k.a. **William L. Blackman,** was born in 1875. In 1910, William (35) and his wife, **Mary Jane Augustine** (31), were living next door to Henry Blackman, William's brother (WLBlkmn1910). They appeared to be living near Grande Ecore or Boutte du Bayou, east of Mansura. They were farmers and had been married 12 years. Mary Jane indicated that she had had 4 children and 2 were living: i.e. **Philger** (9) and **Cleophas** (6), who were living with them. Both parents could read and write.

In 1920, William (45) and Mary Jane (41) were living in the Grande Ecore or Boutte du Bayou area of Mansura (WLBlmn1920). They were home owners and he listed his occupation as "Baptist Minister". He indicated both his parents were born in North Carolina. Living with them were their 2 sons, **Pilger** (19) and **Cleophas** (16), and their daughter, **Betsy** (4). Also living with them was Mary Jane's widowed mother, **Elizabeth Augustine** (70).

William Blackman, throughout his life, was a strong leader in the areas of agriculture, Baptist ministry, education, and civil rights. He was pastor at **St. Paul Baptist Church** in Marksville, **Jerusalem Baptist Church** in Mansura, and **Little Zion Baptist Church** in Long Bridge. Mary Jane Blackman was a well-known and respected educator and church leader in the parish (Blackman).

Their children, **Pilger, Cleophas,** and **Betsy Ann** followed in their parents' footsteps, graduating from college and becoming community leaders in the areas of ministry, farming, construction, civil rights, and education (Blackman):

o **Reverend Pilger Blackman** married **Beatrice Barron** and had a very distinguished career as a minister in the area, especially as pastor of Little Zion Baptist Church in Long Bridge.

o **Cleophas Blackman** married **Carrie Augustine** and became a successful local farmer and carpenter.

o **Betsy Ann Blackman** married **S.L. Bonton.** She became a very well-known and respected educator.

May Blackman, a.k.a. **Mary,** was born in Louisiana in 1878. She married **James Randall** on July 17, 1897 (MayBlaMarr). In the 1900 U.S. census, May (22) and James (35) were living with her parents near Moreauville, LA. They had been married for four years and had two children with them: **Pinkey** (2) and **Edna** (4 months).

In 1910, James (44) and May S. Randall (31) were farmers, living near Moreauville, LA (JamMayRan1910). Living with them were the following children: **Pinky Ann** (11), **Ednis** (10), **Galornize** (8), **James T** (7), **Earl** (5), **Misseck** (5), **Alvorance** (4) **Alice** (3) and **Mabel** (1).

In 1920, James (36) and Mary (32) were living near Moreauville LA (JamMayRan1920). Living with them were the following children: **Edna** (20), **Godonize** (18), **Joseph** (16), **Nussik** (15), **Earl** (15), **Alice** (12), **Mable** (10), **Herman** (8), **Maud** (6) and **Leltry** (5).

In 1930, James J. (64) and Mary S (62) were living north of Bayou des Glaises, near Moreauville, LA (JamMarRan1930). Only one child, their daughter, **Feltry** (18), remained at home.

Thus, the children of James and May Randall were as follows:

o **Pinky Ann** (b. 1899),
o **Edna** (b. 1900),
o **Galornize** (b. 1902),
o **Joseph** (b. 1903),

- o **Earl** (b. 1905),
- o **Messeck** (b. 1905),
- o **Alvorance** (b. 1906)
- o **Alice** (b. 1907),
- o **Mabel** (b. 1909,
- o **Herman** (b. 1912),
- o **Maud** (b. 1914) and
- o **Feltry** (b. 1915).

Thomas Blackman was born in Louisiana and first appeared in the U.S. census in 1900, while still living with his parents (NBlkmn1900). Here, based on his age at that time, his calculated birth year was 1880.

It is not clear what became of Thomas Blackman.

Benjamin Blackman was born in 1888 and appeared as a 12-year-old in the 1900 U.S. census, living with his parents (NBlkmn1900).

In 1910, Benjamin (24) and his wife, **Rosa Joshua** (22), were farmers living near Moreauville, LA (BenBla1910). He indicated this was his and Rosa' first marriage each and they had been married for three years. Living with them were their two daughters: **Cleo** (1.5) and **Navel** (2 months).

In his World War I Draft Registration, Benjamin said that his race was "African" and that he was married and farming for **Fred Scallan** of Mansura (BenBlaWWI). He also said he had a wife and children depending on him.

In 1920, Ben (34) and Rose (33) were living on Long Bridge road near Moreauville, LA (BenBla1920). Living with them were the following children: **Cleo** (12), **Navel** (10), **Windell** (6), **Maple** (4) and **Murry** (2).

In 1930, Ben (43) and Rose (42) were farmers, living near Moreauville, LA (BenBla1930). Living with them were the following children: **Cleo** (22), **Navel** (20), **Mindel** (16), **Maple** (14) **Murry** (12), **Windall** (10), **Benjamin** (8), **Pharston** (6), **Elgrie** (4), and **Garrison** (2). Also living with them was **Lomea Joshua** (65), Rose's widowed mother.

In 1940, Ben (53) and Rose (52) were living in the unincorporated area called Long Bridge, LA (BenBla1940). Living with them were the following children: **Windall** (26), **Benjamin** (18), **Pharston** (16), **Elgrie** (14), **Garrison** (12) and **Edwina** (9).

Ben and Rose's children were as follows:

- **Cleo** (b. 1908),
- **Navel** (b. 1910),
- **Mindel** (b. 1914),

- **Maple** (b. 1916),
- **Murry** (b. 1918),
- **Windall** (b. 1920),
- **Benjamin** (b. 1922),
- **Pharston** (b. 1924),
- **Elgrie** (b. 1926),
- **Garrison** (b. 1928) and
- **Edwina** (b. 1931).

Ida Blackman was born 1891and appeared in the 1900 U.S. census along with her parents. It is not clear what became of her.

Current Status

The Blackman family of Mansura had its beginning in North Carolina, finally arriving in the Mansura area and starting a family after the end of the Civil War. They brought a spirit of vision and leadership to the community that has persisted to this day.

Though few in numbers, they are very visible in the local community through their involvement in the church, local politics and community activities.

Blackman Family Pictures

William, Mary Jane, Pilger, Cleophas and Betsy Ann Blackman

Henry and Emma Blackman and Family

Bayou Tassin as it looks today

Topographical Map Showing Location of St. Paul Church, Catholic Cemetery on Old River Road, Bayou Tassin that Ran Through "Down the Hill" and Old River.

Chapter 6.
The Demouy Family

ARTHUR DEMOUY   LOUISE "ELOISE" DEMOUY

An Introduction to the Demouy Family

The Demouy family of Mansura has been around since the early 1800's. They were Free People of Color and, throughout their early history, owned and farmed land along the road known as the Grande Bayou Lane, north of Mansura.

Their early beginnings can be traced as far back as France. They share parentage with two other well-known families in the area: The **Cadoree** and the **Noguez** families.

The Demouy family members have always been active members of religious organizations, often in leadership roles.

The Demouy family, as it exists today, began with **Louis Demouy** and **Marie Ledeau** around 1850.

Historical Highlights[85]

As discussed in Chapter 1, the state of Louisiana was home to several small pockets of mixed-race people from as early as the late 18th to the early 19th centuries. In Avoyelles Parish, those people included mixtures of African-French, African-Spanish, African-Native Americans, and others.

---

[85] DISCLAIMER: Although the circumstances described in this section are true, there are no specific cases where any of these can be specifically applied to any of the individuals or families described here. However, it is important for the reader to see things as they were then.

Avoyelles Parish held a substantial population of Free People of Color by 1860 that included four Blacks and 46 mulattoes. Many FPC's lived on or near slave plantations and generally performed jobs and had lives that were not much different from the slaves themselves. In some cases, the FPC's were skilled craftsmen such as blacksmiths, carpenters, brick masons, etc. Several owned their own land and a few were slave holders.

Socially, and often physically, mulattoes were caught between two worlds: White and black. In Avoyelles Parish, as in most other areas where large populations of mulattoes lived, they tended to develop their own communities, marry among themselves, and, generally avoided non-work interaction with the black communities. Unfortunately, although they were often children and offspring of members of the nearby white community, they were usually not trusted and shunned by that community.

More complete discussion of these issues is out of the scope of this work. To read more, several books have been published on these topics (Talley), (Gatewood).

It is in this environment that our story of the Demouy (also Cadoree and Noguez) family begins.

Mary Ledeau/LeDeux (1839 – 1899) was believed to have been born in Point Coupee Parish, LA (Cadoree), since several people with the family names, LeDoux, Demouy and Cadoree lived there and in close proximity to each other.

She bore two children prior to her marriage to **Alexandre Noguez** in 1869: **Arthur Demouy** was born in 1852 and, eventually became the earliest documented ancestor to the Demouy family; while **Alcide Cadoree** was born in 1861 and became the earliest documented ancestor of the Cadoree family.

Louis Demouy (1825-1853) was the first person known to have the surname, **Demouy**, in Avoyelles Parish (ArtLouDemMarr). Little is known about him other than that he was born in France (LouDem1). He appears to have had a relationship with Mary Ledeau at some point. From that union, a child, **Arthur Demouy**, was born in 1852 (De Mouy), (LouDem).

Cadoree[86]**,** whose first name has not been identified, appears to be the first person with the surname, Cadoree, in Avoyelles Parish. Nothing is known about him beyond his relationship with Mary Ledeau (ArtLouDemMarr). From that union, a child, **Alcide Cadoree**, was born in 1861. Alcide, and his two wives, i.e. **Minerva Guillot** and **Mary Roberts** are the ancestors of the current Cadoree family.

---

[86] Some references claimed his first name was Cadoree but these have no real factual basis.

Further development of a profile for the Cadoree family is outside the scope of this work.

Alexandre Noguez was a prominent person in Avoyelles Parish in the years following the Civil War (Cadoree). Marie Ledoux and Alexandre gave birth to a girl, **Marie Alexandrine**, in 1865. He married Marie Ledoux in 1869. She brought two children, Arthur Demouy (b. 18520 and Alcide Cadoree (b. 1861) into the marriage.

Alexandre served as the first black sheriff of Avoyelles Parish during that period and was a member of the 1879 Louisiana Constitutional Convention.

The Life of Arthur and Louise Demouy (Cadoree)

Arthur Demouy, the son of Louis Demouy and Mary Ledeau, married **Louise Rocque**[87], who was born in Louisiana, on December 17, 1874 (ArtLouDemMarr).

Louise Rocque (rscott4003) was the daughter of **Gabriel Berzat** and **Marie Chevalier** (See **Berzat Family** in Chapter 4). Gabriel was the son of **Julien Berzat** and **Edvise Joffrion** and brother of **Jean Baptiste Berzat,** ancestor of the Berzat family of Mansura. Marie's family remains unknown.

That marriage was the beginning of the current Demouy family of Avoyelles Parish.

In 1880, Arthur (27) and Louise (24) were farmers living in the Grande Bayou area of Mansura, LA (artdem1880). Living with them were 2 children: **Adolph** (11) and **Elizene** (2).

In 1900, Arthur (47) and Louise (46) were still living in Grande Bayou (artdem1900). Their family had expanded to include the following children: **Adolph** (24), **Elizene** (22), **Henry** (16), **Phillip** (14), **Ella** (12), **George** (11), **Louis** (9), and **Emanuel** (6). They indicated they had been married 25 years and had had 10 children, with 9 surviving[88]. They were farming their own land. Arthur listed his father's place of birth as France and his mother's as Louisiana. Both of Louise's parents were listed as born in Louisiana.

In 1910, Arthur (57) and Louise (54) continued to reside in Grande Bayou (artdem1910). Living with them were the following children: **Ella** (22), **Louis** (18) and **Curtis** (15). Also living with them were 2 granddaughters: **Josephine Berger** (11) and **Rosa Berger** (7).

In 1930, Arthur Demouy (77), now widowed, was living with his son, **Louis Demouy** and Louis' wife, **Irene** (artdem1930). His son, **Adolph**, and family, were living next door.

[87] Some references refer to her as Berzat or Berza. In this work, her name will be Rocque.
[88] It's not clear why only eight are named here.

89

Arthur died on September 3, 1930 in Mansura, LA and is buried in St. Paul Lutheran Cemetery in Mansura, LA.

Louise died on June 19, 1922 in Mansura, LA.

Arthur and Louise Demouy's Children (Cadoree), (michaeldemouy1),

The children of Arthur and Louise Demouy are profiled below:

- **Adolph Joseph Demouy** was born on November 30, 1875 (topalicia). In 1880, Adolph (4) and his sister, **Elizene** (2) were living with their parents, Arthur and Louise Demouy, near Grande Bayou, north of Mansura, LA (artdem1880).

  In 1900, Adolph (24) is still living at home with his parents and seven of his siblings (artdem1900). He was listed as a farm laborer who could read and write.

  In 1904, Adolph married **Margaret "Maggie" Goudeau** (Cadoree).

  In 1910, Adolph (34) and Maggie (35) were living in St. Landry Parish. They had been married 6 years and had three children: **Mary R. (Ruth), Pearl** and **Joseph** (AdolDem1910).

  In 1930, Adolph was living in Avoyelles Parish (AdolDem1930). He was listed as a widow with four daughters: **Pearl** (23), **Blanche** (19), **Louise** (17) and **Agnes** (15).

  In 1940, Joseph/Adolph (64) was listed with two daughters: Pearl (27) and Agnes (22) (ADolDem1940).

  Adolph died on December 26, 1947 (AdolDemDeath).

- **Marie Elizene Demouy** was born on January 1, 1878. She was listed, along with her brother, **Adolph**, living with her parents in the 1880 U.S. census (artdem1880).

  In 1900, Elizene was a single, 22-year-old, farm laborer living with her parents and her seven siblings near Mansura, LA (artdem1900).

  She married **Filmore E. Coco** in 1901.

  In 1910, Elizene (33) had been married to Filmore Coco for nine years (ElizCo). They had had four children and all were alive. Those children were: **Worthie A** (6), **Joseph R.** (5), **Annielou D** (3) and **Filmore E**, Jr. (1 month).

  In 1920, Filmore (44) and Elizene (42) were living in Grande Bayou, north of Mansura (ElizCoc1920). Living with them were the following children: **Wade** (17), **Rodevis** (14), **Lule** (12), **Earl** (10), **Napoleon** (7), **Ethel** (5) and **Simon** (2).

  Marie Elizene Coco died on March 3, 1925 and is buried in St. Paul the Apostle Catholic Cemetery (ElizCocDeath).

Filmore Coco died January 31, 1944 and is buried in St. Paul the Apostle Catholic Cemetery (FilCocDeath).

Filmore and Marie Elizene had the following children:

o **Worthie A** (b. 1904),
o **Joseph R.** (b. 1905),
o **Annielou D** (b. 1907)
o **Filmore E**, Jr. (b. 1910),
o **Napoleon** (b. 1913),
o **Ethel** (b. 1915) and
o **Simon** (b. 1918).

- **Inez Demouy** a.k.a. **Eunice,** was born on July 9, 1880 (jbbarnette153). She married **Pierre Berger** (1875-1902) on November 25, 1897. He passed away on November 23, 1902.

  She married **Scott Normand** (1840 - 1923) on October 6, 1909.

  In 1910, Scott (70) and Eunice (30) were farmers, living in Cocoville, LA (InDem1910). He indicated this was his 3rd marriage while she said this was her second. Living with them were his two step-daughters: **Sybel Berger** (8) and **Ida Berger** (6). Also present was an orphan boy, **Walter Aerr** (16).

  Scott Normand died on October 5, 1923.

  Inez (Eunice) Demouy died in Metairie, LA on September 21, 1950.

- **Henry Demouy**, a.k.a. **Harry Teska** was born in Avoyelles Parish in 1883 (artdem1900). In 1900, Henry T was living at home with his parents.

  He married **Rosina Eloise Berger** (1892 - 1974) in 1905.

  Henry T (29) and Rosina (27) appeared in the 1910 U.S. census, living in Cocoville, LA (HTDemRos1910). They had been married for five years and had had three children, all still alive. Living with them were the following children: **Carlton** (4), **Otis** (2) and **Harry T., Jr.**, (5 months).

  In 1920, Henry (37) and Rosina (37), were farmers, living near Grande Bayou, north of Mansura, LA (HarRozDem1920). Living with them were their four sons and one daughter: **Carlton** (14), **Otis** (13), **Henry Jr.** (10), **Elsom** (7), and **Hazel** (3).

  In 1930, Henry (48) and Rosina (47) were farmers, living near Grande Bayou, in Avoyelles (HenRozDem1930). Living with them were their two children: **Hazel** (13) and **Rosie** (4).

  Henry Demouy died in Alexandria, LA on June 10, 1934 (HarryDemDeath).

  Henry and Rosina had the following children:

  o **Carlton** (b. 1906),
  o **Otis** (b. 1907),

- o **Henry Jr.** (b. 1910),
- o **Elsom** (b. 1913),
- o **Hazel** (b. 1917) and
- o **Rosie** (b. 1924).

- **Phillip Demouy** was born on March 5, 1885 (rscott4003). In 1900, he was a 14-year-old boy, living at home with his parents (artdem1900).

  In 1910, Phillip (25) and his wife, **Josephine**[89] (28), were farmers, living in Okmulgee, Oklahoma (PhilJosDem1910). They had no children.

  In his World War I draft registration, Phillip was a farmer, living in Omulgee, Oklahoma (PhilDemWWI).

  There are no further public records on Phillip Demouy.

  In 1940, Josephine (sic De Morry) was listed as a widow (JosDem1940).

- **Ella Rose** was born in 1887 (rscott4003). In 1900, she was a 13-year-old girl, living with her parents (artdem1900).

  In 1910, she was a 22-year-old living at home with her parents (artdem1910).

  In 1920, Ella (32) and her husband, **Arthur Berger** (29) were living on Liberty Street in New Orleans, Ward 1 (ElArBer1920). Living with them were their two children: **Arthur, Jr.** (3) and **Giselda** (1).

  In 1930, Arthur (40) and Ella (42) Berger were listed in the U.S. Census for New Orleans (EllaArtBer1930). He was listed as a teacher. Living at home with them were the following children: **Anthony** (14), Griselda (10), **Harding** (9) and **Ruby** (7).

  In 1940, Ella (49) and Arthur (49) were living on Allen Street in New Orleans (ArElBer1940). He was a teacher. Living with them were their four children: Grisella (20), Harding (18), Ruby (17) and Arthur Jr. (23). Also present were Arthur Jr.'s wife, **Mary** (21) and their two children: **Wayne** (2) and **Judith** (1).

  Arthur Berger died April 11, 1955 in New Orleans and is buried in Mount Olivet Cemetery and Mausoleum (ElBerDeath).

  Ella Demouy Berger Died on January 28, 1959 in New Orleans and is buried in Mount Olivet Cemetery and Mausoleum (ElBerDeath).

- **George Demouy** was born April 3. 1889 and was listed as living with his parents in 1900 (artdem1900).

  He married **Eunice Coigent** sometime before 1917 (Cadoree).

---

[89] No records of his marriage or who Josephine was, were located.

On his World War draft registration, he had enlisted in Napoleonville, LA (GeoDemDraft). He listed his occupation as Mission Teacher. He said he was married with one child.

In 1920, he was living on Liberty Street in New Orleans with his wife, Eunice, and one child, **Louise** (GeoDem1920). He listed his occupation as "Ship Yards".

In 1930, he and his wife, Eunice, were living on N Tonti Havana Street in New Orleans (GeoDem1930). They had one daughter, Louise, and a son, **Joseph**. He listed his occupation as "Post Office Clerk".

There is no additional public information on George or Eunice Demouy.

- **Louis Ettiene Demouy** was born in Mansura, Louisiana on May 23, 1891 (Topalicia). In 1900, he was living with his parents near Mansura (artdem1900).

In 1910, Louis (18) was living with his parents near Mansura (artdem1910).

Louis married **Irene Prevot** in 1915.

Their son, **Sydney**, was born on September 15, 1916 (Topalicia).

In 1920, Louis (27) and Irene (26) were farmers, living near Mansura (LouIreDem1920). Living with them were their children: **Sidney** (3), **Grace** (2) and **Marshall** (8 months). They were living next door to Louis' parents.

In 1930, Louis (39) and Irene (38) were farmers, living near Mansura, LA (LouIreDem1930). Living with them were the following children: **Sidney** (13), **Grace** (12), **Marshall** (10) and **Louis, Jr.** (2). Also living with them was Louis' father, **Arthur Demouy** (77).

In 1940, Louis (49) and Irene (48) were living in Grande Bayou, north of Mansura (LouIreDem1940). Living with them were the following children: Sidney (23), Grace (22), Marshal (20), Louis Junior (12) and **Germaine** (8).

Irene Marie Prevot Demouy died in Rapides Parish, LA on November 10, 1963 (IreDemDeath).

Louis Ettiene Demouy died on January 15, 1969 (LouDemDeath).

- **Curtis Emanuel Demouy** was born on October 30, 1893 (Mouy). He was listed in the 1900 U.S. Census for Avoyelles Parish while living with parents (artdem1900).

In 1920, Curtis (26) was living with his parents near Mansura, LA (CurDem1920).

In 1930, Curtis Emanuel Demouy had married Alma Goudeau and was listed in the U.S. census for New Orleans (CEDEm1930). Living with them were their two sons, Curtis, Jr. and Jessie E. (Earl); and one daughter, Margie. He listed his occupation as "Grocery Clerk".

In 1940, Curtis and Alma were living on Touro Street in New Orleans along with sons: Curtis, Jr and Jesse; and daughter, Margie (CurtDem1940). He listed his occupation as "Proprietor Clerk" and owned his own home.

Curtis Emanuel Demouy died on April 24 1959 in New Orleans and is buried in Mount Olivet Cemetery, New Orleans, Louisiana.

Current Status

More recently, the Demouy family has gradually moved away from Avoyelles with a few still remaining. Several members became college educated and worked as teachers.

Demouy Family Pictures

George Demouy

Ella Rose Demouy

Adolph Demouy

Ellisanne Demouy

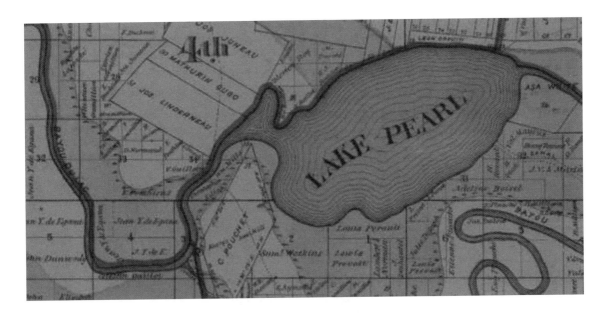

Lake Pearl Pre-Civil War Map (S. Robertson)

Southwestern Edge of Lake Pearl (Today)

Lake Pearl was the site of a large number of pre-Civil War plantations. Many black Mansura families had ancestors who likely were held in captivity near Lake Pearl.

Chapter 7.
The Dupas, Gabriel and Celestine Families

Paulie Celestine, Husband of Mary Dupas

An Introduction to the Dupas, Gabriel and Celestine Families

As will be clear from reading this chapter, the Celestine, Dupas and Gabriel families were joined together by marriage early in their histories. In this chapter, the Celestine, Dupas and Gabriel families will be covered to include as much available information as possible.

For clarity, we will treat each family separately, beginning with the Dupas, because of their slavery aspects. The other two will follow.

1. Dupas

Over the years, the Dupas name has come with various spellings: e.g. Dupas, Dupar, Dupard, and more recently, Duper. Unless specifically spelled a certain way in the official documents used as references in this work, that name will be spelled "**Dupas**".

A search, using Ancestry.com, of the Avoyelles Parish, Louisiana area shows only two people with the Dupart or Dupas name who were born before 1825: **Jacques** and **Roseline Gabriel Dupas**.

Jacque [Dupas], as you will see below, was a slave on one of the plantations in Louisiana. However, which plantation and where it was located is not certain.

While in his younger life as a slave, Jacques apparently fathered at least two children, **Julie** and **Mary**, and likely more. Those two women have been legitimized as children of Jacques Dupas[90] from information on the death records of their children.

An important point that needs to be made here is that at the time that Julie and Mary were born, Jacques, just as other slaves, only went by a single name, "**Jacques**". Consequently, Julie and Mary initially identified themselves as Julie Jacques and Mary Jacques, to define their relationship to their father. Later, especially once slavery was over and the former slaves began adopting surnames, Jacques assumed the name, "Jacques **Dupas**"[91]. All of his children, including Julie and Mary did the same, and became **Julie Dupas**, **Mary Dupas**, **Charles Dupas**, etc.

Emily was a slave on one of the local plantations in the Mansura area. She has been identified as Jacques' slave "wife" and the mother of the two children, Julie and Mary. Her name appeared on Mary's death certificate, which indicated that Mary's father was Jacques Dupas and her mother was a woman named **Emily**.

Additional work is needed here.

2. Gabriel

Roseline Gabriel was a slave held on one of the Louisiana plantations from the early 1800s. Many slaves used their father's sole name, e.g. Jacques, as their last name once slavery ended. Unfortunately, Roseline's last name, Gabriel, was shared as a first name by several slaves in the Mansura, LA area, as shown in Table 7 below:

---

[90] A summary of this information was kindly provided by Shirley Whitmore and Allie Jackson, Jacques Dupas' great-great-grandchildren.
[91] There are no records indicating where the name, Dupas, or it other spelling, Dupart, originated.

TABLE 7. SLAVES NAMED GABRIEL

Child/Slave	Mother	Date of Birth	Slave Holders	Comments	References
Gabriel	Rose	9/20/1824	Pierre Goudeau		St. Paul Baptisms
Gabriel	Mela	10/24/1844	Valery Moreau		St. Paul Baptisms
Hilaire	Meline	oct 1833	Laurent Normand	**Gabriel**: Godfather	St. Paul Baptisms
Celestine	Celeste	2/1/1831	Laurent Normand, Sr. Vve.	**Gabriel**: Godfather	St. Paul Baptisms
Gabriel		1827	Laurent Normand		1860 Probate Sale
Gabriel		1819	Laurent Normand, Sr., Vve.		1848 Probate Sale
Gabriel	Marie	1854	JBte Lemoine		1860 Probate Sale

As a result, it is not possible to positively identify any one of them as a possible father of Roseline Gabriel. Also, since she was believed to have been born before 1825, her father would have been born around 1800 and none of the slave babies being baptized in Table 7 were born that soon.

Only three people shared the last name, Gabriel, in the decades following the end of slavery (See Below). It has generally vanished from the Mansura area. However, Roseline Gabriel made it possible for her descendants to identify a direct connection from the 20th century in the U.S. all the way back to Africa.

3. Celestine

The Celestine name appeared in Avoyelles Parish following the Civil War. However, it described a very large family that originated during the early 1800's.

The Celestine family became joined to the Dupas family as a result of the marriage between **Hyppolite "Paulie" Celestine** and **Mary Dupas**.

Pierre Celestine (55) and his wife, **Lize** (48) appeared in the 1870 U.S. Census for Avoyelles Parish (PierLize1870). Living with them were the following 13 people: **Gustave** (25) and his wife, **Victoria** (22), **Julie** (22), **Ernest** (14), **Marcelin** (13), **Marceline** (13), **Alexis** (10), **Hippolytus** (5), **Elvert** (1), **Joseph** (2), **Ernestine** (6/12), **Louisa** (2), and **Edouard** (3/12). Based on ages, there are clearly more than one family there but the census report does not provide enough information to determine which might be which.

Gustave Celestine, the husband of **Victoria Celestine**, was a mulatto who was born in Louisiana in 1845. He served in the Union Army from April, 1864 to October, 1865 (GusCelMil).

In 1880, Gustave and Victoria were living between Marksville and Mansura, LA. They indicated that both they and their parents were born in Louisiana. Living with them were the following children: **Joseph** (12), **Octave** (7), **Octavine** (6), **Eliza** (4), **Jean Bte** (2) and **Edward** (7/12).

Hypolite "Paulie" Celestine[92], who became the husband of Mary Dupas (See Below), was listed in the 1870 U.S. census as being born in about 1840, making it possible for him to have been Gustave' brother (MarElCel1870).

Historical Highlights

Jacques Dupas was born in Louisiana around 1809 (jacdup1880). The St. Paul baptismal records lists a slave named **Jacques**, being held by farmer Felix Marcott (ConsDes1837), who was present as the godfather of a child named **Bastien** who was baptized at St, Paul, on March 5, 1837. The child's mother was **Victoire** and standing as godmother, along with Jacques, was a female slave named **Rosette**, also held by Felix Marcott. Jacques Dupas would have been 22 years old and Roseline Gabriel would have been 17 years old at that time. Thus, it is possible that the slaves, Jacques and Rosette, could have been Jacques Dupas and Roseline Gabriel. **Further study is needed**.

Jacques and Emily

Jacques was the father to at least two girls, **Julia** and **Mary.** Their mother was a slave named **Emelie.** No further records of Emelie were found.

The children of Jacques and Emelie, are profiled below. The reader will notice that there is much less information about them than on the children of Jacques and Roseline[93].

o   **Julie Jacques** was born in Louisiana around 1835 (JulJacLife). Her parents were Jacques and Emily (i.e. Jacque Dupas and Emily). She married **Elie Ricard** at Sacred Heart Catholic Church in Moreauville, LA on September 16, 1869 (JulJacMarr).

In the 1880 U.S. census[94], Elie (47) and Julie (34) were living in the vicinity of Long Bridge, LA (ElJulRic). He was a farm laborer and she was a housekeeper. Living with them were their four daughters: "J" = **Julia** (20), "P" = **Paulina** (19), "D" = ?? (12), and "J" = ?? (7).

In the 1900 U.S. census, Eli (70) and Julie (65) were living near Long Bridge, LA (EliJulRic1900). Living with them was their grandson, **Cass Ducote** (10). They indicated that they had been married for 45 years. Julie said that she had given birth to 9 children and 7 were still alive at that time.

In the 1910 U.S. census, Julia, a 70-year-old widow, was living in Long Bridge, LA with her daughter, **Mary** (40) and her son-in-law, **Andre Telemaque**(37) (JulRic1910). Living with Mary and Andre were their Telemaque children: **Rayfield** (14), **Loula** (13), **Earlist** (11), **Adolia** (10), **Alex** (8), **Suzzie** (5)

---

[92] He is not the **Hyppolytus** listed as one of **Pierre Celestine's** family.

[93] A good bit of the information on the children and grandchildren of Jacque Dupas and his slave wife, Emelie, was kindly provided by **Shirley Whitmore**, the daughter of **Austin** and **Verta Alford Marks**.

[94] This 1880 census was recorded using only the first initials and last names of the citizens. Some family members can still be recognized based on their first initials, ages and relationship to each other.

and **Auston** (1). Andre and Mary had been married for 15 years and she said that she had given birth to 10 children and all were living. This was Andre's first marriage and Mary's second.

Julie and Elie had the following children (Kimble), (wanda_j1956):

- **Ozilia Ricard** (1857 – 1918) – Married **Joseph Lee** on February 15, 1872 and, after his death, married **Louis Lonzo** on December 13, 1877.

- **Julia Ricard** (1861 - ??) – Married **Charles Holmes** on October 28, 1880 and moved to Okmulgee, Oklahoma during the early 1900s;
- **Marie Adela Ricard** (1869 -1925) – She first married **Leon Ducote** on January 21, 1888. She divorced Leon and left the Catholic Church during the early 1900s. She and Leon had three sons: **Cass**, **Preston** and **Leman**.

  She then married **Andre Telemaque** (See above). They had a total of seven children (See Above).

- **Paulina Ricard** (??) – Married **Jacob Keller**. Died at an early age.

- **Usilla Ricard** – Married **Isham or Isom Carter** on April 7, 1872 in Avoyelles Parish.

Elie Ricard died in 1902 in Long Bridge, Louisiana (Kimble).

Julie Ricard died in 1910 in Long Bridge, Louisiana (Kimble).

- **Mary Jacques** was born on March 6, 1840 in Moreauville, Louisiana (JulJacLife). Her parents were Jacques and Emily (i.e. Jacque Dupas and Emily).

Mary married **Hypolite "Paulie" Elphage Elam Celestine** on September 22, 1870 (A. Williams).

In the 1870 U.S. census, Marie (28) and her husband, Elam (30), were living near Long Bridge, LA (MarElCel1870). Living with them were the following children: **Josephine** (10), **Paulin** (6), **Dorsin** (3) and **Louis** (1/12). Also present was **John Briges** (20), a farm laborer.

In the 1880 U.S. census Mary and Elam were living near Long Bridge, LA (MarElCel1880). Living with them were the following children: Paulin (17), Dorsin (14) and "E" = Emile (10). It's not clear what became of Josephine. Louis must has died during the 1870-1880 decade. Another son, **Carlin**, was born in 1885.

The children of Mary and Hypolite "Paulie" Celestine were as follows (Vanitah):

- **Josephine Celestine** (1860 - ???) – Married **Robert Rawlings** (worthysister)
- **Paulin Celestine** (1863) – Unknown Fate
- **Dorsin Celestine** (1867 – 1942) – Married **Maria Zelia Swan** on November 28, 1889. They had a total of nine children: **Hillery Benton**, **Early "Eli"**, **Ophelia**, **Normand**, **Josephine**, **Davis**, **Israel**, **Loretha** and **Louise** (worthysister).
- **Jane Celestine** (1870 – 1935) – Married **James Owens Bazile** (arj1961)
- **Louis Celestine** (1870 -) – Fate Unknown

- o **Emile Celestine** (1870 – 1952) – Died, Cotton Port, LA, November 12, 1952
- o **Carlin Celestine** (1885 – 1928) – Married **Josephine Solle Smith** (nikamilton). They had 4 children: **Stella**, **Leola**, **Elvira** and **Percy**.

As is so often the case, there are stories that are carried down through the various generations and originating in slavery[95]. In this case, it is more of a description of the lives and difficult times of Mary and her husband, Paulie:

*Mary and Paulie were slaves of the **Valiste Rabalais** family near Pearl Lake[96]. They remained there until the end of the Civil War. After the war, Paulie became a share cropper on the old **Oscar Bordelon** property. He lived to be 115 years old, dying peacefully in 1932 after such a difficult life.*

Hippolite was determined to free himself from slavery and often ran away. In one particular case, he was able to swim across the Atchafalaya River, only to find the slave holder waiting for him on the other side. He was returned and beaten badly.

Mary was known to have many scars on her back from the terrible whippings she got from the slave-holders. Interestingly, her sister, Julie, didn't have scars.

Mary died on February 12 1920 in Avoyelles Parish and is buried in Old Zion Baptist Church Cemetery in Cottonport, Louisiana (MarCel).

Jacques and Roseline Dupas

Roseline Gabriel became **Jacques Dupas'** wife once the war was over. He was already the father to Julia and Mary, the children of a slave woman named Emelie.

Roseline Gabriel was born in Louisiana around 1820 (RosGab1880). Her father, whose name is lost, was born in Africa (RosGab1900). **Jean Gabriel**, who was born in 1829 and resided 2 houses away from Jacques and Roseline in 1870, was likely her brother (JeanGab1870). **Celestine Gabriel**, who was born in 1838 and married **Joseph Magloire** (See McGlory Family, Chapter 10) at St. Paul on February 23, 1871 (CelGabJoMag1871), was living with Jean in 1870 and is likely the sister of Jean and Roseline.

A 4th Gabriel was **Marie Gabriel**, who married **Cyriaque Francisco** on 11/16/1893 (See Francisco Family Chapter). Little else is known about her.

Jacque Dupas and Roseline Gabriel were married on December 15, 1870 (JulDuPRosGabMarr). As part of their marriage, they declared 6 children: **Charles**, **Angelie**, **Irma**, **Rose**, **Lorenza**, and **Julien**.

In the 1870 census, Jacques (61) and Roseline (50) were living in Avoyelles parish, near Long Bridge or Moreauville (JacRosDup1870). Living with them were **Charles** (22), **Angile** (21), **Irma** (18), **Rose** (16), **Sezmie** (a.k.a. "**Lorenza**") (14) and **Julien** (10).

---

[95] Based on a story appearing in the Avoyelles Parish Weekly News as related by Percy Celestine.
[96] Based on stories told by Percy Celestine, the grandson of Mary Dupas Celestine.

Jacques, a.k.a., "**Jacob**" and Roseline appeared as farmers living in the Long Bridge-Moreauville, Louisiana area in the 1880 U.S. census when Jacques was 65 and Roseline was 60 years old (JacRosDup1880). All of their children had left home by then.

Jacques died in Mansura on October 25, 1880 at the age of 80 and is buried in the St. Paul Cemetery in Mansura, Louisiana (JacDup1880).

In the 1900 U.S. census (RosGab1900), Roseline Gabriel (80) was living in the area of Grande Bayou, near Mansura, Louisiana, with her son, **Julian Dupas** (39), his wife, **Josephine** (33), and their children: **Wilson** (13), **Aurelia** (11), **Pierre** (9), **Ophelia** (7), **Wallace** (3), and **Lones** (2). She declared that her mother was born in Louisiana but **her father was born in Africa**.

Roseline Gabriel Dupas died on November 5, 1900 at the age of 95 and is buried in St. Paul's cemetery in Mansura (RosGabDup1900).

In this section, the children of Jacques and Roseline Dupas will be profiled:

- **Charles Dupas** was born in Louisiana in 1848. He first appeared in the 1870 U.S. census as a 22-year-old man, living with his parents, Jacques and Roseline Dupart, and his five siblings.

  Charles married **Eupheme Day** on December 27, 1877 (ChDupMarr1). Service was performed by Rev. J. E. Chauvin, Witnesses: Charles Holley, Ernest Celestine, Jean Baptiste Day

  In the infamous 1880 U.S. census (Only first initials listed), Charles Dupas (28) was a farmer, living near Moreauville, LA. Living with him was his wife, **"P" Day** (25), his son, **"A" Dupas** (8) and his daughter, **"C" Dupas** (3).

  Charles married **Victorine Davis** in Avoyelles Parish on December 23, 1884 (CharVicMarr).

  It's not clear when Charles and Eupheme died or whether they had adult children.

- **Angele Dupas** was born in Louisiana about 1850. She was listed as one of the children declared at the time of her parents' marriage (JulDuPRosGabMarr). She only appeared in the 1870 U.S. census where she was listed as a 21-year-old girl, living with her parents (JacRosDup1870).

  No further information on her was found.

- **Irma Dupas** was born in 1852 in Louisiana. She was listed as one of the children declared at the time of her parents' marriage (JulDuPRosGabMarr). She appeared in the 1870 U.S. census where she was listed as an 18-year-old girl, living with her parents (JacRosDup1870).

  Irma married **Jean Baptiste Luke (Luc)** in Avoyelles Parish on February 15, 1872 (IrmDupMarr). She became **Irma Luc**.

In the 1880 U.S. census, Irma and Jean Baptiste were living in Grande Bayou, northeast of Mansura. Living with them were the following children: **Rosina** (7), **Francois** (5) and **Jean Baptiste** (1) (IrLuc1880).

Jean Baptiste Luc died on August 6, 1885 and is buried in St. Paul the Apostle Catholic Cemetery in Mansura (StPaulBurlV).

Irma married **Louis Berzat**, the oldest son of Jean Baptiste Berzat (See Luc and Berzat Families, Chapter 4) on July 30, 1889 (IrDupMarr2).

In the 1910 U.S. census, Irma (49), now a widow, was living in Moreauville, LA with her son, **Joseph P.** (20). Also living there was Joseph's nephew, **Clifton Augustin** (9) (IrmDup1910).

It is not clear when Irma died.

- **Rose Dupas** was born around 1854 in Louisiana. She also was one of the children claimed in their parents' wedding.

  No further records of Rose were found.

- **Lorenza Dupas** was born about 1860 and married **Jean Pierre James** in Avoyelles Parish in 1875 (See **James Family Chapter**).

  In the 1900 U.S. Census, they had the following children living with them: **Levi** (18), **Julian** (15), **Joffrion** (14), **Eugenie** (11), **Eloise** (10), **Mathilda** (7), **Eugene** (6), **Irma** (4), **Pierre** (3), **Angelica** (2) and **Celestine** (7/12). Their oldest daughter, **Mary Elizabeth** (22), was not present in the 1900 census since she had married **Willie Walton** on January 10, 1895 (ElJamWilWalMarriage1895).

  Jean Pierre James died in Mansura on August 11, 1927 (JPJamDeath1927).

  In the 1930 census, Lorenza (70) was living with her two grandsons, **Preston Titus** and **Cilton Sampson** (LorJam1930).

  She died during the 1950s while living with her daughter, Angelica, in Mansura, LA.

  - **Julian Dupas** was born in Louisiana around 1860. He was one of the children claimed as part of his parents' marriage (JulDuPRosGabMarr). He appeared as a 10-year-old, living with his parents in the 1870 U.S. census (JacRosDup1870).

    In the 1880 U.S. census for Avoyelles Parish, Julian was a 17-year-old single head-of-household, living in Grande Bayou (JulDup1880). Living nearby were his parents, Jacques and Roseline Dupas and his sister, Irma Luc.

    Julian married **Mary Francisco** on December 22, 1885 in Avoyelles Parish (JulDupMarFranMarr).

    In the 1900 U.S. census, Julian (39) and **Josephine** [Last name unknown] (33) were living near Mansura, LA (JulJosDup1900). Living with them were the following children: **Wilson** (13), **Aurelia** (11),

Pierre (9), **Ophelia** (7), **Wallace** (3) and **Lonus** (2). Also present in the house was Julian's mother, Roseline Gabriel (80).

In the 1910 U.S. census, Julian (49) and Josephine (45) were living in the vicinity of Mansura (JulJosDup1910). He and Josephine had been married for 25 years and had 9 children, 7 of whom were still alive. Living with them were the following children: Aurelia (21), Pierre (18), Ophelia (16), Wallace (14), Lones (12) and **Rosa** (8). **It is not clear what became of Wilson.**

In the 1930 U.S. census, Julian (69) and Josephine (64) were living in Grande Bayou (JulJosDup1930). Living with them were their four **Francisco** grandchildren: **Ambroise** (11), **Melville** (8), **Wilson** (6), and **Lucilia** (3).

Julian Dupas died on August 14, 1937 in Mansura, LA (JulDupDeath).

Julian's children with either Mary or Josephine were as follows:

o **Wilson** (b. 1887),
o **Aurelia** (b. 1889),
o **Pierre** (b. 1891),
o **Ophelia** (b. 18937),
o **Wallace** (b. 1897) and
o **Lonus** (b. 1898).

Current Status

The Dupas and Celestine families of Avoyelles Parish continues to thrive, although many members now live in other parishes and states. Descendants of Jacques and his wives, Emily and Roseline, have made contributions to our society in various types of endeavors such as athletics, business, education, manufacturing, the military and the theater.

They are hard-working people who also like to stop and have fun. Most are deeply religious and kind-hearted.

There is no doubt that Jacques, Emelie and Roseline would be proud to see their accomplishments after being free for over 150 years.

Dupas Family Pictures

Mary Ricard,
Granddaughter of Jacques Dupas

Lones Dupas

Mansura During 1927 Flood

Prior to the Flood of 1927, a number of black families lived along the top of the Mansura Bluff, a 20-foot high plateau that ran from Grande Bayou to Boutte Des Bayou.

When the flood arrived, the Mansura Bluff became a lake front with flood waters rising to near the top where the black community resided.

Boats, ships, barges and every other type of vessel were used to transport flood refugees to shore at various points along the bluff.

The flood damaged much of the road and other structures such as the hand-made stairs that were located at the bottom of the bluff. The destruction of this part of the "Down the Hill" infrastructure was the beginning of the end for that area.

Thanks to Charles Riddle for Use of Tarver Flood Pictures

Chapter 8.

The Francisco Family

Paul and Octavie Francisco

An Introduction to the Francisco Family

The Francisco family is one of the largest African-American families that began in the Mansura area. Their known ancestors date back to the early 1800's, some with parents who were born in Africa.

Today, they flourish throughout the country and have made contributions in many areas including education, military, business, sports, and politics.

The name, Francisco, is either French or Spanish and is derived from the English name, **Francis**. However, a search of Ancestry.com showed no white person in Avoyelles Parish with that name prior to the Civil War.

Historical Highlights

The earliest documented records of the Francisco family members were found in an Avoyelles Parish Probate Sale of Slaves who had been held by **Manette Gauthier**, the widow of **Joachim Juneau**. The Juneau family had resided inside the town of Mansura until Manette's death in 1863.

Following her death, and there being no adult heirs to claim ownership of her possessions, a probate sale was conducted on October 13, 1863 (FranciscoProbSale). In addition to her home and other possessions, 15 slaves were also sold to various slave holders:

TABLE 8. MANETTE GAUTHIER SLAVE SALE

Name	Age	M/F	B/W/M	Buyer
Augustin	35	M	B	Joseph J. Juneau
Jean Baptiste	28	M	M	Joseph J. Juneau
Aimee	30	F	B	Valerian Moreau, jr.
Philice	7			Valerian Moreau, jr.
Alicia	5			Valerian Moreau, jr.
Emile	3			Valerian Moreau, jr.
Durelie	1			Valerian Moreau, jr.
Alexander	24	M	B	Edgar E. Cochrane
Julienne	18	F	B	Vital Gremillion
Helena	16	F	B	Leandre Roy
Elodie	14	F	B	Emile J. Bordelon
Lucille	12	F	B	Joseph J. Juneau
Rosa	11	F	B	Hyacinthe Richi
Valentine	11	F	B	Marcelin Dufour
Leocadie	9	F	B	Ludger Lemoine

From **Table 8**, the following conclusions can be reached:

- The slave, **Julienne**, being sold to **Vital Gremillion,** was born in 1845, based on her age in 1863 (45). Julienne Francisco, who later became **Julienne Pryor** by her marriage to Samuel Pryor (See Below) was also born in 1845 (JulPryor1900). **This is reasonable evidence that these two Juliennes are the same person.**

- Similarly, the slave, **Leocadie**, being sold to **Ludger Lemoine**, is likely **Locadia Francisco**. The ages of both are the same (Both born in 1854) and the unusual names are so similar that **it seems very likely that these two people are the same.**

- The case of the slave, **Lucille** (Born in 1851), being sold to **Joseph L. Juneau**, is not so clear. If her age is compared to that of the other two people with similar names who were related to the Franciscos, i.e. **Luce** (Born in 1858) and **Lucille** (Born in 1863), in the discussion below, **there is no match. Further study is needed here.**

An extremely intriguing entry in the St. Paul baptismal records is that of a 1-month-old girl named **Julie**, whose mother, **Laysa**, was held in captivity by **Joachim Juneau**, the husband of Manette Gauthier (See Above). Julie was born on March 26, 1845, the same year that **Julienne Francisco Pryor** was born. Also, as discussed above, she was born and held on the same plantation as the slave Julienne (who may have been the same person as Julienne Francisco Pryor!). Thus:

- Based on age, similar names, and being on the same plantation, it is very possible that the baby, Julie, is the same person as the slave, Julienne, being sold in the probate sale above.
- And, as stated above, the slave, Julienne, could be the same person as Julienne Francisco, the future wife of Samuel Pryor.

If these conclusions are correct, then the mother of Julienne Francisco has been tentatively identified as the slave, **Laysa**. **More research is needed here.**

Post-Civil War Francisco Family Records

The post-slavery records of the Francisco family began with three men:

- **Julien Francisco** (b. 1808);
- **Francois Francisco** (b. 1821);
- **Sylvain Francisco** (b. 1830).

It is not clear if they were brothers and there is no evidence to indicate that there might be other siblings.

In this work, each of these gentlemen and their families will be discussed separately. Any information regarding their relationship will be presented as is.

----

1. Julien Francisco

Julien Francisco was born in Louisiana around 1808 (JulFran1900). In the 1880 census (JulFran1880), he was 67-years-old, married to **Josephine Thomas** (40) LAGHN.usGHN.org [97] and living near Marksville. They had living with them: one son, **Paul** (18), and two daughters: **Lucille** (13) and **Lovinia** (12). Julien indicated that his father was born in Louisiana but his **mother was born in Africa**.

Their neighbors included several **Thomas** families, possibly relatives of Josephine. The members of the family next door, headed by **Louisa Thomas**, all claimed that their **father was from Africa** (JulFran1880).

One of their neighbors was a single parent named **Locadia Francisco** (25), (See Above), who lived two houses away and had 1-year-old, twin boys, **Alexandre** and **Alexis Francisco**. Based on her age (25), Locadia would have been born in 1855 and would have been 8 or 9 in 1863, when the Manette Gauthier probate sale shown in **Table 8** occurred.

In that 1863 probate sale, the slave being sold, Leocadie, was 9, the same age that Locadia Francisco would have been. This further supports the idea that both the slave, Leocadie, and

---

[97] The record of their marriage indicates that it occurred on December 21, 1888 - LAGHN.USGHN.org

Locadia Francisco were the same person. **She could have been Julian and Josephine's daughter, based on their relative age, but there is no proof.**

In 1900, Julian (92) was living with his daughter, **Lucille** (37) and her husband, **Valentine Augustine** (38) (JulFran1900).

In 1910, Julian, now 107[98], was still living with Valentine and Lucille (JulFran1910). He died sometime around 1913. It is not clear where or when Josephine Francisco died.

Julian and Josephine's children were as follows:

- **Paul Francisco** – Paul married **Octivie Bontemps**, a French-speaking mulatto from Mansura, on June 9, 1886 in Avoyelles Parish LAGHN.USGHN.org. Their children appear to have been born while they were living in Evergreen, Louisiana[99].

   In the 1900 census, Paul (42) and Octavie (30) were living near Mansura, LA (PaulFran1900). They had been married for 14 years and had had 7 children with 5 surviving at the time. Paul could read and write but Octavie could not.

   Living with them were their 2 sons, **Arkange** (12) and **Isadore** (10), who were in school, and their 2 daughters: **Virginie** (7) and **Elizabeth** (5), who were too young to attend school. Also, living with them was their niece, **Roselia Evans** (14) and their nephew, **Jules Washington** (10).

   Paul eventually moved his family to Creek, Oklahoma (PaulFran1910). From there, some of his descendants, including **Isadore** (a.k.a. **Zedore**) moved to California (Francisco).

- **Lucille Francisco** – Lucille married **Valentine Augustine** around 1880. They had no children. Her father, Julian Francisco, lived with them until his death sometime after 1910. During this time, Lucille's "nephew", **Joseph C. "Gollie" Francisco**, also, resided with her and Valentine (JulFran1910). Valentine died on June 18, 1924 (ValAugdeath). Lucille died on August 13, 1928 (LucFranDeath).

   Her nephew, **Joseph "Gollie" Francisco,** is believed to be the son of **Latrina** (or **Lavina**) **Guillot**, a Choctaw Indian who died when he was born[100]. His father is believed to have been **Abel Francisco**. Gollie was raised by Lucille Francisco Augustine, a.k.a. "**Taunt Lo**".

- **Lovinia Francisco** - No further records of Lovinia Francisco were found for this study.

----

2. Francois Francisco

---

[98] Probably census taker error.
[99] Private communication from Karen Francisco.
[100] Information provided by James Francisco, Gollie's grandson.

Francois Francisco was born in Louisiana around 1821 and both his parents were born in Louisiana. **Delphine Matta** was born in Louisiana about 1833 (Topalicia). She may have been previously married to a Civil War veteran by the name of Bazile Nero.

France (49) and Delphine (37) Francisco appeared in the 1870 U.S. census (FranDelFran1870). Here, they were farmers who appeared to be living near Mansura. Living with them were the following children: Five boys (**Fulgence** (18), **Francois II** (13), **Lovincia** (5), **Abel** (1) and **Hilaire** (9)); and two girls: (**Virginie** (16) and **Augustine** (11)). Their youngest son, **Shelby**, was not yet born (b. 1874).

The children listed in 1870 seem to be in two groups:

o   Fulgence (18), Virginie (16), Francois II (13), Augustine (11) and Hilaire (9) and
o   Lovincia (5) and Abel (1).

This suggests that they might not all be full siblings .

It is not clear when Francois and Delphine separated. However, Francois married **Clementine Steven Kemper,** a Native American[102], on February 13, 1877 in Marksville, LA (FranClemMarr). Witnesses were: Onezime Sampson and Alfred barker. They declared one child named **Joseph**.

In the 1880 census, Francois (54) and Clementine (44) were farmers near Mansura, LA (FranClemFran1880). Living with them were four boys: **Loventia** (14), **Abel** (12), **Azia** (4)[104] and **Pierre** (1). Also residing with them was his 12-year old stepson, **Joseph Smith**.

Living nearby was Francois' son, **Fulgence** (26) and Fulgence's wife, **Marie** (24). Fulgence and Marie had one daughter, **Maria** (5), and two sons, **Savoy** a.k.a. "**Sway**" (2) and **Marcelin** (1). **Francois II** (20) was listed as a boarder in the home of **Harris Humphrey** (FranFranII1880).

Based on their ages, it seems reasonable to assume that Azia (Isaiah?) and Pierre were the children of both Francois and Clementine, while the others may have been products of a previous relationship.

Interestingly, in 1880, Delphine appeared to be living next door to Francois, between his house and their son, Fulgence's house. Her surname was once more her maiden name, **Martha** dit **Matta**. Residing with her was her three sons: **Hilaire** (17), **Shelby** (5) and **Camille** (8 months); and her daughter: **Lucille** (20)[105]. Delphine Francisco died on July 3, 1904 and is buried in St. Paul's cemetery in Mansura (DelpDeath).

---

[102] From Family History provided by James Francisco.
[104] Likely **Isaiah**.
[105] Lucille and Augustine are the same age, suggesting that they might be the same person.

In the 1900 census, 70-year old Clementine was now a widow (ClemFran1900). Francois had died in Mansura on December 9, 1898. Living with her were her daughter **Angelica** (16), her son, **Isiah** (24), Isiah's wife, **Marie** (22), and Isiah and Marie's two boys, **Alzida** (5) and **Tarleton** (3).

Clementine's son, **Pierre** (21), lived next door along with his wife, **Elizabeth Augustin** (20), their son, **Joseph C** (1), and Elizabeth's mother, **Eulalie Alexandre** (64). They appeared to be living in the vicinity of Grande Ecore[106].

Francois' Children with Delphine:

- **Fulgence** was born in 1852. He married **Marie Reason** on May 1, 1873 in Avoyelles Parish, Louisiana (FulFranMarriage). They had 9 children: **Maria** (b. 1875), **Savoy** (b. 1878), **Marcelin** (b. 1879), **Walter** (b. 1882), **Olive** (b. 1889), twins: **Cleovis** and **Cleophus** (b. 1890), **Angela** (b. 1893) and **Leonard** (b. 1895). He died in Avoyelles Parish on December 23, 1929 at the age of 83 (FulFranDeath).

   In 1930, **Marie** (79) was living in Mansura with her son, **Marcelin Francisco** and her daughter, **Dora** (MarFran1930). Also, living with them were Dora's grandson, **Cleveland Murry**, and Marcelin's niece, **Bernice Francisco**. Marie died in Avoyelles Parish on October 20, 1936 at the age of 84 (MarFranDeath).

- **Virginie** was born in 1854. She appears to have married a **Lonzo**. She died on January 3, 1925.

- **Francois II** a.k.a. **Edgar Francois Francisco,** was born in 1857. He (20) was listed as a boarder in the home of Harris Humphrey (FranFranII1880). He married **Josephine Normand** on November 13, 1883 in Avoyelles Parish.

   Their children were as follows: **Marceline** (b. 1893); **Aldege** (b. 1895); **Aurelia** (b. 1896); **Florence** (b. 1898); **Mary** (b. 1899); **Jebertie** (b.1900); **Arthur** (b. 1901), and **Obrian** (b. 1907).

- **Augustine** was born in 1859. No further records of her were found.

- **Hilaire** was born in 1861. No other information was found on him.

- **Lovincia** (Or **Loventia**) was born in 1865. He married **Clara Parker** in 1883, **Helen Nero** in 1890 and **Honora Elmer** in 1896. In 1900, he appeared in the US Census married to Honora Francisco. They had been married four years. Residing with them, beside the children listed below, was his aunt, **Rachel Baker** (b. 1840).

   Lovincia appears to have had three sets of children:

   o With Clara - **Widdy** (b. 1886), **Armina** (b. 1890),

---
[106] Based in proximity to residents who had known locations

- o With Helen - **Edward** (b. 1891),

- o With Honora - **Cornelius** (b. 1898), **Frank** (b. 1899).

No further records of Lovincia were found.

- **Abel** was born in 1869. He married **Lovinia Guillot** on February 14, 1893 in Avoyelles Parish (AbelFranMarriage). He married **Maria Sampson** on November 16, 1896 in Avoyelles Parish (AbelFranMarriage2).

  In 1910, Abel (29) and Maria (25) appeared in the U.S. Census with the following children: **Joseph G** (b. 1897), **Delfie** (b. 1899) and **Curby** (b. 1900). Abel Francisco died on February 25, 1936 (AbelFranDeath).

- **Shelby** was born in 1875. He married **Marie Augustine** on February 4, 1896. He married **Rosa Washington** in 1898. Both Shelby and Rosa indicated this to be their second marriages.

  Their children were as follows: **Kirby** (b. 1900); **Hester** (b. 1902); **Felix** (b. 1906); **Percy** (b. 1910; **Antoine** (b. 1913); and **Hillary** (b. 1914).

Francois' Children with Clementine:

- **Azia**, a.k.a. **Isaiah**, was born in 1876. In 1910, he had been married to his wife, **Delphine**, for five years and had no children (AziaFran1910). In 1930, Isaiah (54) and Delphie, a.k.a." **Aunt Da**" (48) were farmers near Hessmer who owned their home (IsaiFran1930).

- **Pierre** was born in 1879. He married **Elizabeth Augustine** on January 26, 1898. In 1900, he (21) was living near Hessmer with his wife, Elizabeth (20), his son, **Joseph C.** (1) and his mother-in-law, **Eulalie Alexandre** (PierrFran1900).

Francois' Child with Clarisse Pryor:

In 1871, Francois Francisco had a child name **Cyriaque Francisco** with Claire Clarise Pryor (Topalicia). No records were found to indicate that they were married.

In 1900, Cyriaque (29) and his wife, **Angela Berzat** (23) **Francisco** lived near the residence of Sylvain and Francoise (SylFran1900), suggesting that Cyriaque could be a close relative. Living with them was one child: **Emile** (1).

In 1910, Cyriaque (39) and Angela (33) had the following children living with them: three boys (**Emile** (11), **Preston** (3) and **Alsida** (1.5)) and two girls (**Angella** (8) and **Leone** (5)) (cyrang1910). They had been married 15 years and Angella had had four children (All alive). Cyriaque indicated that this was his second marriage[107].

---

[107] Cyriaque had married Marie Gabriel on November 16, 1893. Marriage was performed by Father J.E. Chauvin of St. Paul's parish.

Angelle Berzat Francisco, died in Mansura in 1927; **Cyriaque** died on August 10, 1944 in Avoyelles.

Emile died in 1969 in Mansura. **Preston** died in 1957 in New Orleans. **Leone** married **Clarence St. Romain** in Mansura. She died in 1999.

----

3. Sylvain Francisco

Sylvain Francisco (SylFran1900) was born in Louisiana in 1830 and declared that **both his parents were born in Africa!** He died on February 1, 1904 and is buried in St. Paul's cemetery (M. Bordelon).

Sylvain's wife, **Francoise Francisco**, was born in 1844 and stated that she was born in Louisiana but her parents were born in Virginia.

Sylvain and Francoise indicated that they had been married for 38 years (m. 1862) and had had seven children and three were still alive in 1900.

There were a few additional Franciscos living in the Mansura area during the mid-to-late 1800s who appear to have been descendants of Sylvain and Francoise Francisco. Unfortunately, the information on these individuals is inconsistent. For example:

- **Mose Francisco** was listed as the son of **Sylvain Francisco** on his Social Security application in November, 1944 (SylFranDeath). He was born in Avoyelles Parish on February 1, 1875. His spouse was listed as **Francis Pryor**.

   No further records of Mose or Francis were found for this study

- **Sylvar Francisco** was listed as the son of **Sylvain Francisco** on his Social Security application in March, 1938 (SylFranSS). He was born in Mansura, LA on September 19, 1866. His mother was listed as **Francis Pryor** (!).

No further records of Sylvar or Francis were found for this study.

Current Status

Over the past 50+ years, the Francisco family has grown in many ways:

- The size of the Francisco family has increased considerably, adding several new generations over that period;
- The number of branches in the Francisco family has grown with members now living in several states, including Texas, California, Illinois and, of course, Louisiana.
- Franciscos have participated in various religious and civic organizations in roles such athletic coaches and elected government officials.
- Franciscos have made important contributions in other areas that include education, business, the military and sports.

Francisco Family Pictures:

Isador "Zedore" Francisco

Paul Francisco

Joseph "Peechu Doo" Francisco

Children of Francois Francisco: Front Row, L-R Seated - Olefus (Oliver), Marie Claire Murray, Joseph; 2nd Row Standing -Edward Hadley, Arthur, Jeff Hargrove Jr., Florence Sampson; Louis Hargrove, Obrana

Kirby and Benita Francisco

Joseph "Gollie" Francisco

A country wedding in Grande Ecore, ca. 1950. Note the normal wedding refreshments: wine and cake.

Most wedding receptions were held outside at the home of the bride.

Chapter 9.
The James Family

ELOISE JAMES

An Introduction to The James Family

The James family of Mansura was one of the largest families in the area. Their name has persisted due to their having so many male children in every generation from as far back as 1870. They are a group of hard working people who are always willing to stand up for what they believe in.

The exact origin of the name, James, in Avoyelles Parish, is unknown. However, its prominence in the Bible, i.e. the apostle James, King James Bible, etc., makes it a likely choice for a Christian man seeking a name. However, very few slaves with the name, James, appeared in the Avoyelles Parish, pre-Civil War records.

While there are other James family members in the Mansura area whose ancestors migrated there from other areas of the state, this work will focus on the James family of Mansura that evolved from the marriage of **William James** and **Rosalie Gustin**.

Historical Highlights

William James was born in Louisiana around 1830 (WillJam1800). In the St. Paul Baptismal records is the baptism of a slave named **William** on October 26, 1832 (ConsDes1837). His mother was a slave named **Ayme** who was being held by **Laurent Normand, Sr.** of Hydropolis[111]. William's godfather was a Free Man of Color named **Joseph** and his godmother was a slave named **Louise**, who was being held by the widow of **Pierre Normand**.

The closeness in birth year of William, the slave (1832) and William James' stated birthyear to the census takers (about 1830) and the fact that the slave William was held on a plantation in or near Mansura makes it possible that he is the same person as William James. **More study is needed here**.

Rosalie Gustin was born in Louisiana around 1835. The origin of the name, "Gustin" is not clear, although it could be a variation of "Augustine", which was pronounced "*o gees tan*" or just plain, "*gees tan*" in French.

The St. Paul records show the baptisms of two babies named **Rosalie**, one in 1832 and the other in 1838. Since Rosalie Gustin's stated birth year (1835) lies between these, it is not possible to make any assumption about which of these children may have been her. Also, there are several variations of that name in the church records, e.g. Rosa, Roseline, Rossell, etc., making it difficult to determine if one of them could be the same person as Rosalie James (ConsDes1837).

William James and Rosalie Gustin's marriage is recorded in the St. Paul Catholic Church in Mansura, Louisiana as having occurred on September 30, 1866 (WilJamRosAugMarr1866). As part of their marriage, the couple legalized 7 children[112]: **Jean Pierre** (14), **Celestine** (??), **Jean Baptiste** (??), **Lucille** (7), **Augustin** (4), **Rosalie** (3), and **Pauline** (New Born).

Interestingly, an Avoyelles Parish Rebate Sale in 1860 had shown the sale of a slave mother named **Celeste** and her two children, **Augustin** (3-months, mulatto/M) and **Jean Pierre** (10-years, B/M) to **Eliza Bordelon**, the widow of Laurent Normand (JeanPSale). They had been held on the plantation belonging to Laurent Normand, the same plantation where William appears to have been held.

The following observations can be made from the above information:
   o The slave, Celeste, had two children with the same names as two of the children claimed by William and Rosalee: Jean Pierre and Augustin;
   o The slaves, Jean Pierre and Augustin, and their mother, Celeste, were held on the same plantation as William;
   o The slave, Jean Pierre (born in 1850) and Jean Pierre James (born in 1852), were nearly the same age;
   o The slave, Augustin, was listed as a mulatto, while Jean Pierre was listed as black;

---

[111] Near area called Cocoville.
[112] The ages of the claimed children listed here were calculated based on their ages in later records. Any inaccuracies are due to known difficulties that uneducated slaves had in keeping track of time.

- The slave, Augustin, (born in 1860), may not have been the same age as the child, Augustin (born in 1863 - 1868) (AugJam1880), (AugCleoJam1900), claimed in the marriage of William and Rosalee.

This all suggests the following:

- Jean Pierre James could have been the slave, Jean Pierre, sold in the Normand rebate sale;
- Celeste may have been Jean Pierre's mother, not Rosalee,
- William may have been the father of Jean Pierre and Augustin.
- Jean Pierre and Augustin were not full siblings,
- **Further work is needed**.

William (50) and Rosalie (45) appeared in the 1880 U.S. census (WilRosJam1900) along with 5 daughters: **Lucille** (21), **Rosalie** (17), **Paulina** (14), **Josephine** (8), and **Mary** (2); and 5 sons: **Augustin** (18), **Alphonse** (13), **Adolphe** (10), **Abel J** (6), and **Cesaire** (3). **Jean Pierre James** did not appear in William's 1880 household because he had married **Lorenza Dupas** in 1875 and had his own household (See Below).

In the 1900 U.S. census, William (67) and Rosalie (60) were living in Mansura along with one son, **Evariste** (20) and one grandson, **Samuel** (10) (WilRosJam1900).

Rosalie Gustin James died at the age of 72 in Mansura on April 7, 1905 (M. Bordelon). William James died at the age of 94 in Mansura on May 29, 1927.

William and Rosalie's Children:

- **Jean Pierre James** and **Lorenza Dupas James** appeared in the 1900 U.S. Census (JPLorJam1900). He indicated that he was born in Louisiana around 1852. She was born in Louisiana around 1862. They had gotten married in 1875. They were living in Mansura along with their 6 daughters: **Eugenie** (11), **Eloise** (10), **Mathilda** (10), **Irma** (4), **Angelica** (2), and **Celestine** (7 months); and 5 sons: **Levi** (18), **Julian** (15), **Joffrion** (14), **Eugene** (6), and **Pierre** (3).

Their oldest daughter, **Mary Elizabeth** (22), was not present in the 1900 census since she had married **Willie Walton** on January 10, 1895 (ElJamWilWalMarriage1895).

Jean Pierre and Lorenza James were described as being two very colorful people by those who remembered them. They both loved to drink liquor and were frequently drunk. They kept several of their grandchildren whose parents worked the fields around Mansura. Some memories of them are as follows:

- *Lorenza, a.k.a. "Mama" or "Taunt Lo" was a small woman who was extremely feisty. **Herman Augustine**[113] told how she fixed very rudimentary food for her grandchildren, such as chitterlings, cabbage, beans and rice and sweet potatoes. When it was time to eat, the children were made to sit on the floor along the wall with their legs spread, while she fixed their meals in a small metal pan. She would then say, "Chan!" meaning "Here!" and would then slide each child's pan across the floor, landing it between their legs, where they ate it.*

---

[113] Her Grandson

○ *According to **Beulah Walter**, the granddaughter of Lorenza and Jean Pierre, very Saturday all of the girls helped clean the house and did laundry while the boys did outside chores like feeding the animals, chopping wood and attending to the garden. On more than one occasion, after the girls had brought in the laundry from the clothes lines, Taunt Lo would sneak outside with some of the girls' underwear and put it back on the clothes lines just when the boy friends were arriving for courting, leading to much embarrassment among the girls in her house.*

○ ***Beulah Walter** remembered how she was so wishing to leave that house that when **Oliver Prier** came for his third courting visit, she had all her possessions already tied in a small bundle. He arrived in a buggy and took her straight to the Justice of the Peace in Hessmer, where they were married.*

In the 1910 census, Jean Pierre (58) and Lorenza (48) were living near Grande Ecore, outside of Mansura, LA (JPLorJam1910). Living with them were their 3 daughters: **Irma** (12), **Angelica** (12), and **Celestine** (9) and their son, **Pierre** (13). Their son, **Julian James**, lived 2 houses away.

Jean Pierre James died in Mansura on August 11, 1927 (JPJamDeath1927).

In the 1930 census, Lorenza (70) was living with her 2 grandsons, **Preston Titus** and **Cilton Sampson** (LorJam1930). She died during the 1950s while living with her daughter, Angelica.

Jean Pierre and Lorenza's Children:

○ **Mary Elizabeth** (b. Jan,1878) – Married **Joseph Walton** January 10, 1895 in Avoyelles Parish. They had 6 children: **Minerva**, **Joseph**, **Widdy**, **Florence**, **Beulah** and **Viola**. She died sometime before 1910 in Avoyelles Parish.

○ **Levi** (b. Aug. 20, 1880) – Although he was listed either as a widower or divorced, there are no records of his marriage or children.

Levi was executed in the Avoyelles Parish jail on April 4, 1924 for murder. As the story goes, he was the last person seen walking along the railroad tracks near Mansura with a woman who had just come to town. When her body was discovered near the tracks, he was arrested, tried and hanged. Many people doubted his guilt and some still do. His was the last execution in the Avoyelles Parish jail.

○ **Joffrion** was born on February 10, 1885 (JoffJamBirth). He married **Celestine Antoine** (See Her Picture Below) in about 1920, although he may have had an earlier wife. Joffrion (a.k.a. "*Nonc Vont*") and Celestine (a.k.a. "*Chute a' Vont*") were fixtures around the town of Mansura, usually traveling around in his horse-drawn buggy with her at his side. His right leg was always propped up on the front wall of the buggy since he had had it partially amputated by a cane knife wielded by an angry local woman earlier in his life. It is not clear if either had children. Also, both appear to have died during the 1960-70 but the public records need locating.

○ **Julian** was born in 1885 in Avoyelles Parish, Louisiana. He married **Marie Victoria Day** (b. April, 1886) in 1908 (See Her Picture Below). He had a total of 9 children. Julian died on December 25, 1931 in Mansura, LA.

- o **Eugenie** was born in Mansura, Louisiana in 1889 (EugJam1910). She married **Forest Titus** in Mansura in 1905. They appear to have had 1 daughter, **Illinois** (b. 1906) and two sons, **Preston** and **Merlin**.

  Eugenie died on July 19, 1915. It is unclear what became of her daughter, Illinois, when she died. Preston, who was three years older than Merlin, ended up living with his grandparents, Jeanpierre and Lorenza. Merlin, ended up living with **Giles** and **Emma Augustine** (MerTit1930). There may have been two other boys, **Jack** and **Joseph**, but there are no written records of them[114].

  In 1920, Forest was married to **Olivia Sampson** and they had 3 children: **Hazel, Lester** and **Feltus** (ForTit1920). He eventually moved to Port Arthur, Jefferson County, TX where he died on June 9, 1936 (ForTitDeath).

- o **Eloise** was born in January, 1890 (JPLorJam1900) (See Her Picture Above). She married **Modella Augustine** in Mansura, LA in 1907 (ElJam1910). They had a total of 10 children (**See Augustine Family**) (ElJam1930). She died in Mansura, Louisiana in 1946.

- o **Mathilda** was born in Mansura, LA in 1893(JPLorJam1900). No further public records of her were found.

- o **Eugene** was born in 1894(JPLorJam1900) (See His Picture Below). He married **Grace Alexander** in Mansura, LA on July 25, 1915. They had 8 children: **Lange, Morris, Leroy, Joe, Evens, Daltry, Marshall** and **Lewis**. Grace died in Mansura, LA in 1960 and Eugene died in April, 1980 in Mansura, LA. Both are buried in St. Paul the Apostle Cemetery.

- o **Irma** was born in Mansura, LA in 1896(JPLorJam1900). She had three children: **Joseph, Loretta** and **Herman Tassin** (IrmaJam1920). She died on August 9, 1939 in Mansura, LA.

- o **Pierre** (a.k.a. Peter) was born on March 23, 1896 in Mansura, LA(JPLorJam1900). He married **Maggie Augustine** in Mansura, Louisiana in 1916. He was the father of 11 children. He died on December 15, 1967 (PierrJamDeath).

- o **Angelica** was born on March 25, 1897(JPLorJam1900) and died on April 5, 1970. She had one child, **Rebecca**.

- o **Celestine** was born in 1989(JPLorJam1900) (See Her Picture below). She married **Preston Prier** in 1918. They had two children: **Harold** and **Hilry** (**See Prier Chapter**). She died in February, 1978.

- **Augustin** and **Cleophine James**. Augustin James was born between 1863 and 1868 in Avoyelles Parish (AugJam1880), (AugCleoJam1900). He married **Cleophine Anderson** in Avoyelles Parish on December 23, 1885 (AugCleJamesMarriage).

---

[114] From family stories told by Beulah Prier and Herman Augustine.

In the 1900 census, they were living near Grande Ecore, outside of Mansura, LA (AugCleoJam1900). Augustin (32)[115] and Cleophine (27) had living with them, 3 daughters: **Edna** (15), **Theresa** (9), and **Josephine** (6).

Augustin (47) and Cleophine (42) were listed as living in Grande Ecore, near Mansura in the 1910 census (AugCleJam1910). Living with them were 2 daughters: **Josephine** (16) and **Victoria** (12); and 3 sons: **Manuel** (10), **Hurby,** a.k.a. **Herbert** (5) and **Buvens** (1). Augustin's birth year was listed as 1863.

In the 1920 census, Augustin (57) was living east of Mansura with his wife, "**Cladal**" (49) and his 3 sons, **Joseph, Herbert,** and **Buvens** (AugCleoJam1920).

Augustin died on October 14, 1925 in Avoyelles Parish at the age of 61 (AugJamDeath1925).

Augustine and Cleophine's Children:

o **Josephine** was born 1884. She married **William Sampson** on January 17, 1892;

o **Hurby,** a.k.a. **Herbert James**, was born in 1895. He married **Effie Daranda** in 1928. They eventually had two children: **Warren** and **Catherine**.

o **Beuvens** was born in 1899. He married **Lella ????** in 1929. They had at least one child: **Marshall James**.

o There are no clear records of what became of **Edna, Theresa, Victoria, and Manuel James**.

• **Alphonse** and **Aurelia James.** Alphonse James was born in 1867 in Avoyelles Parish. He married **Aurelia Sampson** on December 19, 1889 in Avoyelles Parish. They were listed as living in Grande Ecore, near Mansura in 1900 (AlpAurJam1900). Living with them were their daughter, **Alphonsine** (8), and 3 sons: **Alfred** (5), **Louis** (3), and **Edward** (2).

Alphonse died in Avoyelles Parish on February 5, 1937 (AlpJamDeath).

Alphonse and Aurelia James' Children:

o **Alphonsine** was born in 1892. She married **Gilmore Murry** in 1911.

o **Alfred** was born September 18, 1897 and died on July 20, 1940 (AlfJam). No further records of him were found.

o **Louis** was born in 1897, based on age in 1900 US Census (AlpAurJam1900). No further records of him were found.

o **Edward** was born in 1898, based on age in 1900 US Census record (AlpAurJam1900). There are no further public records of him in Avoyelles Parish.

---

[115] This suggests he was born in 1868.

- **Abel** and **Ellen James.** Abel James was born in 1874. He married **Ellen Prinell** on December 17, 1896 (AbEllJamMarriage). They were living in Grande Ecore, near Mansura, in 1900 (AbEllJam1900). They had only one child, a daughter named **Viola** (1). Here, Abel indicated that his father, William, was born in Virginia, while he and his mother were born in Louisiana.

  Abel and Ellen were living next door to Abel's niece, **Mary [Elizabeth James]**, and her husband, **Joseph Walton** in 1900.

- **Rosalie James** died in Mansura on February 14, 1882 at the age of 18. She is buried in St. Paul's Catholic Cemetery (RosJam2burial).

- **Evariste James** died in Mansura on January 18, 1903 and is buried in St. Paul's Cemetery (EvarJamBur).

- **Lucile James** died in Moreauville, LA on January 14, 1929 (LucJamDeath).

No further records of Celestine, Jean Baptiste, Adolph, Cesaire, Lucille, Paulina, Josephine, or Mary James were found for this study. This author would greatly appreciate any additional information that might come from the readers of this work.

Current Status

Members of the James family have always been hard workers, especially during the days when farming was a way of life.

Since the decline of farming, they have expanded into other areas, including business, education, medical fields and the military.

Their family members can be found throughout Louisiana as well as California, Illinois, Texas and Washington state.

James Family Pictures

| Celestine James | Eugene James | Marie Victoria Day | Celestine Antoine |

This type of structure, called "The Lot", was a common feature of many of the larger Share-cropper operations found throughout the Mansura area.

Here, the tenants could not only get feed for the animals, but could also use some of the equipment there to grind corn into corn meal and grits, and coffee beans into ground coffee. They could also file the hoes and plow points.

The Lot usually had a common water well for the use of the tenants as well as storage space for their farm equipment, fertilizer and seeds.

Chapter 10.
The McGlory Family

Helen McGlory

An Introduction to The McGlory Family

The McGlory family is likely one of the oldest families in the Mansura-Marksville area. While that family grew to a very large group at one time, the numbers of local residents bearing that name has diminished over time, with only a few small groups remaining.

However, the McGlory family has grown from its roots in Louisiana slavery, to develop large branch families in many areas. Those families were involved in several fascinating stories that have been carried down through the generations, making them one of the most interesting families to study.

The current name, "McGlory", has had various spellings and pronunciations over time. The earliest was "Magloire" which later was changed to "Maglaire". The final spelling, "McGlory" appeared in the early 1900's as the English language began to replace the earlier French.

The McGlory family appears to have begun in the earliest days of the Louisiana slaves trade, around the time of the Louisiana Purchase. By then, hundreds of African slaves were being brought into the state as the French and American farmers ventured farther and farther west.

An interesting public record shows the purchase by Mansura slave holder, Pierre Normand, Sr. of an 18-year old male slave named ***Magloire*** in New Orleans (MagSlave). The purchase, occurring on May 7, 1812, was from Louis Esnault for the price of $500. *Magloire* was listed as being from the Congo and spoke Benue-Congo[118].

The special significance of Magloire, the slave, is that he may be a key link from the McGlory family Avoyelles Parish to a **specific location in Africa**.

In any case, Magloire and the other early arrivals from Africa represent people who, somehow, **managed to survived the journey from Africa to Mansura**.

Historical Highlights

In this section, a few pieces of documentation will be used to provide a structure on which to develop the profiles of members of the McGlory family:

- First of all, an Avoyelles Parish Probate Sale resulting from the death of slave holder, **Jean Baptiste Lemoine,** was held on November 9, 1860 and is shown in **Table 9** (JBLemSale). The table shows the names of the slaves being sold (any children are right justified), their age at the time of the sale, their gender, their calculated birth years and who the buyers were.

TABLE 9. AVOYELLES PARISH PROBATE SALE OF SLAVES

Slave	Age	M/F	Birth Date (Calc'd)	Buyer
Julie	60	F	1800	Jerome Lemoine
Julien	40	M	1820	Celise Ducote, wd. J.V. Lemoine
Francois	37	M	1823	Joseph W Cappell/ Aristide Cappell
Joseph	22	M	1838	Zelien Gauthier
William	20	M	1840	J.V.Rabalais
Vital	18	M	1842	Ambroise Lemoine
Celeste	30	F	1830	wd. Celeste Ducote, JBte. Lemoine
Antoine	9	M	1851	wd. Celeste Ducote, JBte. Lemoine
Julie	7	F	1853	wd. Celeste Ducote, JBte. Lemoine
Marie	26	F	1824	Mrs. Hypolite Laborde
Gabriel	6	M	1854	Mrs. Hypolite Laborde
Arthemise	23	F	1837	Mrs. Paulin Lemoine
Estelle	4	F	1856	Mrs. Paulin Lemoine
Rosina	2	F	1858	Mrs. Paulin Lemoine
Adelaide	13	F	1847	wd. Celeste Ducote, JBte. Lemoine
Madeline	8	F	1852	C.L. Gauthier,
Felicien	14	M	1846	Zenon Laborde
Gustave	13	M	1847	Alcee Roy

---

[118] The **Benue–Congo** group of languages constitutes the largest branch of the Niger–Congo language family, both in terms of sheer number of languages, of which Ethnologue (2009) counts 900, and in terms of speakers, numbering perhaps 350 million. Spoken Sub-Saharan Africa, from Nigeria east and south - Ref. Wikipedia

- Secondly, the St. Paul Marriage records show the marriages of 6 men with the last name, **Magloire**, between 1869 and 1871. These are shown in **Table 10** below:

TABLE 10. MAGLOIRE MARRIAGES AT ST. PAUL (MAGMARR)

Name	Spouse	Marriage Date	Birthdate[119]	References (Page/Sheet)
Jean Louis	Josephine Augustine	7/8/1869	1817	155/46
Joseph	Celestine Gabriel	2/23/1871	1841	213/49
William	Mary Thomas	9/22/1870	1842	197/48
Felicien	Arthemise Gibbs	2/23/1869	1847	138/45
Leon	Rose Williams	7/8/1869	1847	154/46
Joseph	Marguerite Baker	9/15/1870	1850	196/48

Some key observations that can be made by comparing the two tables are below:

- The names of three slaves (i.e. **Joseph**, **William** and **Felicien**) that are enlarged and in bold in **Table 9** are the same names as some of the Magloire people who got married in **Table 10**.

  Also, their ages, determined from later census searches for **Joseph Magloire**, **William Magloire** and **Felicien Magloire**, were within 2 years of the ages given for the respective slaves at the time of the sale, strongly supporting the belief that these are the same people.

  Thus, at least three of the slaves who were sold during the probate sale in **Table 9** were very likely members of the Magloire family;

- The first entry in **Table 10**, **Jean Louis Magloire**, was determined to be much older (b. 1817) than the other Magloire men getting married during that period. An obvious conclusion from this is that he could be either their father, uncle or other older relative.

- The five Magloire men in **Table 10** who were born within 9 years of each other (i.e. Joseph, William, Felicien, Leon and Joseph, might be brothers or first cousins. They could have been Jean Louis Magloire' family.

We will study each of these men individually.

The Magloire Men

[119] In this table, the reader will note the birthdates were determined separately by researching the U.S. Census records for each of these men and calculating their birthdates from the information given in those census records.

In this section, this author hopes to locate as much information as possible on each of the "Magloire men" who appear in **Table 10**. This should make it possible to understand how they might be related to each other and how their ancestors were trapped in slavery:

- **Jean Louis Magloire**, who was identified as the oldest of the Magloire men who were shown in **Table 10** as married during the period 1869-1871, will be considered as the earliest confirmed Magloire in the parish.

  He married **Josephine Augustine** on July 18, 1869 and is listed in the records of St. Paul the Apostle Catholic Church (JLMagMarr).

  "J.L." Magloire (53) and **Josephine Magloire** (33) appeared in the 1870 U.S. Census, living near Marksville along with a one-year-old girl, **Celise** (JLMag1870). His date of birth was listed as 1817. All three of them were described as mulattoes who were born in Louisiana.

  No further information on them was found.

- **Joseph Arnat Magloire** was born about 1841 and married **Celestine Gabriel** on February 2, 1871 as recorded in the records of St. Paul the Apostle Catholic Church.

  Joseph Magloire served in Company C, U.S. Colored Troops 73rd Infantry Regiment during the Civil War under the alias, **Joseph Margass** (JosMagPen). His widow, **Celestine Magloire**, filed for his pension on June 15, 1900.

  Celestine Gabriel was believed to have been born in Louisiana between 1839 (CelGab1900) and 1842 (JosMag1870). She had two known siblings, **Rosaline Gabriel** and **Jean Gabriel** (See Dupas – Gabriel - Celestine Family Chapter above).

  The St. Paul Baptism Records show the baptism of a slave child named **Celestine**, who was born on February 1, 1831 (ConsDes1837). Celestine was the child of a slave woman named **Celeste**, who was held captive by Gertrude Normand, the widow of Laurent Normand Sr. of Hydropolis, near Mansura.

  Interestingly, the slave Celestine's godfather was a slave, named **Gabriel**, who was also held by the widow Normand. At the death of Gertrude Normand in 1848, a slave by the name of Gabriel (29) was sold to Barthelemy Normand in a probate sale (GabSale). This slave would have been 12 in 1831, at the time of Celestine's birth, making it possible for him to have been Celestine's brother.

  Also, sold in that same 1848 Probate Sale was a 60-year-old black female named Cileste (Celeste??). She would have been 43 at the time of Celestine's birth and 31 at the time of Gabriel's birth. This makes it possible for her to have been the mother of both Celestine and Gabriel. **More work is needed here.**

  In the 1870 census, Joseph and Celestine were farm laborers, living near Marksville, Louisiana (JosMag1870). Living with them were the following children: **Arnet** (9), **Eliska** (7), **Alicia** (3), and **Aristide** (2).

In 1880, Joseph (39) and Celestine (39) were still living near Marksville with the following children: **Gervais** (19), **Eliska** (12), **Alicia** (11), **Arestide** (8), **Ludger** (8), **Octavy** (6), **Alfred** (3), and **Rebecca** (1) (JosCelMc1880).

In 1900, Joseph (62) and Celestine (61) were living near Hessmer (CelGab1900). Living with them were their daughter, Rebecca (25), their son-in-law, **Alfonce Bello** (22), their grandson, **Jean B.** (12), and their granddaughter, **Josephine** (10).

The children of Joseph and Celestine were:

- **Gervais Arnat** - Gervais, Joseph and Celestine's son, married **Victorine Berzat**, the daughter of Jean Baptiste and Josephine Berzat (**See Luc-Berzat Chapter**), on May 19, 1881, as is recorded in the records of St. Paul's Catholic Church in Mansura, Louisiana[122]. They became farmers on their own land located inside the town of Mansura. They had 4 children between 1881 and 1888: **Helen** (1881), **Victoria Beulah** (1884), **Joseph Armond** (1886), and **Lula** a.k.a. "Ola" (1888).

  - ❖ **Helen** was shown in the 1920 census, married to **Poland Guillory** and living between Mansura and Hessmer (PolHelG1920). They had 3 children living with them: **Jessie** (9), **Lones** (8), and **Laura** (5). They were farmers. Helen and the 3 children could read and write.

  - ❖ **Victoria** eventually married **Eddie Hollis** and lived in Mansura (VicEdHol1940).

  - ❖ **Lula** eventually married **Willie Walton** and lived out her life in Mansura.

- **Elisca Magloire** – Eliska married **Homer Guillory**, the son of Hyppolite Guillory and Pauline Fontenot in Avoyelles Parish on October 10, 1881 (ElisMag).

  In 1900, Homer (34) and Eliska (30) were living near Hessmer, LA (ElisHom1900). Living with them were the following children: **Erylica** (17), **Celisca** (14) and **Prudent** (2). Also present was a boarder, **Exavier Lonzo** (22) and mother, **Elizabeth Bello** (65).

  Eliska Guillory died on November 29, 1941.

  Homer Guillory died on November 28, 1921.

- **Aristide Magloire** – Aristide married **Clara Lonzo** in Rapides Parish, Louisiana on March 11. 1893 (ArMagClaLonMarriage). In the 1910 census, Aristide (40) and Clara (36) were farmers, living near Hessmer, Louisiana (ArisClaMag1910). Living with them were their son, **John W.** (14), their 2 daughters, **Josephine** (4) and **Lauranza** (7 months), and their 2 nieces, **Rose Lonzo** (18) and **Josephine Lonzo** (10).

  Aristide died on July 27, 1930 at the age of 63 (ArisMagDeath).

---

[122] Marriage Certificate issued by St. Paul the Apostle Catholic Church, Mansura, LA

o **Alfred Magloire** (23) and his wife, **Mary** [Unknown last name] (21) appeared in the 1900 census, living near Hessmer (AlfMarMag1900). Living with them was their son, **Arthur** (3) and their 2 daughters, **Claire** (2) and **Virginie** (8 months). They were living next door to Alfred's parents, Joseph and Celestine Magloire.

o **Ludger Magloire** (28) and his wife, **Alicia Pryor** (25) were shown in the 1900 census living near Hessmer (LudAliMag1900). Living with them were their 2 sons, **Joffrion** (6) and **Andrew** (4), their daughter **Alida** (10 months), a servant girl, **Angela Washington** (13), and a boarder, **Anotele Washington** (4).

o **Rebecca Magloire** married **Alphonse Bello**. They were listed in the 1900 census (AlpRebBell900) as living with her parents, Joseph and Celestine, along with their children: **Jean Baptiste** and **Josephine Bello.**

o **Willie McGlory** - Willie was born in 1895 (WilMarMcG1920). He and his wife, **Mary Moore**, appeared in the 1920 U.S. census, living in Ward 8 of Avoyelles Parish (Near Moreauville-Plaucheville area). Living with them was their 10-year-old, son, **Ollan**, and a 20-year-old boarder, **Dellis Giles**.

In 1930, Willie and Mary, along with their 20-year-old son, **Olan**, were living in Glenmora, Rapides Parish, Louisiana (WilMarMcG1930).

In 1940, Willie and Mary were still residing in Glenmora. He was described as a Baptist minister and owned his own home (WilMarMcg1940).

o **Henry McGlory** - Henry and his wife, **Letty**, appeared in the 1920 U.S. census, living in Spring Hill, Louisiana (HenLetMcG1920). Living with them were their 3 daughters: **Beula** (19), **Floristine** (16), and **Anistine** (11). Also living with them was Henry's nephew, **William Opten** (8). Henry was described as a saw mill laborer.

• **William Magloire** was born in about 1840[123] and married **Mary Thomas** on 9/22/1870 at St. Paul Catholic Church.

In the 1870 U.S. Census for Avoyelles Parish (WilMag1870), William (28) was listed as living near Marksville, LA with his wife, **Marie** (25) and two children: **Camelia** (2) and **Onil** (9). Also, living with them was a young female, **Marie Cole** (21).

In the 1900 U.S. Census, William (55) and Rose (55) were listed as living in Moreauville, LA (WlMag1900). Living with them was their grandson, **Willie Joshua** (16).

In the 1910 U.S. Census, William (65) and Rose (65) were living near Moreauville, LA (Wilmag1910). They were living alone. They indicated that they had had only one child, who was alive at that time.

• **Felicien Magloire** was born in 1847 in Louisiana. He married **Arthemise Gibbs** on February 23, 1869 at St. Paul's Catholic Church (See **Table 10**, Above).

---

[123] Calculated from U.S. Census records.

A male slave by the name of Felicien was sold from the estate of Jean Baptiste Lemoine to Zenon Laborde as part of a probate sale on November 9, 1860. Felicien was listed as 14-years-old at the time (b. 1846).

Felicien and Arthemise Magloire appeared in the 1870 U.S. census living in Subdivision 6 of Avoyelles Parish (FelMag1870). Here, he was listed as being 22-years-old while she was 20. Living with them was a 7-month-old male named **Alcide** and a second person named **Arthemise Magloire**[124], who was 37-years-old.

In the 1880 U.S. Census, Felicien (33) and Arthemise (32) were living near Marksville, LA and had the following children residing with them: **Alicide** (10), **Landry** (9), **Theopile** (7) and **Eugene** (5) (FelMag1880). Also, residing with them was a 25-year-old mulatto male, named **Gabriel**[125] (See **Table 9**, above).

No additional public records on Felicien or Arthemise Magloire could be found for this study. The following information was located regarding their children:

o **Alicide Magloire** was born in 1869 (FelMag1880). He appeared to have moved to Luther, Oklahoma where he appeared in the 1900 U.S. Census. He was married to **Almatina Stephens** and they had six girls: **Ellen** (11), **Sarah** (12), **Lillie** (7), **Emma** (4), **Effie** (5), **Lucy**; and one son, **Preston** (2).

o **Landry Magloire** was born in 1871 (FelMag1880). He married **Nancy Hamilton** on January 9, 1896 in Avoyelles Parish (LanMagMarr). In the 1910 U.S. Census, Landry and "**Anna**" are living in "Grand Cotes", Avoyelles Parish, LA (LanMag1910). They had the following children living with them: **Mathews** (6), **Ida** (5) and **Arick** (4).

o **Theopile Magloire** was born in 1873 (FelMag1880). He married **Emma Lonzo** on February 4, 1895 (TheoMagMarr).

o **Eugene Magloire** was born in 1875 (FelMag1880).

• **Leon Magloire** was born in 1847. He married **Rose Williams** on 7/8/1869 (See **Table 10**, above).

Leon (33) and Rose (26) appeared in the 1880 U.S. Census for Avoyelles Parish along with their three daughters: **Anne Marie** (7), **Elizabeth** (5) and **Julia Rebecca** (2). They were farmers, living near Marksville, LA.

In the 1900 U.S. Census for Avoyelles Parish, Leon (54) was now married to **Clementine** (58) and living near Marksville, LA (LeonMag1900). Living with them were their three daughters: **Zoe Matilda** (16), **Josephine** (13) and **Isabella** (9). Also, living with them were their grandchild, **Hildon Lockwood** (9) and his mother, **Marie Magloire** (74).

In the 1910 U.S. Census, Leon (72) and Clementine (68) were living near Marksville, LA (LeonMag1910). Living with them was their daughter, **Rosebella** (19),

---

[124] An Arthemise appears in the probate sale (Table 9) but her age doesn't match that of this Arthemise.
[125] Is this the same Gabriel listed as Marie's son in the 1860 slave sale?

No further information available on them was found.

- **Joseph Magloire** is listed as having gotten married to **Marguerite Baker** in the records at St. Paul the Apostle Catholic Church on September 15, 1870 (JosMarr1970). In the 1880 U.S. Census is a couple with the names and ages: **J. Magloin** (30) and **M. Magloin** (25), who could be Joseph and Marguerite (JM1880).

  The 1900 U.S. Census for Rapides Parish shows a widowed **Joe McGlory** residing alone in Alexandria where he is described as a "White Washer" (JoeMag1900). There is no further information on either Joseph or Marguerite.

Current Status

Over the past 50 years, the McGlory name has generally vanished from Mansura. Small groups bearing that name reside in or near Marksville, LA. Others have lived in Michigan and other states.

The McGlory family made important contributions in the areas of construction, transportation and the military.

McGlory Family Pictures

SISTERS: HELEN, VICTORIA AND LULA McGLORY

Current Old River Road, in the vicinity of Grande Bayou and "Down the Hill".

Following the Civil War, Marie Charlot, the matriarch of the Oliver family, purchased a large tract of land bordering Old River Road on the south (Right) side.

Later, that land became subdivided among several of the black and mulatto families who resided along that road.

Chapter 11.

The Oliver Family

Marie Charlot

Introduction to the Oliver Family

The Oliver family of Mansura is, and has always been a relatively small family, compared to large families such as the James and Sampson families. Nevertheless, their hard-working and good-natured styles has always earned them respect. Their commitment to the church and the community makes them a very important asset to any activities related to those areas.

The Oliver name had its origin in France as the given name, **Olivier**, where it was brought to England by the Normans in 1066.[127] As with other Louisiana names, over time, the Olivier name gradually was changed to the more English-sounding, Oliver.

---

[127] From FamilyTree.com

A search using Ancestry.com did not show any white persons in Avoyelles Parish with the names Olivier or Oliver prior to or soon after the Civil War.

From the 1870 U.S. Census to the most recent records, the Oliver family members have been farmers located on Old River Road, near the area called Grande Bayou.

Historical Highlights

Bazile Olivier, born around 1812, is the earliest confirmed person with the Olivier surname. He and his wife, **Honorine**, were born in Avoyelles parish. They were married there and had as many as 11 children. Following Bazile's death sometime before 1900, Honorine and several of her children moved to the Oklahoma City area where they made their permanent homes. A number of their children appear to have passed away before 1900.

Louis Olivier was born about 1840 in Avoyelles Parish, LA (LouOli1870). He and **Marie Charlot** were married on May 9, 1868 in Avoyelles Parish. Over time, they became the parents of nine children. Louis died sometime in 1886. Marie died on July 29, 1918 in Avoyelles Parish (MarOliDeath).

Although Bazile is clearly old enough to have been Louis' father, there is no documented evidence to prove this. For clarity, the families of Bazile and Honorine Olivier and that of Louis and Marie Olivier will be treated separately.

----

1. Bazile and Honorine Olivier

Bazile Olivier claimed to have been born in Louisiana in 1812 in his 1870 U.S. census records (BasHonOliv1870). He claimed that his parents were also born in Louisiana.

Not much confirmed information about Bazile Oliver exists. **More study is needed here.**

Honorine Francois claimed to be born in Louisiana around 1836 (BasHonOliv1870) or 1830 (BasHonOli1880). The St. Paul Baptism Records list the baptisms of three female slave babies with the name, "Honoroe" and one with the name, "Honoroine. All had birth years close to that specified by Honorine Olivier in those 1870 and 1880 census records:

Unfortunately, there is not enough information available to suggest that one of those babies was the same person as Honorine Olivier.

More study is needed here.

Bazile Olivier and **Honorine Francois** were married on January 6, 1877 in Avoyelles Parish (BasHonMarr).

Bazile (58) and Honorine (36) appeared in the 1870 U.S. Census for Avoyelles Parish, Louisiana (BasHonOliv1870). Living with them were five young people: **Rose** (17), **Victorine** (15), **Paul** (10), **Louis** (8) and **Gustave** (2). Clearly, all but Gustave were born during slavery, although there is no evidence as to whether or not they were slaves or free people

By 1880 (BasHonOli1880), Bazile (65) and "**Norine**" (50) were farmers, living in Grande Bayou, next door to Jean Pierre James and his family. They had the following children living with them: **Gustave** (17), **Octavie** (13), **Zinon** (9), **Louise** (7) and **Sophie** (3).

There is a record of the death of a Basile Olivier that occurred in New Orleans on October 5, 1887 (BasOlivDeath). **Further study is needed to prove that this was the Basile Olivier from Avoyelles.**

In the 1900 U.S. Census for the Oklahoma county of Lincoln, Norine was a 72-year-old, living in the town of **Wellston**, with her daughter, **Octavia**, and Octavia's husband, **Oliver Nesow** (NorOli1900). She indicated that she had had 11 children and that 6 remained alive.

The Children of Basile and Honorine Olivier

Basile and Honorine listed a total of nine children in the 1870 and 1880 census records. However, she indicated that she had had a total of 11 in the 1900 census for Wellston, Oklahoma. At that time, six remained alive. However, only three had records that could be located for this work:

- **Paul** – Was born in 1855 and appeared as a 10-year-old boy[128] in the 1870 census (BasHonOliv1870). He married **Cecelia Holmes** in Avoyelles Parish on July 4, 1878 (PaulCecMarr).

  In the 1880 U.S. Census, Paul (23) and Cecelia (25) were living between Cocoville and Marksville, in the area near the Tunica Indian village (PaulOli1880). Living with them were their two sons: **Fabius/Eluster**[129] (1) and **Zervon** (6).

  At some point between 1880 and 1900, Paul and his family moved to Oklahoma and remained there, working as farmers (Bradley).

  Paul (44) next appeared in the 1900 U.S. census for Deep Fork, Oklahoma (PaulOli1900). Here he was living with his wife, **Cedonia** (46)[130], and five children: **Eluster** (21), **Lesetti** (20), **Wittan** (15), **Purene** (12) and **Joseph R** (5).

  In 1910 (PaulOliv1910), Paul was still living in Deep Fork, Oklahoma. Only his wife, Cedonia, and one of his children, Joseph R., remained.

  By 1930, Paul was a widower, living alone in Deep Fork, Oklahoma (PaulOliv1930).

---

[128] Probably an error by the parents or the census takers.
[129] All of the later records refer to their son, **Eluster**, who was born at the same time as that recorded for Flavius. This suggests that they are the same person (Bradley).
[130] It's not clear when Cecelia became Cedonia. However, their ages match, indicating they could be the same person.

Paul died in Oklahoma City, in January, 1934 (PaulOlDeath). He is buried in Wilbourn Cemetery.

- **Gustave** – Appeared in the 1870 U.S. Census as a two-year-old boy, living with his parents, Bazile and Honorine(BasHonOliv1870) and in the 1880 census as a 13-year-old boy, doing the same.

  Gustave (31) next appeared in the 1900 U.S. Census for Wellston, Lincoln, Oklahoma (GusOli1900). Living with him were his wife, **Nora Oliver** (30), and six children: **Fred** (10), **Winston** (9), **Lola** (6), **Lewis** (4), **Lida** (2) and **Cordwell** (9/12).

  In the 1920 U.S. Census, Gustave (51) and Nora (50) were still living in Wellston, Lincoln, Oklahoma (GusOli1920). Living with them were their nine children: **Winston H** (28), **Louis B R** (24), **Cardwell S** (20), **Rustine M** (18), **Theodore T** (16), **Lordon L** (14), **Eldonia V** (12), **Meldon V** (10) and **Twelvy Z** (6).

  In 1930, Gustave (61) and Nora (60) remained in Wellston (GusOli1930). Living with them were their two daughters: **Melton** (19) and **Twelvy** (16).

  In 1940, Gustave L (71) and Nora V (70), were living in Wellston with their granddaughter, **Loretta Oliver** (16) and grandson, **Hughes** (15) (GusOliv1940).

- **Octavia** – Appeared in the 1880 U.S. Census for Avoyelles as a 13-year-old girl, living with her parents, Bazile and Honorine Oliver (BasHonOli1880). She married **Camile Normand,** the son of **Francois** and **Celestine Normand** of Mansura, LA on January 22, 1898 (OctCamMarr).

  It is not clear what became of Camile Normand. However, Octavia (23) appeared in the 1900 U.S. Census for Wellston, OK, married to **Oliver Nesow** (25) (NorOli1900). Octavia and Oliver had the following children living with them: **Clifton** (3), **Leona** (2) and **Lawrence** (5 months). Also, living with them was her mother, **Norine**.

  In the 1910 U.S. Census for Wellston, Oklahoma, Octavia (29) and Oliver (30) "Nero"[131] were listed as farmers, having the following children living with them: **Clifton** (13), **Leona** (11), **Lawrence** (10), **Roy** (7), **Arthur** (3) and **Pearl** (0) (OlivNero1910).

  In the 1920 U.S. Census for Wellston, Oklahoma, Oliver (52) was now listed as married to **Flora** (33) (OliNero1920). They had the following children living with them: **Arthur** (13), **Pearl** (8), **Linnwood** (6) and **Herbert** (4).

The Rest of Basile and Honorine Olivier's Children

The children below were born to Basile and Honorine Olivier and listed in the 1870 or 1880 U.S. censuses. **Further study is needed to determine what became of them.**

- **Rose** – Was born in 1853 and appeared as a 17-year-old girl in the 1870 census (BasHonOliv1870).

---

[131] Apparently, Oliver's original surname was misspelled, "Nesow" in the 1900 census.

- **Louis** – Appeared in the 1880 U.S. Census as a seven-year-old boy, living with his parents, Bazil and Norine (BasHonOli1880) .

- **Victorine** – Was born in 1855 and appeared as a 15-year-old girl in the 1870 census (BasHonOliv1870). .

- **Zinon** - Appeared in the 1880 U.S. Census as a nine-year-old boy, living with her parents, Bazil and Norine (BasHonOli1880).

- **Louise** - Appeared in the 1880 U.S. Census as a seven-year-old girl, living with her parents, Bazil and Norine (BasHonOli1880).

- **Marie Ann** - Appeared in the 1880 U.S. Census as a five-year-old girl, living with her parents, Bazil and Norine (BasHonOli1880).

- **Sophie** - Appeared in the 1880 U.S. Census as a three-year-old girl, living with her parents, Bazil and Norine (BasHonOli1880).

----

2. Louis and Marie Olivier

Louis Olivier and Marie Charlot were both born in Avoyelles Parish during slavery.

They were married in Avoyelles Parish following the Civil War, in which Louis served, and settled down to raise a family and farm the land in the vicinity of Grande Bayou. All of the current, local Olivers appear to be their descendants.

Louis Olivier was born about 1840 in Avoyelles Parish, LA (LouOli1870). His parents were both born in Louisiana but their identities remain unknown[132].

Louis Olivier enlisted in the U.S. Army on April 15, 1864[133] in "Avril" Parish for a term of three years and was assigned as a laborer to the 2nd Regiment U.S. Colored Light Artillery where he

---

[132] Louis was a very common slave name, making it nearly impossible to identify one who might be Louis Olivier. Similarly, no slave with the name, Louis, was sold in an Avoyelles Probate sale.

[133] As noted in *Back Through the Veil, Book1* (Prier), a significant number of African-American slaves from the Mansura and Marksville areas, Louis Olivier among them, had the courage to escape their enslaved lives and join the Union army as it passed through Avoyelles Parish during the spring of 1864. After serving with honor in several campaigns, once the war was over, these men showed incredible courage in returning to a home town that was populated by angry Whites, many of whom were hostile to the federal government and, especially towards the former slaves. whose freedom had cost them their life styles and the lives of many of their friends and family members.

was stationed at Vicksburg (LouOliMil). He was described in his military record as being 24 years old, 5 feet, 10 inches tall with black complexion, black eyes and black hair.

Louis Olivier, on returning home, became a farmer in Grand Bayou (LouOli1870). His home was located in the vicinity of those belonging to **Pierre Sampson**, **Rudolph Berger** and **Julien Saucier**, other black men who had also served in the Union army.

Marie Charlot was a Native American who may have been born in St, Landry in 1832. She may have been the 18-year-old, "mulatto" woman who appeared in the 1850 U.S. census for that area, living with a 57-year-old mulatto female whose name was Sophie Desmers (MarChar1850).

From her picture (See Above), she appears to have had strong Native American facial features. She could have been born on one of the many local Indian villages that were found throughout Avoyelles, Point Coupee and St. Landry Parishes at that time (Northrup).

Marie later purchased a large tract of land in Grande Bayou that ran from the current location of the Oliver family homes to the western edge of the area called "Down the Hill". That land was later subdivided into several smaller farms along the south side of "Grande Bayou Road".

Marie is believed to have "married" to **Isadore Rabalais** (1831-1902) and was the mother of his son, **Oliver**, (See below) (C. M. French).

She also bore a son, **Paul Marius Lehmann** (b. Mar 1864), for Jewish immigrant **Isaac Lehmann** of Lembach, Alsace[134]. Isaac was killed by Confederate sympathizers about a month following Paul's birth.

Marie raised the two children, Oliver and Paul, bringing them into her marriage to Louis Olivier in 1868.

Louis Olivier and **Marie Charlot** were married on May 9, 1868 in Avoyelles Parish, Louisiana and their marriage recorded at St. Paul the Apostle Catholic Church (LouMarMarr). As part of that marriage, they claimed two children: **Jermone** (b. 1859), **Olivert** (b. 1861).

[At this point, it remains unclear where Jermone came from and what became of him later. Also, despite family history to the contrary, there are no records of Paul Lehman in the Olivier family except his sub-tutoring oath (See Below).]

Over time, they became the parents of the following additional children: **Ernestine** (b. 1871), **Estelle** (b. 1873), **Angelica** (b. 1875), **Josephine** (b. 1876), **Edward** (b. 1881), **Leonce** (b. 1883), and **Eunice** (b. 1885).

In the 1880 census, everyone in that household but Louis was described as a mulatto (LouMar1880).

---

[134] Information from a posting on Avoyelles Parish Genealogy Society group page on Facebook by Sheldon Roy, 10/12/2017.

Louis died sometime in 1886. A oath to provide sub-tutoring for his children (**Ernestine, Estella, Josephine, Octavie, Ursin, Edward** and **Leonard**) by **Paul M. Lehman** was signed on August 9, 1886 (LouOlideath).

Marie died on July 29, 1918 in Avoyelles Parish (MarOliDeath).

The Children of Louis and Marie Charlot

- **Jermone** appeared in the 1870 U.S. Census as a 12-year-old boy, living with his parents, Louis (38) and Marie (30) (JerOliv1870). Also present was his brother, Olivier (9).

  He appeared in the 1880 U.S. Census as a 21-year-old man, living with his parents (LouMar1880). Also present were his siblings: Oliver (19), Ernestine (9), Estelle (7), Angelica (5) and Flavie (2).

  No further records of **Jermone** were found for this study.

- **Oliver** appeared in the 1880 U.S. Census as a 19-year-old man, living with his parents (LouMar1880).

  He later appeared as a 36-year-old man, living with his mother, Marie, and six siblings: **Ernestine** (29); **Estelle (27), Josephine** (24), **Edward** (19); **Leonce** (17) and **Eunice** (15) in the 1900 U.S. census (JosOliv1900).

  In the 1910 census, Oliver and his brother Leonce (27), were living with their mother, Marie (OlivRab1910). He was now listed as 46-years-old **Olivert Rabalais.** Their large age difference suggested that he and Leonce were actually half-brothers.

  Oliver Rabalais died on May 23, 1947 (Ballard).

- **Ernestine** appeared in the 1880 U.S. Census as a nine-year-old girl, living with her parents (LouMar1880).

  In 1900, she was living with her mother, Marie, and five siblings (ErnOli1900).

  She married **Ozemie Fontenot** around 1908 (ErnOzeMar). They had one child, **Clifton Joseph**, who was born in 1909.

  Ernestine passed away in Mansura, Louisiana in 1958.

- **Estelle** appeared in the 1880 U.S. Census as a seven-year-old girl, living with her parents.

  In 1900, she was a 27-year-old single woman, living with her mother, Marie (60), and five of her siblings (See Above) (ErnOli1900).

  Estelle married **Celestin Hebert** in 1902.

In the 1910 U.S. Census, she (36) and Celestin (40) were living in Mansura (EstCelHeb1910). Living with them were the following children: **Joseph** (7), **Chester** (5), **Clarence** (5), **Marie** (4) and **Louis** (1).

By 1930, Estelle was a married head-of-household, living inside Mansura, with the following children (EstHeb1930): Chester (24), Clarence (24), **Beatrice** (22), **Jimmy Hebert** (18) and **Mabel** (13).

In 1940, Estelle (66) and Celestin (69) were living in Mansura on the Cotton Port Highway (EstCel1940). Living with them were their son, Jimmy (28) and their daughter, Mable (23).

- **Angelica** appeared in the 1880 U.S. Census as a five-year-old girl, living with her parents (LouMar1880). No additional records of her were found for this study.

- **Josephine** appeared in the 1900 U.S. Census as a 24-year-old girl, living with her mother, Marie (60) and five siblings (See Above) (JosOliv1900).

  She died on March 3, 1909 (JosOlivMarr).

  *[In the 1880 U.S. census, a five-year-old girl named "**Flavie**" appeared living with her parents (LouMar1880). There are no further records of her. However, since she would have been the same age as Josephine in the 1900 census (See Above), but was not present then, it appears likely that **Flavie** and **Josephine** were the same person].*

- **Edward Louis** appeared in the 1900 U.S. census as a 19-year-old farm laborer, living with his mother, Marie, and five siblings (See Above) (JosOliv1900).

  Edward married **Martha Pierre** of Moreauville, LA (Reed).

  In 1910, Edward (28) and Martha (22) were farmers, living near Mansura, LA, along with their only child, **Wilbert E.** (7 months) (EdMar1910). They were living next door to his mother, **Marie**, and her two sons, **Leonce** and **Oliver**[135].

  For the next two decades, Edward and Martha worked as farmers in the Grand Bayou area, along with their son, Wilbert.

  In 1930, Wilbert (20) was married to **Catherine Carmouche** (19) (wilCat1930) and they had one child living with them, **Augustine [Prevot]** (6).

  Edward Louis Oliver passed away in Rapides Parish, LA on November 10, 1960 at the age of 80 (EdOlDeath).

  Martha Oliver passed away in 1971 at the age of 83. She is buried in St. Paul the Apostle Cemetery, in Mansura, LA (MarOlDeath).

---

[135] Oliver reappears as Olivert Rabalais, a 46-year-old mulatto. Since he and Jermone were significantly older than their siblings, it is likely that they were from an earlier marriage.

- **Leonce** appeared as a 17-year-old farmer in the 1900 U.S. census, living with his mother, Marie, and five siblings (See Above) (JosOliv1900).

  In the 1910 census, Leonce (27) was living with his mother, **Marie** (68) and his half-brother, **Oliver Rabalais** (46) (OlivRab1910).

- **Eunice** appeared as a 15-year-old farmer in the 1900 U.S. census, living with her mother, Marie, and five siblings (See Above) (JosOliv1900).

  She married **Martin Jean Batiste** (See Batiste Family Chapter).

Current Status

The Oliver family of today has continued to live their lives as they learned to from their parents and grandparents. They are firm believers in the value of how your appearance effects the way others see you:

> "Keep your image clean outside you home";
> "Watch how you live"
> "Respect yourself"
> "Watch who you hang around with".

They have made important contributions in the areas of:

- Business,
- Support for the Church and
- Helping others when you can.

Oliver Family Pictures

Edward Oliver

Wilbert and Catherine Oliver

Faces in the crowd attending the dedication of the new Our Lady of Prompt Succor Church in Mansura in May, 1938.

Many of the people mentioned in this book were likely present at this historic event.

Chapter 12.

The Prier Family

Oliver Peter Prier

Introduction to the Prier Family

The Priers have always been a family of wanderers, many moving away as soon as they reached the age when either they or their parents felt they were sufficiently mature. Some of the early Priers moved to Opelousas, Lake Charles, and other cities in Louisiana. Later, others made their homes in Alexandria, Shreveport, Beaumont, Houston, Chicago, and many other faraway places.

Despite the family's traveling ways, Avoyelles Parish remains the home to a large number of Priers.

The Prier name is derived from the old English word, **Prior**, which was the name for the church official just below an **abbot**. It later became a description for a person with the qualities of a prior.

Just like other local African-American surnames, the Prier name has gone through several changes over the years. The earliest ancestors spelled their name Pryor. Later, other variations included Prior, Pryer, and Prya, finally, becoming "Prier" by the mid-20th century.

This chapter will explore the history of the Prier family whose members lived in or near Mansura, using all available records that have been vetted to a satisfactory level of credibility. If there are records, oral histories, etc. that cannot be verified using commonly available records or credible sources, these will be either excluded or their questionable accuracy noted.

Toward the end of this chapter, information on various **Priors**, who resided in the Bunkie and Cheneyville, Louisiana areas will be reviewed. Unfortunately, no records were found to help determine whether they are related to the Mansura Priers.

Historical Highlights

There are a few shreds of evidence suggesting which slavery plantations some members of the Prier family might have begun their journeys to freedom from. Although these sources are very sketchy, in many cases, this book will still explore these and attempt to draw some conclusions from that information.

It is generally believed, among Prier genealogists, that the Prier family members of today are descendants of **Moise** or **Moses Pryor**[136]. This is the approach that this study will use. **Different views are more than welcome.**

Moise Pryor

Moses/Moise[137] – Moses or Moise Pryor is believed to be the first person in the Prier family tree in the Mansura area. As will be seen, there is some confusion as to whether there was one or two Moise Pryors. However, for this work, it is assumed that there were two: **Moise Pryor I** and **Moise Pryor II**.

Let's look at the raw information:

- The first mention of someone named **Moise** in the Avoyelles parish area was during the Catholic baptism of a slave baby, **Jeanne**, born on October 17, 1823 (Church). Jeanne's mother was **Susane**, a slave held captive by a slave holder named **William Blondel**.

  The baptism was performed by a Catholic priest on October 26, 1825. Present at Jeanne's baptism was Jeanne's godfather, a slave named **Moise,** and her godmother, a slave named **Desire'**.

---

[136] i.e. Harold Taylor
[137] Although the name, Moses, is found in several informal family genealogy studies, in the official records, he is referred to as Moise. The difference between the two names is likely a result of local pronunciation of French names by illiterate former slaves.

While nothing is known about the two slave godparents participating in Jeanne's baptism, to be a Catholic godparent **today**, one generally must be an adult, (i.e. 16 years old or greater)[138]. Thus, since the baptism occurred in 1825, one can conclude, based on current Cannon Law, that Moise and Desire' had to have been born at least 16 years earlier, i.e., no later than **1809**.

Since it is a common belief among many in the Prier family that the original Moise was born in Virginia around 1800[139], it is possible that the Moise named in the baptism record could be the same one as in the Prier family history (See Below).

He will, therefore, be referred to as **Moise I** because of his name being the first to appear in the local Mansura records.

Much additional work is needed here!

- The second piece of information on the Moise I/Moise II issue is the probate sale of a slave by the name of Moise and his family on March 20, 1860, at the death of **Laurent Normand, Jr**. of Cocoville, LA (Moi/PrySale). Here, 43 slaves were sold, including a black male named **Moise** (40), his spouse, **May** (25), and two children: **Mary Jane** (3) and **Lucy** (6 months). Moise, May and the two children were sold together to **Eliza Bordelon**, the widow of Laurent Normand, Jr. of Cocoville, LA.

  Based on his age at the time of the sale, (i.e. 40), this Moise would have been born around 1820. Moise I, on the other hand, would have been at least 60 by then, likely too old to be a recent parent.

  This second Moise is, therefore, referred to as **Moise II**.

- The third piece of information is an Avoyelles Parish marriage record that shows the marriage of **Moise Pryor** and **Mary Smith** on June 6, 1867 (MoiMarPryMarriage). The marriage took place on the grounds of the plantation previously owned by **Lucien Dominique Coco**.

  If one assumes that May and Mary are the same person (**Not Proven!**), then the newlywed couple could be the same people as Moise and May, listed in the slave sale above.

  The conclusion is that this person now married to Mary Smith could be **Moise II**.

- Finally, the death certificate of John Pryor (See Below) says that his parents were Moses Pryor and Casey Batiste (JohnPriDeath).

From the above information, it appears that:

- There could have been two **Moise Pryors (Moise Pryor I** and **Moise Pryor II)**;

- **May** could have been Moise II's slave wife;

- Moise Pryor did marry **Mary Smith**;

---

[138] As stated in Canon 874 and required by the Diocese of Austin: Must be at least 16 years of age. Must be a baptized Catholic who has completed the sacraments of Eucharist and Confirmation. May not be the parent of the child being baptized. If married, must be married in the Catholic Church, regularly attending mass on Sunday, and living their Faith. The two godparents do not have to be married to one another. A baptized non-Catholic may not be a godparent but may serve as a witness along with a Catholic godparent.

[139] Information provided by Harold Taylor in his Prier Family Tree.

- Moses Pryor and Casey were the parents of John Pryor.

Based on the above discussion, family history and a few public records, the discussion in this book will proceed on the assumption that Moise Pryor I was the father of the other local Pryors and had the following children (It is equally possible that he was not related to them at all:

- **Moise Pryor II** (born 1820-26)
- **Claris** (born 1834)
- **Samuel** (born 1836)
- **John** (born 1845)
- **Eleanor** (born 1848)
- **James** (Born 1872: See the Discussion Below)

In any case, it is known that Claris, Samuel, John and Eleanor were siblings[140]. Based on the age spread of the children, it is quite possible that Moise II, Claris, and Samuel had the same mother, while John and Eleanor could have shared a different one. James seems to have been a special case where **much additional work is needed.**

Unfortunately, no additional records were found regarding Moise Pryor I, his birth or death.

The Children of Moise Pryor I

- **Moise I** – Moise I appears to have been born in about 1820, based on his age (40) at the time of the Laurent Normand probate sale, described above (Moi/PrySale)

  As mentioned above, a slave by the name of **Moise** (40), his spouse, **May** (25), and two children: **Mary Jane** (3) and **Lucy** (6 months) were sold to **Eliza Bordelon** on March 20, 1860, at the death of slave holder, **Laurent Normand, Jr.** of Cocoville, LA (Moi/PrySale).

  Moise Pryor married **Mary Smith** on June 6, 1864 in Avoyelles Parish, LA (MoisPryMarr). It is possible that May and Mary were the same person but **there is no proof.**

  Moses Pryor and **Casey Baptiste** were the parents of John Pryor, as indicated on John Prier's death certificate. The fact that they had different last names suggests that they may not have been married.

  No additional records on Moise or Mary were located.

- **Clarice** – Clarice Pryor was born about 1834 and lived her entire life in the Mansura, LA area. Not many records exist about her except the following:

---

[140] This is based on Family Histories, Public Records, etc. as will be shown below.

- ○ Clarice Pryor married **Marcelin Joseph** on September 5, 1889 (MarJosClarPryMrriage)[141].
- ○ In about 1871, she had a child, Cyriaque Francisco, for Francois Francisco (See Francisco Family Chapter).

- ○ **Claris Pryor** died a widow at the age of 83 on July 7, 1917 in Mansura, LA (ClarPryDeath). Her death certificate indicated that her parents were **Moise Pryor** and **I. Dolay.** She would have been born in 1834. Cyriaque Francisco told the medical examiner that Claris' father was Moise Prier and her mother was I. Dolay.

- • **Samuel** (a.k.a. **Toussaint**) **Pryor** – Nothing much is known about Samuel's parents other than that they were both born in Louisiana. Here are a few pieces of information that might help define his life better:

  - ○ On **Emile Prier's** Death Certificate, his son, **Simon Prier**, indicated that Emile Prier's father was named "**Tousin Prier**" and his mother was "**Juline Francisco**" (SamPrideath).

  - ○ At the death of **Zenon Lemoine** of Cocoville, on December 12, 1850, a probate sale of his property was held and 76 slaves were sold (SamPrySale). Among them was a 12-year-old black male named "**Toussaint**". He was sold to Villeneuve Roy. His birth year would have been **1838**.

  - ○ In the 1880 U.S. Census for Avoyelles Parish, Samuel Pryor (44) was listed as married to Julienne Francisco (45) (SamPry1880). His age here indicated that his birth year was **1836**, close to that shown in the Zenon Lemoine probate sale for "Toussaint".

  - ○ This strongly indicates that **Samuel Pryor** might have been "**Toussaint**" the slave of **Zenon Lemoine**.

Samuel Pryor and **Julienne Francisco**[142] were married in Avoyelles Parish on April 25, 1881 (SamPryJulFranMarr). Their Catholic wedding was witnessed by A. Sampson and Fulgence Francisco. As part of their marriage, they declared six children: **Aurelian, Emile, Onile, Florida, Alica** and **Florestine**.

They appeared as husband and wife in the 1880 U.S. census living near the Mansura-Hessmer highway on a road called by many "The Gremillion Cotes". Samuel was 44 and Julienne was 45 at the time.

They were farmers and were living next door to several Francisco families headed by brothers and, possibly, parents of Julienne. Residing with them, in 1880, were their three sons: Aurelian (12), Emile (10) and Onil (8); their three daughters: Florida (6), Alicia (4) and Floristine (2); Julienne's sister, **Lucille "Luce" Francisco** (21) and Samuel's "brother", **James Pryor** (8)[143].

It is not known when or where Samuel died. However, in the 1900 census (JulPry1900), widowed Julienne Pryor was still living near the Mansura-Hessmer highway[144] with her widowed daughter, **Florestine** (26) and Florestine's 2 children: **Anna Lou** and **Beulah**. Also present was an orphan, **Eddie Jones**.

---

[141] The parish marriage records show the marriages of Marcelin Joseph to a "Clarie" Pryor and an Elaine Pryor on that same day.

[142] Julienne Francisco was born in Avoyelles Parish, Louisiana around 1835 (SamPry1880). It remains unclear if her father was Julian or Francois Francisco, despite some evidence, cited above (See Francisco Family profile) that he could be. Her mother is unknown.

[143] It is difficult to believe that James Pryor was truly Samuel's brother because of their large differences in ages (Samuel was 44, James was 8).

[144] Via proximity to Robert Chatelain and Eddie Normand families

Living nearby were Julienne's sons, Oneal and Aurelian along with their families as well as several Francisco families.

Samuel and Julienne's children married as follows:

o **Emile** married **Mary Louise Nicholas** (a.k.a. Neco or Nicaud) on February 4, 1894 (EmJulPryMarriage). He died on October 12, 1931 (EmPryDeath). They had 5 sons: **Sam**, **Simon**, **Pennison**, **Preston**, and **Oliver**[145]; and 2 daughters: **Mary Ida** and **Marielouise**.

o **Oneal** married **Maria Francisco** on February 6, 1894 (OnMarPryMarriage). He died on April 15, 1925 (OnPryDeath). They had 2 children: **Wade** and **Rosa**.

o **Florestine** married **Mathew Bourgs** on December 31, 1894 (FloPryMatBouMarriage). She died in Alexandria on August 20, 1939. They had 2 children: **Anna Lou** and **Beulah**.

o **Florida** married **Thomas Fox** on December 15, 1887 (FlorPryThomFoxMarriage). They had 4 children: **Beulah**, **Marie L.**, **Kirby and Curly**.

o **Alicia** married **Ludger Magloire** on October 5, 1893 (AliPryLudMagMarriage). They had 2 sons, **Joffrion** and **Andrew**, and a daughter, **Alida**.

o **Aurelian** married **Ernestine Magloire** on December 8, 1887 (AurPryErnMagMarriage). He died April 19, 1926 (AurPryDeath). They had 2 sons: **Adelma** and **Landry**; and 4 daughters: **Adela**, **Mathilde**, **Winnie** and **Eva**.

• **John** – John Pryor was born around 1850 in Louisiana. He was one of the more interesting members of the Pryor family. He lived an itinerant life, traveling through Louisiana, and, possibly, Texas, as he plied his trade as a traveling preacher. As a result, he had at least three wives and many children.

At the time of his death in Mansura, Louisiana, on January 1, 1930, his wife was listed as **Mary Jackson** (JohnPriDeath).

Records indicate that John married **Lucy Owing** on February 13, 1872 (JoPryLucOwMarriage).

There is also a marriage record showing a **John Prier** becoming married to **Rosa Gauthier** on Sep 30, 1880 (JoPrRoGauMarr). John (30) and Rosa (28) appeared in the 1880 census, living near Mansura. Living with them was their 4-year-old son, **Thomas** (JoRoPry1880).

John Prior (65) was listed in the 1920 census, living with his nephew, **Emile Prior**, in Mansura (JoPri1920).

John Prier[147] died in Avoyelles Parish on January 1 1930 at the age of 85. From this, he would have been born in 1845.

---

[145] This author's father

[147] In the 1930 census, a **John Davis** (91) was living with his "nephew" and Emile Prior's son, **Oliver Prier** (JoPri1930). Unfortunately, it is not **completely clear if John Davis and John Prior were the same person**. In any case, Oliver Prier named his next child, who was born the year following John Prior's death, **John Byron Prier**[147]. Since there are no earlier records of a John Davis in the Prier family, an obvious choice is to assume that there was some sort of census-taker error, here. However, **additional study is needed to determine who John Davis was**.

John's children included the following[148]:

o **Thomas** - Born 1876 in Avoyelles Parish (ThomPry1880). His mother was **Rosa Gauthier**.

o **Nevada** - Born May 22, 1893 in Long Bridge, Avoyelles Parish. She had been living at 3028 Sumpter, Street when she died on July 28, 1943 in Houston, Texas (NevGivDeath). Her death certificate indicated that she was a widow from Long Bridge, LA and that her father was John Pry. Unknown mother

o **Bonita** - Born 1896 in St. Landry Parish. Her mother was **Virginia Martin**.

o **Alverta** - Born May 27, 1898 in St. Landry Parish, Louisiana. Died August 1977 in Beaumont, TX. Her mother was **Virginia Martin**.

o **Rosa** - Born August 20, 1900 in St. Landry Parish, Louisiana. Died February 23, 1951 in Beaumont, Texas. Her mother was **Virginia Martin**.

o **Cora** - Born October 22, 1904 in St. Landry Parish, Louisiana. Died March 1, 2002 in Beaumont, Texas. Her mother was **Virginia Martin**

o **Lydia** – Born 1905 in St. Landry Parish, Louisiana. Her mother was **Virginia Martin**.

o **Solomon** - Born in St. Landry Parish, Louisiana. His mother remains unknown. He is believed to have died in Texas and was buried in Opelousas, LA.

• **Eleanor Clara "Classie" Pryor** – Clara Prier was born in June, 1848, in Mansura, LA[150]. Clara, eventually, married **Philogene Telemaque** in Avoyelles Parish[151]. Eventually, all Telemaques changed their surname to "**Marks**".

Clara and Philogene had the following **Marks** children[152]:

o **Willie Joshua** - Born March, 1877 in Mansura, Louisiana. He married **Sarah Botley** on January 5, 1903 in Opelousas, Louisiana. He died on September 2, 1933 in Opelousas, Louisiana.

o **John Telemaque** - Born June 27, 1883 in Mansura, Louisiana. He married **Pearl Taylor** on October 19, 1911 in St. Landry Parish, Louisiana. He died in 1963 in Beaumont, Texas.

o **Cornelia Adams** -Born April 27, 1884 in Mansura, Louisiana. She married **Judas Adams**. She died January 1, 1980 in Opelousas, Louisiana.

After a separation from Philogene, Clara moved to St. Landry Parish, where she married **Stephen Fisher** on November 18, 1896 (ClaTelSteFisMarr).

Eleanor Clara "Classie" Pryor died in Opelousas. LA on October 24, 1924 at the age of 85 (ClaFisDeath).

• **James Pryor**, was shown as an 8-year-old boy, living in the household of Samuel and Julienne Pryor in the 1880 census (SamPry1880). He was described as Samuel's brother, although

---

[148] From Rhoda Prier – Verified by Harold Taylor.

[150] Moses Pryor Family Tree, Harold Taylor, owner

[151] A number of slaves were bought and sold in Louisiana with the name, Telemaque, who were listed as being from the Congo region of Africa[151]. One, in particular, was described in a November 3, 1807 sale of a 12-year-old male named *Telemaque* from Francois Tournier of Avoyelles Parish, Louisiana to Martineau Landreneau[151]. He was sold as part of an inventory that included "2 plantations, implements, beasts and slave" for the price of $8500. Telemaque spoke "Benue-Congo" as his primary language. There is no clear way to link the Telemaque family to the slave, *Telemaque*. Over time, the name, Telemaque, was shortened to Marks

[152] Moses Pryor Family Tree, Harold Taylor, owner

Samuel was 44 at the time. While it is possible, **further research is needed to confirm their relationship and whether James could be Moise's son as well.**

No additional records on James were found.

Miscellaneous Priers in Avoyelles Parish

In addition to the Prier (or Pryor, Prior) family members in the Mansura, LA area, there were several families with those names in the Bunkie and Cheneyville, LA areas during the Reconstruction Period. Unfortunately, there is not enough information available to tie any of them to the Priers in the Mansura area. For example:

- **Henderson Prior** (74) and his wife, **Minnie** (71), appeared in the 1900 U.S. census (HenPri1900). They had been married 33 years and had had 14 children. Henderson indicated that he was born Tennessee, his mother in Virginia and his father in Tennessee. Minnie was born in Louisiana, as were her parents.

  Living with them was their widowed son, **Peyton** (40) and who appear to be his children: **Mary** (13), **Martha** (12), **James** (11), **Lottie** (10), **Jarvis** (9), **Octavia** (4) and **Gertrude** (1).

- **Madison Prior** (41) and his wife, **Mary** (38), appeared in the 1900 U.S. census (MadPri1900). Living with them were their six sons: **James M.** (13), **David E.** (11), **Samuel** (9), **Abraham** (8), **Willie** (6) and **Moris** (4).

  Living next door to them was **Louis Prior** (34), single head-of-household.

- Interestingly, a World War I Draft Registration shows a record for 21-years-old **Moses Prior** of Bunkie (MosPriDraft). He indicated that he was a farmer on the Haase plantation there and his next of kin was **Mary Prior**.

More work is needed to understand how these Priors might be related to the Mansura Priers.

Current Status

Over the past 60 years, the Prier family has grown in size and has spread out across the state and country with some members spending time in other countries.

During the 1950's, members of the Prier's began working in non-farm-related areas such as the military, becoming nuns and acquiring trade skills such as plumbing and construction. A few began attending college.

Since then, members of the Prier family have established roots in Texas, California, Illinois and several other states, working in areas such as academics, manufacturing and retail.

In Avoyelles Parish, descendants of Moise Prier can be found in all aspects of the community, including involvement in the church, leading local government, and fulfilling roles as solid citizens.

Prier Family Pictures

Simon Prier   **Preston Prier**   **Ella Prier,**   **Ola Prier James**

100 years old.

Children of John Pryor: Bonita, Alverta and Rosa

Historic Mansura Scenes

Chapter 13.
The Sampson Family

Woodruff Sampson

Introduction to the Sampson Family

The specific origin of the Sampson name, as it pertains to that family in Avoyelles Parish, is unknown. However, due to it being the same as that of the biblical figure, Sampson, and the fact that many slaves were given such biblical names, it is possible that it is derived from a slave who was given the name, "Sampson". That slave, and his children, would have used Sampson, as their last name, once slavery was over, and a family name was born.

An alternate possibility is that the original slave's name was Sam. In this case, Sampson was developed by acknowledging the fact that a child was Sam's son, or "Samson" or "Sampson".

In this work, only those family members whose names were spelled "Sampson" are studied. Another family, with the spelling, "Samson" may have had residents in Pointe Coupee Parish and are not related to the Sampsons of Avoyelles Parish[158].

Also, in this work, there will be three different men with the name: "Alfred Sampson". To make it possible to distinguish one from the others, roman numerals are added at the end of each name. These numerals will be added in the chronological order in which the individual Alfred was listed. Thus, the "Alfred" born in 1832 will be called **Alfred Sampson I**, the Alfred born in 1862 will be called "**Alfred Sampson II**", while the Alfred in 1876 will be called "**Alfred Sampson III**".[159]

Historical Highlights

Benjamin Sampson, Sr., who was the first black person in Avoyelles Parish with the surname, **Sampson**, was born in North Carolina around 1775 (BenMelSam1880). He was believed to have been a Free Person of Color (FPC)[160] and was referred to as a West African (Vedhapudi).

From **North Carolina**, Benjamin Sampson was believed to have lived in **Virginia**, then traveled to Louisiana, settling, first, in **Grande Couteau** in St. Landry Parish and then in Avoyelles Parish[161].

The references below appear to verify some of this story if it is possible to prove that this is the same Benjamin Sampson who resided in Avoyelles Parish, Louisiana in 1880:

- The 1830 U.S. Census for the **Eastern District of Virginia** shows a household headed by a male Free Person of Color (FPC) by the name of Benjamin Sampson (BenSam1830). In the household were:
  - one male under 10,
  - three males between 10 and 24,
  - one male between 55 and 100,
  - one female between 10 and 23,
  - one female between 24 and 36 and
  - one female between 55 and 100.

- The 1840 U.S. Census for **Sussex County, Virginia** shows a household headed by a male FPC by the name of Ben Sampson (BenSamp1840). In his household were:
  - one male between 10 and 24,
  - one male between 56 and 100,
  - one female between 10 and 24, and
  - one female between 55 and 100.

  Living next to Ben Sampson was an FPC by the name of **John Sampson**. John's household included:
  - two males under 10 years of age,

[158] Information provided by Elaine Sampson, formerly of Marksville, LA
[159] Woodruff Sampson's son, Alfred, who is not included in this work, would have been **Alfred IV.**
[160] Based on Family History provided by Elaine Sampson, as told to her by her father, **Cilton P. Sampson, Sr.**
[161] Based on Family History provided by Elaine Sampson, as told to her by her father, **Cilton P. Sampson, Sr.**

- one male between 36 and 55,
- two females under 10 years of age,
- one female between 10 and 24, and
- one female between 36 and 55.

Based on his stated age (105) in the 1880 U.S. Census, Benjamin should have been 55 in 1830 and 65 in 1840. Thus, he could have been the man between 55 and 100 in each of the 1830 and 1840 censuses. The woman in the 55-100 range could have been his wife.

Further study is needed here.

There were no further records of Benjamin Sampson Sr. until 1880. Here, he and his wife, **Melice**, were living alone in the Mansura-Moreauville area (BenMelSam1880). He gave his age as 105 here while Melice listed hers as 80. His calculated birth year was **1775**, based on his age here.

They were living 2 houses away from **"Olysim"** Sampson, possibly their son, and his wife, **Marie Louise**. Benjamin said that he and his parents were born in **North Carolina**. Melice said that she and her parents were from LA.

Benjamin Sampson, Sr. died in Avoyelles Parish on June 4, 1881 (BenSamDeath).

Melice Sampson, Benjamin Sampson Sr.'s wife, was born in Louisiana around **1800**. No additional records indicating where she was born, who her family was or when she died were found for this study.

Benjamin Sampson, Jr. (71) and his wife, **Rachal** (69), appeared in the 1870 U.S. Census for Avoyelles Parish, LA (BenRacSamp1870). He is believed to be the son of Benjamin Sampson, Sr. and Melice[162]. Here, Benjamin Jr. indicated that he was born in **Virginia**. His calculated birth year was **1799**, based on his age here.

Rachal Sampson, Benjamin Jr.'s wife was born around 1802 in Illinois (BenRacSamp1870). There are no records of her being moved to Louisiana. One source claims that her name was **Rachael Marachell Green** (Topalicia). However, this middle name is likely a contraction of "Ma Rachal", or "Mother Rachal".

There are a few pieces of information that could have some bearing of Rachal's identity:

- There was a slave woman named **Rachal** listed as the godmother to a slave child, named **Roselle**, who was baptized in St. Paul's records on December 30, 1832 (Church). Roselle's mother, **Emelie**, was held by **Pierre Normand** of Mansura and Rachal was being held in slavery by **Colin Lacour** of Mansura.

- On July 14, 1854, a probate sale was held to dispose of the assets belonging to the late **Colin Lacour** of Avoyelles Parish. Among the assets sold were three slaves: **John** (36), **Pierre** (40) and **Rachal** (55). Rachal was sold to **Valery Dufour**.

---

[162] From Sampson family history provided by Elaine Sampson.

Based on her age (55) at the time of this sale, the slave, Rachal, would have been born in **1799**, nearly the same birth year as calculated based on Rachal Sampson's given age in the 1870 U.S. census (See Below).

Two conclusions can be drawn from the above information:

- The godmother, Rachal, was likely the same person as the slave, Rachal, who was sold from Colin Lacour's estate in 1854.

- Based on age comparison, the slave, Rachal, sold in the Lacour probate sale was possibly the same person as Rachel Sampson.

- **Therefore, the slave godmother held by Colin Lacour in the 1832 baptism and sold in the 1854 probate sale could possibly have been Rachel Sampson, the wife of Benjamin Sampson.**

The Lives of Ben and Rachel Sampson

Ben (71) and **Rachel** (69) **Sampson** first appeared the 1870 census, living between Moreauvillle and Mansura, Louisiana (BenRacSamp1870). Living with them was a 15-year-old black male named **Valery Stanton**.

They were living next door to **Alfred Sampson I**, possibly their son (See below), and his wife, **Margueritte**. Another possible son, living a few houses away, was "**Leymis**" **Sampson**, a.k.a. **Onzimie** or **Olysim** (See below), and his wife, **Marie Louise**.

Rachal died in Avoyelles Parish on March 25, 1888 at the age of 86 and is buried in St. Paul's Catholic Cemetery (BenSamDeath).

Benjamin Sampson, Jr.'s death records are not located.

Children of Ben and Rachal Sampson

In this section, an attempt will be made to tie together the various people in the Mansura area who used the last name, Sampson, from the mid-1800s forward. The main assumption here is that those whose birth years fell within a relative narrow time span could be either siblings or first cousins.

Benjamin Sampson, Sr. was born in 1775 and Benjamin Sampson, Jr. was born in 1799. Based on their age difference (24 years), it is likely that they were, possibly, father and son. **[Not Proven!]**

The next Sampson born in Avoyelles Parish was **Austin Samson**, born in 1828 (See Below). Benjamin Sampson, Sr. was 53 years older than Austin while Benjamin Sampson, Jr. was 29 years older than Austin. Thus, it is more likely that Benjamin Sampson, Jr. was Austin's father. **[Not Proven!]**

The next step is to determine whether there were other Sampson men who could have been Benjamin, Sr.'s children. Austin's siblings or children of Benjamin Sampson, Jr.

Table 11, below, lists a group of men who appeared in the various local public records, e.g., U.S. Census for Avoyelles Parish, with the surname, Sampson. They are listed in the order of their calculated birth years, in an attempt to determine whether these could be grouped together as possible siblings, or cousins. Such groupings might be a family, e.g., of Ben and Rachel Sampson.

TABLE 11. COMPARISON OF CONTEMPORARY SAMPSON MEN

Name	Year Born	Spouse	Year Married	Born In	Father Born in[163]	Mother Born in[123]
Austin	1828[164]	Susane Allison	1872	Louisiana	Virginia	Virginia
Olysim	1830[165]	Marie Louise Martin	1885	Louisiana	Not Stated	Not Stated
Alfred I	1832[166]	Marguerite Ford	1871	Louisiana	Louisiana	Louisiana
Arvene	1833[167]	Josephine Pierite	1868	Louisiana	Virginia	Mississippi
Pierre	1842[168]	Marie Alexander	1870	Louisiana	Louisiana	Louisiana

It can be seen that the men in **Table 11** do form a relatively narrow birth year group, i.e. 1828 - 1842, that could be a single family. Unfortunately, the fact that they were born well before the end of slavery, a time when there were few records of slave families, makes any legal connections between them difficult to define.

An attempt was made in **Table 11** to see whether there was consensus among those men as to where their parents were born. From earlier, Benjamin Sampson, Sr. indicated in the 1880 census that he (and his parents) were born in North Carolina (BenMelSam1880). Also, the 1830 and 1840 U.S. censuses show a Benjamin Sampson living in Virginia.

By comparison, in the 1870 census (BenRacSamp1870), Benjamin Sampson, Jr. said that he was born in Virginia. This offers the possibility that Benjamin Sr. was born in North Carolina and later moved to Virginia, where Benjamin Jr. was born. **Unfortunately, there is not enough information available to form a good conclusion**.

To determine whether there were Sampson women present during the first half of the 19th century who could have been children of either Benjamin Sampson, Sr. or Jr., a search of Ancestry records for Avoyelles Parish was done from 1820 to 1850.

[163] Based on information each person gave to census takers.
[164] Based on his age in 1880
[165] Based on his age in 1880
[166] Based on his age in 1870
[167] Based on his age in 1880
[168] Based on his age in 1880

In this case, only one person, **Lucenda Sampson,** a Free Woman of Color, was found (LucSamp). She (40) was working as a cook for **Oliver P. Normand** in 1880[169]. She indicated that she, her parents, and her daughter, **Mary** (10), were all born in South Carolina. Living with her were the following additional children, all of whom said that they were born in Louisiana and their parents were born in South Carolina: **Palmyra** (8), **Azzo** (6), **Brazile** (5), **Oceanna** (4), **Minerva** (3), **Nellie** (1), **Florence** (4) and an unnamed infant (2 months). All of these latter children were listed as servants. **There is no proof that Lucenda Sampson was related to any of the Sampson men in Table 11.**

When the profiles of each individual listed in the **Table 11** are studied in detail, some specific relationship information will emerge. These men and their families will be profiled below in the order of their birth.

Austin Sampson (52) and his wife, **Susane Allison** (35), appeared in the 1880 U.S. census, living near Mansura, Louisiana (AusSuSam1880). No specific public records were found of their marriage or what Susane's last name was[170].

No records were found in this study indicating how Austin was related to either Benjamin Sr. or Jr. He was, however, born around 1828 while Benjamin Jr. was born around 1800, an age difference that makes it possible for him to be Benjamin Jr.' child.

Some of Austin and Susane's neighbors in 1880 were Franciscos, Berzats, and Pryors, making it likely that they were living off the Mansura-Hessmer highway. Living with them were their two daughters, **Fannie** (13) and **Mimie** (4) and their son, **Alfred II** (6) (See the discussion above on using Roman numerals to distinguish the various Alfreds).

In 1900, Austin (72) and Susan (58) were shown living near Grande Ecore, east of Mansura, Louisiana (AusSuSSam1900). They were living alone and had been married for 27 years. Their son, **Alfred II**, was living a few houses away. Susan indicated that she had had six children and three were still alive. Austin stated that he was born in Louisiana but both his parents were born in **Virginia**. Susan stated that she was born in Alabama, her father was born in Virginia, and her mother was born in South Carolina. No further records of Austin and Susan or of their daughters, Fanny and Mimie were found.

Austin and Susan's son, Alfred II (25)[171], and his wife, **Mary Hollis** (23), appeared in the 1900 U.S. census, living near Grande Ecore (AlfMarSam1900). They had been married for three years and had two sons: **Woodruff** (2) and **Milton** (5 months).

---

[169] The story of the romance and ensuing drama between Lucenda Sampson and Oliver P. Normand and their children is the subject of a brief dramatization appearing in Ancestry.com (https://www.ancestry.com/mediaui-viewer/tree/75282541/person/32316553569/media/e664b873-9e94-479e-9965-e385cb5f4898). It is out of the scope of this work.
[170] Susane's last name, Allison, was assumed based on the fact that her father's name was Lockwood Allison. Her married Ann Judson Hartwell on August 12, 1845 in Perry, AL. – Elaine Sampson
[171] The designations: Alfred I, Alfred II, etc. will be used here to keep track of the different Alfred Sampsons with the same name.

In the 1910 census, Alfred II (35) and Mary (34) were farmers, living near Grande Ecore, outside of Mansura, Louisiana (AlfMarSam1910). Their family had increased and now included four sons and two daughters: **Woodruff** (12), **Milton** (9), **Carrie** (7), **Roosevelt** (5), **Indiana** (3) and **Wesley** (0).

The children of Alfred II and Mary Sampson were:

- **Woodruff** (b. 1898),
- **Milton** (b. 1901),
- **Carrie** (b. 1903),
- **Roosevel**t (b. 1905),
- **Indiana** (b.1907,
- **Wesley** (b. 1910)
- **Mayo** (b. 1912)
- **Sam** (b. 1915) and
- **Anthony** (b. 1919).

Alfred Sampson I was born in Louisiana around 1832. He married **Marguerite Ford** in Avoyelles Parish, Louisiana on February 22, 1871 (AlSamMarFordMarriage). At the time of their marriage, the couple acknowledged three children: **Paul, Paulina,** and **Aurelia.** Witnesses were: **Onezime Sampson, Arvenne Sampson,** and **Felicien Maglorie. Thus, there appeared to be some sort of close relationship between Alfred I, Onezime, and Arvene, possibly as brothers.**

Alfred I (38) and Marguerite (29) were living next door to Benjamin Jr. (71) and Rachal (69) in 1870 (BenRacSamp1870). Since Benjamin Jr. was born around 1800 and Rachal in 1801, while Alfred I was born in 1832, **it is possible that Alfred I could be their son.** Living with Alfred I and Marguerite were three children: **Paul** (7), **Paulini** (6) and **Aurelia** (1). They appeared to be living near Mansura, LA.

In 1880, Alfred I (48) and Marguerite (37) were living near the town of Mansura, likely in Grande Ecore (AlfMarSam1880). Living with them were their four sons: **Paul** (17), **Thomas** (9), **Ferdinand** (4) and **Felix** (2) and their four daughters: **Paulina** (15), **Aurelia** (11), **Martilia** (6) and **Anna** (2 months). They were living next door to **Arvene Sampson**, likely Alfred I's brother (See Below) and his family. Alfred I stated that both his parents were born in Louisiana.

Alfred I died on July 16, 1887 in Avoyelles Parish (AlfSamDeath).

In the 1900 census, Marguerite had been married to **Marcelin Celestine** for 11 years (MarSam1900). Living with her and Marcelin were her two youngest sons from her marriage to Alfred I, **Ferdinand** (24) and **Felix** (22). Marguerite indicated that she was born in July, 1844 and that her parents were from Louisiana.

Living next door to Margueritte and Marcelin was Alfred I and Marguerite's son, **Paul Sampson** (37), his wife, **Marie (Victoria) Lavalais** (33), their five sons: **Winfred** (13), **Winter** (11), **Wade** (9), **Wamer** (6) and **Ben** (1); and their daughter, **Pauline** (3).

On the opposite side of Marcelin and Marguerite's house was Marguerite and Alfred I's other son, **Thomas Sampson** (28), his wife, **Emma Augustine** (24) and their three sons: **Michel** (4), **Curtis** (3) and **Addison** (1).

Alfred I and Marguerite's children and grandchildren were as follows:

- **Paul** (m. **Marie Lavalais**) - Wade, Warner, Icy, Ben, Delphie, Jane, Eunice, Jeanette
- **Paulina** – No additional information found.
- **Aurelia** (m. **Alphonse James**) – Alphonsine, Alfred, Louis and Edward.
- **Thomas** (m. **Emma Augustine**) - Michel, Curley, Joseph, Mary, Octavia, Lena, Vincent, Ethel, Mildred, Hazel, Marguerite and Philip.
- **Martilia** – No additional information found.
- **Ferdinand** – No additional information found.
- **Anna** - No additional information found.
- **Felix** - No additional information found.

Arvene (a.k.a. Arsene, Irwin, Irvin)[172] **Sampson** was born in Louisiana around 1833 and was believed to be the son of Benjamin Jr. and Rachal Sampson (AlSamMarFordMarriage). As before, the 33-year gap between Arvene and Benjamin Jr. and Rachal's ages makes it possible for him to be their son.

Arsene and his wife, **Josephine Thomas**, first appeared in the 1880 census, living as farmers near Grande Ecore in Mansura, Louisiana (ArvSamJosPie1880. Living with Arsene (47) and Josephine (34) were their two sons: **Joseph** (11) and **Pierre** (8) and their two daughters: **Eugenia** (5) and **Amaimte** ?? (2). Also present were Josephine's children from a previous marriage: two sons, **Oge' Francisco** (19) and **Cleopha Francisco** (18), and her daughter, **Josephine Francisco** (13). Living next door was Alfred Sampson I (Arvene's brother?) and Alfred I's wife, Marguerite.

In 1900, **Irwin** (68) and Josephine (55) Sampson and their 2 sons: **Ones** (20) and **Landry** (18) were living in the town of Mansura (IrwJosSam1900). Next door to them was **Pierre Sampson** (50) and his family (Irwin's brother?). Here, Irwin indicated that he was born in Louisiana but said that his father was born in **Virginia** and his mother in **Mississippi**. He listed his birth as April, 1832. Josephine said that only her father was born in **Virginia**.

Arsene died in Avoyelles Parish on March 2, 1922 (ArsSamDeath). There is no record of Josephine's death.

The descendants of Arvene and Josephine Sampson are:

---

[172] Using different names: i.e. Arvene, Arsene, Irwin, Irvin, seems common within the Sampson family and others.

- **Ones** (m. **Marie Augustine**) – Joseph, Annielou, Calvin, Willow, Mary, Martin, Martha, Florence, Celina, and Mable.
- **Pierre** (m. **Mary E. Parker**) – Carrison, Leon and Mccloskey.
- **Landry** – Moved to Tulsa Oklahoma. Not clear if he had a family there (LandSampDraft).
- **Joseph** - No records were found to indicate what became of him.

Olysim[173] (a.k.a. Onezeme, Ozimme, or Leymis) **Sampson** was born in Louisiana in May, 1840. His parents could have been Benjamin Jr. and Rachal Sampson, based on the age analysis above. He married **Marie Louise Batiste** (Topalicia).

"**Leymis**" (39) and **M. Louise** (30) first appeared in the 1870 U.S. census living near Mansura, Louisiana (LeyMarSam1870). Living with them were the following seven boys: **Placide** (12), **Alfred III** (8), **Joseph** (5), **Marius** (3), and **Clarence** (1); and one girl, **Julienne** (14). Also present was a farm laborer, **C. Sampson** (16).

In 1880, Olysim, now called "**Onezeme**" (50), and **Mary L.** (40) were living near Mansura or Grande Ecore, Louisiana (OnzMarSam1880). Living with them were their 7 sons: **Alfred III** (18), **Joseph** (15), **Marius** (12), **Clarence** (11), **Lovincia** (8), **Jean Baptiste** (5), and **Wallace** (1 month); and two daughters: **Flavie** (10) and **Sidonia** (2).

Olysim married **Marie L. Martin** in Avoyelles Parish on September 22, 1885 (Topalicia).

In the 1900 census, Onezeme (60) and Marie L. (48) were living in Grande Ecore, near Mansura, LA (OneMarSam1900). Living with them were their 4 sons: **Oneal** (12), **Jules** (11), **Simon** (9), **George** (7); Onezeme's stepdaughter, **Marie Augustine** (16), and their grandson, **Alcide** (14).

In the 1910 census, "**Ozimme**" (79) and Marie L. (51??) Sampson were living on either the Cottonport or Long Bridge roads (OziMarSam1910). Living with them were their son, **George** (16) and daughter, **Annie** (12). From the census notation, it appears that Ozimme had been married three times while Mary L. has been married twice.

Onezeme Sampson died at the age of 94 in Avoyelles Parish on December 31, 1923 (OneSamDeath). In the 1920 census, 95-year-old **Marie Bilmore** was living with her son, **Simon**, in Hessmer, Louisiana.

Onezeme and Mary Sampson's descendants include the following children (Their spouses) and grandchildren:

- **Placide** (m. **Sydonia Lavalais**) – Died in 1934 in Baton Rouge.
- **Alfred III** (m. **Leontine ??**) – Clarence, Hilry, Mary Lee, Glacite, Author, Bennadez.
- **Joseph** (m. **Ernestine ??**) – Estella, Walter, Loney, Wilton, Curry and Lessie.
- **Marius** (m. **Amanda Lavalais**) – Harriet, Paul, Jean Baptiste, Kennie, Herman

---

[173] Olysim is an example where name spelling can create severe complications. Here his name appears to be spelled at least 5 different ways (i.e. Olysim, Onezeme, Ozimme, Ozimme, or Leymis). Each different spelling is highlighted here to call attention to that difference.

- **Clarence** (m. **Elizane Lavalais**) – Harry, Hillary, Sydney, Theresa, Louis, Annatole, Lesta and Felta.
- **Flavie – No records found.**
- **Lovincia** (m. **Florida Titus**) – Audrie, Syble, Ethel.
- **Jean Batiste** (m. **Mary Augustine**) – Joseph, Pauline.
- **Sidonia** (m. **?? Augustine, divorced**) – No record of children found.
- **Wallace** – No records found.
- **Oneal** (m. **Mary ??**) – Wilfred, Evelina, Rosetta, Welton.
- **Jules** – No records found.
- **Simon** (m. **Carina ??**) - Raphile, Joseph, and Curry.
- **George** – Died 1918.
- **Annie** (m. **William Rogers**) - Moved to Alexandria.

Pierre Sampson was born in Louisiana around 1842 (PieMarSam1880). As with the other listed Sampson men, his age difference from Ben and Rachel Sampson (About 42 years) makes it possible that he could be their son, but there is no documentation to prove it.[174]

Pierre enlisted in the 49th U.S. Colored Infantry on April 15, 1864, a month before the Battle of Mansura and served under the alias, Pierre Washington. He was discharged in 1865 (PieSampVet).

Marie Lemoine[175] was born in Louisiana around 1850. Her parents were also born in Louisiana. Pierre and Marie were married around 1870 (PieMar1900).

In the 1880 U.S. census, Pierre (38) and Marie (30) were farmers, living in the vicinity of Grande Bayou, near Mansura, Louisiana (PieMar1880). Living with them were their 4 sons: **William** (12), **Horace** (10), **Leonce** (7) and **Wilson** (4); and their daughter, **Sidonia** (3). Marie was described as a mulatto while Pierre was described as black.

In the 1900 census, Pierre (50) and Marie (48) had been married 30 years and were living near Mansura, LA (PieMar1900). Living with them was their daughter, **Angela** (18) and their son, **Jules** (15). Living next door was their widowed son, **Leonce** (26), his son, **Overton** (3) and Leonce's sister, **Josephine** (8). Living nearby was Pierre and Marie's son, **Wilson Sampson** (23), his wife, **Jennie** (20), and their daughter, **Clara** (1). They had been married 2 years.

In the 1920 census, Pierre (71) and Marie (62) were farmers, living on the Large road, near Mansura, LA (PieMarSam1920). Living next door to them was **Carrison Sampson** (21), his wife, **Angelica** (23), their son, **Cilton** (1), and their 2 daughters: **Marie** (9 months) and **Viola** (1 month).

---

[174] There are 3 slave children who were baptized in the St. Paul records between 1838 and 1845 with the name, *Pierre*. There is, however, no additional evidence to clearly link any one of them to Pierre Sampson, who claimed to have been born in 1842.

[175] Provided by Elaine Sampson

Pierre Sampson died in Avoyelles at the age of 82 on April 8, 1927 (PieSamDeath). His descendants include the children of:

- **William** (m. **Josephine James**) - Henry, Alphonse, Louis, Leonie, Sydonie, Florence, Benita and Sydonia
- **Horace** (m. **Maria Linder**) - Julia, Josephine, Felix, Olive, Larina, Polan, Clifton, Louisiana, and Houston;
- **Leonce** (m. **Mary St. Romain**) – Joseph, Preston, Culberth, Laudress, Laura, Carrie, Cilton, and Lester;
- **Wilson** (m. **Eugenie Bowman**) – Clara, Carrie, Bertha, Waval, and Joseph.
- **Sidonia** (m. **Ferdinand St. Romain**) – Ida, Batterson, Pierre and Paul.

Current Status

The Sampson family is huge. It consists of large branches in Avoyelles Parish as well as in various parts of Louisiana. Numerous smaller groups exist in several other states.

From its beginnings in the mid-nineteenth century, that family has experienced explosive growth due to their dedication to the family and the large numbers of male children born in most of their family groups.

Sampson Family Pictures

Mayo Sampson   **Lester & Pearl Sampson**   **Louis & Florence Sampson**

Summary

Although a relatively small number of families were studied in detail in this work, several important observations can be made:

- Unlike what is commonly believed, the number of generations from the middle of the 20th century back to the first arrivals from Africa was relatively small. In nearly every case where the first arrival from Africa was identified, he or she was no more than a great-great-great-grandparent of someone alive today.

- The African-American population of Mansura are the descendants of three basis groups: Africans, Europeans and Native Americans. In fact, the actual number of these earliest ancestors is very small, especially for the Europeans and Native Americans.

- Surprisingly, there were a small number of mixed race slave holders in the Mansura area, with one significantly large slave holder.

- A large amount of official information exists that allows African-Americans to trace their families' roots back through the local slavery plantations.

- Nearly all racial groups lived difficult lives in the Mansura area. Most people were farmers and generally at the mercy of the environment, weather and pests. As a result, disease and the resultant shortened lifespan was the norm. However, Native-Americans and African-Americans seemed to have the worst of it since not being landowners kept them in constant peril of starvation due to lack of credit.

- Very few people remained single much past 20 years-old. Presumably, there was pressure to become independent and less a burden on their families. However, mulatto females tended to remain single longer than others, perhaps reflecting their desire to find mates who resembled themselves.

- As people got older, the normal process was for them to move in with their children or other relatives or to acquire a house nearby.

Appendix A. Slaves Held by Jean Pierre Lemoine

Name	Birth Year	Place of Origin	Document Date	Seller	Buyer	Price	Notes
Solomon (B/M)	1781	Tennessee	9/19/1809	Jesse Benton	Pierre Lemoine	4000	In Group of 11 Slaves
Adam (B/M)	1788	"	"	"	"	"	"
Dewey (B/F)	1785	"	"	"	"	"	"
Nancy (B/F)	1789	"	"	"	"	"	Mom and boy
Charlotte (B/F)	1788	"	"	"	"	"	Mom, 2 Boys
Philis (B/F)	1780	Louisiana Creole	6/12/1815	Widow George Baron	"	1343	Mom, 2 boys and 3 girls
Fann (B/F)	1790	African	5/15/1809	Marshall William	"	1100	Group of 3 slaves: Mom and young child
Fawn (B/F)	1790	African	"	"	"	"	Fawn and Child, Jude
Jude (B/F)	1790`	Virginia	"	"	"	"	Individual
Francois (B/M)	1783	Rapides	8/30/1801	Louis Deville	"	1925	Individual
Abraham (B/M)	1790	Unknown	5/5/1810	William H. Ashley	"	2500	In Group of 6 Slaves
Jenny (B/F)	1787	Unknown	5/20/1810	"	"	"	Mom, boy and girl
Lindor (B/M)	1779	Africa	3/17/1809	Isabelle Rabalais, dec.	"	700	Deceased Mistress
Patience (M)	1781	Unknown	10/9/1809	Pierre Lemoine	Jean Philippon	600	Individual
Unknown (B/M)	1785	Jamaica	10/13/1809	Alexandre Cathelin	Pierre Lemoine	500	Individual
Tobie (B/M)	1788	African or European	6/22/1812	Pierre Lemoine	Guillaume Benito	1125	In Group of 2 Slaves
Cook (B/F)	1790	African or European	"	"	Guillaume Benito	"	"
Manette (B/F)	1788	African	6/20/12	"	Pequet & Lacroix	570	Mother and 2 children

Appendix B. Slaves Sold in Zenon Lemoine Probate Sale, 1850

Slave	Age	M/F	Buyer
Ursin	46	M	Moncla, Joseph
Gustin	23	M	Juneau, J.
Dorsin	21	M	Coco, F.B.
Sostine	19	M	Lemoine, Hillaire
Louise	17	F	Rabalais, Jean Bte.
Jacques	3	M	Lemoine, Jean Pierre
Constance	29	F	Gremillion, Ceran
Jean Pierre	10	M	Gremillion, Ceran
Avis	6	M	Gremillion, Ceran
Pavis	6	M	Gremillion, Ceran
Andre'	5	M	Gremillion, Ceran
Celestine	2.5	F	Gremillion, Ceran
Auguste	12	M	Armand, D
John	34	M	Richi, Z
Elizabeth	10	F	Coco, Jean Bte.
Azilia	8	F	Richi, Z
Octave	5	F	Richi, Z
Celestine	4	F	Richi, Z
Phillippe	22	M	Marshall, Horace
Pierre	66	M	Rabalais, Jean Bte.
Kitty	47	F	Rabalais, Jean Bte.
Francois	?	M	Rabalais, Jean Bte.
Julie	5	F	Rabalais, Jean Bte.
Bailey	19	M	Rabalais, Martin
Mary	13	F	Bordelon, Valery
Valery	29	M	Rabalais, Martin
Marceline	22	F	Rabalais, Martin
Unnamed	1		Rabalais, Martin
Olivier	?		Rabalais, Martin
Honore'	11	M	Gremillion, Fellician
Magdeline	7	F	Gremillion, Ceran
Toussaint	12	M	Roy, Villenueve
Barthelemy	38	M	Poret, Isadore
Aimie	45	F	Mayeux, Linon
Narcisse	5	M	Mayeux, Linon
Bertheline	11	F	Courvillion, Symphorism
Lafleur	33	M	Gremillion, Ceran
Laure	32	F	Coco, Jean Bte.
Julien	2	M	Coco, Jean Bte.
Alphonse	2	M	Coco, Jean Bte.
Petit John	11	M	Riche, Zerbin
Caroline	15	F	Ormand, Dorsaint

Congo	58	M	Coco, Jean Bte.
Missa	22	F	Lemoine, Hillaire
Infant	2		Lemoine, Hillaire
Ned	22	M	Rabalais, John V.
Nanette	22	F	Rabalais, Rene'
William	18m	M	Rabalais, Rene'
Philis	6		Rabalais, Rene'
Charles	24	M	Matheus, M.M.
Cresoy	22	F	Lemoine, Hillaire
Ludger	3	M	Lemoine, Hillaire
Amilie	2	F	Lemoine, Hillaire
Marcelin	20	M	Rabalais, Jean Bte.
Henriette	30	F	Riche', Zerbin
Cecile	7	F	Riche', Zerbin
Quiney	27	F	Bordelon, Vergiss
Pauline	8	F	Bordelon, Vergiss
Eugene	16	M	Richi, Zerbin
Albert	31	M	Armand, Dorsaint
Marianne	37	F	Armand, Dorsaint
Eulalie	7	F	Armand, Dorsaint
Fanny	5	F	Armand, Dorsaint
Celeste	8	F	Armand, Dorsaint
Baptiste	22	M	Armand, Dorsaint
Quiney	18	F	Armand, Dorsaint
Infant	?	?	Armand, Dorsaint
Hilaire	12	F	Guillot, Valery
Rose	24	F	Rabalais, Rene'
Antoine	4	M	Rabalais, Rene'
Clarice	2	F	Rabalais, Rene'
Infant	1		Coco, Jean Bte.
George	28	M	Coco, Jean Bte.
Rachal	22	F	Coco, Jean Bte.
Georgina	3	F	Coco, Jean Bte.
Infant	4m		Coco, Jean Bte.
Julian	18	M	Coco, Jean Bte.

References

1860, Avoyelles Slaves. "1860 Slave Schedules." *1860 United States Census: Slave Schedules*. Marksville, LA: Ancestry.com, 1860.

1880 U.S. Census. "1880 U.S. Federal Census, Avoyelles Parish, Ward 2, 003." *1880 U.S. Census*. n.d.

1880, U.S. Census. *U.S. Federal Census, Avoyelles Parish, LA, Ward 3*. Census Report. Washington DC: `U.S. Census Bureau, 1880.

1930, U.S. Census Bureau. *U.S. Federal Census, Avoyelles Parish, LA, Ward 3, Dist. 8*. Census Report. Washington DC: U.S. Census Bureau, 1930.

AbelFranDeath. "Abel Francisco." *Louisiana, Statewide Death Index, 1819-1964*. Mansura, LA: Ancestry.com, 25 February 1936.

AbelFranMarriage. "Abel Francisco." *Louisiana, Marriages, 1718-1925*. Marksville, LA: Ancestry.com, 14 February 1893.

AbelFranMarriage2. "Abel Francisco Marriage to Maria Sampson." *Louisiana, Marriages, 1718-1925*. Marksville, LA: Ancestry.Com, 16 November 1896.

AbEllJam1900. *U.S. Federal Census, Avoyelles Parish, LA, Ward 3, Dist. 0014, Family No. 189*. Census Report. Washinton DC: U.S. Census Bureau, 1900.

AbEllJamMarriage. "Louisiana, Marriages, 1718-1925." 17 December 1896. *Ancestry.com*. <http://search.ancestry.com/search/db.aspx?dbid=7837>.

Ad, Commercial. *Cochon De Lait Festival*. Mansura Chamber of Commerce, Mansura, LA. Advertising Poster.

AdAug1880. "1880 United States Federal Census for A. Augustin, Louisiana Avoyelles Not Stated 004." Marksville, LA: Ancestry.com, n.d.

Administration, National Archives and Records. *U.S., Civil War Pension Index: General Index to Pension Files, 1861-1934 forLouis Oliver*. Provo, UT: Ancestry.com, 1890.

Affairs, Records of the Department of Veterans. "1890 Veterans Schedules for Louis Olivier, Family Number 66." 2005. *Ancestry.com*.

AgBerzDeath. "Agnes Berzat in the U.S., Find A Grave Index, 1600s-Current." *Find A Grave Index, 1600s-Current* . Provo, UT, USA: Ancestry.com Operations, Inc., 2012. . Mansura, LA: Ancestry.com, 7 December 1971.

AlDrouin1900. *U.S. Federal Census, Avoyelles Parish, Ward 3, Dist. 0014, Family No. 8*. Census Report. Washington DC: U.S. Census Bureau, 1900.

AlfJam. "Social Security Claim for Alfred James, August 23,1940." *U.S., Social Security Applications and Claims Index, 1936-2007*. Ancestry.com. U.S., Social Security Applications and Claims Index, 1936-2007 , 2015.

AlfMarMag1900. *U.S. Federal Census, Avoyelles Parish, LA, Ward 4, Dist. 015, Family No. 135*. Census Report. Washington DC: U.S. Census Bureau, 1900.

AlfMarSam1880. "Alfred and Marguerite Sampson in 1880 U.S. Census." *U.S. Federal Census, Avoyelles Parish, LA, Ward 003, Family No. 51*. Washington DC: U.S. Census Bureau, 1880.

AlfMarSam1900. *U.S. Federal Census, Avoyelles Parish, Marksville, LA, Dist. 0014, Family No. 259*. Census Report. Washington DC: U.S. Census Bureau, 1900.

AlfMarSam1910. *U.S. Federal Census, Avoyelles Parish, LA, Ward 3, Dist. 0016, Family No.142*. Census Report. Washington DC: U.S. Census Bureau, 1910.

AlfSamDeath. "Alfred Sampson Death Certificate." 11 June 1936. *LA Statewide Death Index, 1900 - 1949 on Ancestry.com, Certificate 6872, Vol. 16*.

—. "St. Paul the Apostle Catholic Church Burial Records, Book V (1886-1905)." *Burial Record*. Mansura, LA: Diocese of Alexandria, 16 July 1887.

AliAug1900. "1900 United States Federal Census for Pierre Francisco, Louisiana Avoyelles Police Jury Ward 03 District 0014 , Family 272." *Twelfth Census of the United States: Schedule No. 1 - Population*. Mansura, LA: Ancestry.con, 1900.

AliBatDeath. "Alice Batiste." *U.S.Social Security Death Index, 1935-2014*. Marksville, LA: Ancestry.com, July 1984.

AliPryLudMagMarriage. "Marriage of Alicia Pryor and Ludger Magloire." *Avoyelles Parish Marriage Certificate*. Marsville, LA: Avoyelles Parish Clerk of Court, 5 October 1893.

AlpAurJam1900. *U.S. Federal Census, Avoyelles Parish, LA, Ward 3, Dist. 0014, Family No. 237*. Census Report. Washington DC: U.S. Census Bureau, 1900.

AlpJamDeath. *Alphonse James - LA Statewide Death Index 1900-1949*. New Orleans, LA, 5 February 1937. Database.

AlpRebBel1900. *U.S. Federal Census, Avoyelles Parish, LA, Ward 4, Dist. 0015, Family No. 136*. Census Report. Washington DC: U.S. Census Bureau, 1900.

AlSamMarFordMarriage. "Marriage of Alfred Sampson and Marguerite Ford." *Avoyelles Parish Marriages, 1871*. Marksville, LA: Avoyelles Parish Clerk of Court, 22 February 1871.

AlZoNormand1900. *U.S. Federal Census, Avoyelles Parish, Ward 3, Dist. 0014, Family No. 17*. Census Report. Washington DC: U.S. Census Bureau, 1900.

AmbInez1940. "Ambrose Batiste." *1940 United States Federal Census for Inez Batiste, Louisiana Orleans New Orleans 36-369, Family 352*. New Orleans, LA: Ancestry.com, 1940.

AmbInez1956. "U.S. City Directories, 1822-1995 for Ambrose Batiste ." *Louisiana New Orleans 1956 New Orleans, Louisiana, City Directory, 1956* . New Orleans, LA: Ancestry.com, 1956.

AmbInezBap1930. "Ambrose Baptiste." *1930 United States Federal Census for Inez Batiste, Louisiana Orleans New Orleans (Districts 1-250) District 0217* . New Orleans, LA: Ancestry.com, 1930.

amycollins0921. "Zenon LEMOINE." n.d. *Ancestry.com*. Internet. 2 December 2016.

Ancestry.com. n.d. <http://www.ancestry.com/>.

Ancestry.com. "Lucien Dominique Coco." *Hunting For Bears, comp.. Louisiana, Marriages, 1718-1925*. Ancestry.com Operations Inc. Provo, 2004.

AndAug1880. "1880 United States Federal Census for A. Augustin , Louisiana Avoyelles Not Stated 004 , p.48." *1880 U.S. Census for Avoyelles Parish*. Mansura, LA: Ancestry.com, n.d.

AndrAug1870. *1870 U.S. Federal Census, Avoyelles Parish, LA, Subdivision 6*. Washington DC: Census Bureau, 1870.

Anonymous. *Purchase of Christian captives from the Barbary States*. Wikipedia.org, Unknown. Painting. <https://en.wikipedia.org/wiki/Catholic_Church_and_slavery#/media/File:Purchase_of_Christian_captives_from_the_Barbary_States.jpg>.

Archives, National. "U.S., Colored Troops Military Service Records, 1863-1865." 2007. *Ancestry.com/National Archives and Records Adminsitration.*

ArElBer1940. "1940 United States Federal Census for Ella Berger, Louisiana Orleans New Orleans 36-159, Family 16." *Sixteenth Census of the United States: 1940 Population Schedule*. New Orleans, LA: Ancestry.com, 1940.

ArisClaMag1910. *U.S. Federal Census, Avoyelles Parsh LA, Ward 4, District 0017, Family No. 75*. Census Report. Washington DC: U.S. Census Bureau, 1910.

ArisMagDeath. "Death Certificate for Aristide Magloire, Certificate No. 11245, vol. 26." *Louisiana Statewide Death Index, 1900-1949*. New Orleans: State of Louisiana, 27 July 1930.

ArMagClaLonMarriage. "Louisiana Marriages, 1718-1925, Aristide Magloire and Clara Lonzo." *Marriage Certfcate*. Alexandria, Rapides Parish, LA, 11 March 1893.

ArsSamDeath. *Arsene Sampson Death Record, Certificate No. 2346*. 2 March 1922. Ancestry.com.

artdem1880. *1880 U.S. Federal Census, Avoyelles Parish, LA, Subdivision 6, Family No. 125*. Census Report. Washington, DC: Census Bureau, 1880.

artdem1900. *1900 U.S. Federal Census, Avoyelles Parsih, LA, Ward 3, Dist. 0014, Family No. 181*. Census Report. Washington DC: Census Bureau, 1900.

artdem1910. *1910 U.S. Federal Census, Avoyelles Parish, Ward 3, Dist. 0016, Family No. 68*. Census Report. Washigton DC: U.S. Census Bureau, 1910.

artdem1930. *1930 U.S. Federal Census, Avoyelles Parish LA, Ward 3, Dist. 7, Family No. 44*. Census Report. Washington DC: U.S. Census Bureau, 1930.

Artist, Commercial. *Broadside advertsing sale of slave with 10 individuals listed*. New Orleans, LA, 1835.

Artist, Our Special. *Our colored troops at work -- the 1st Louisiana native guards disembarking at Fort Macomb, Louisiana*. WikiMedia.org. *OurColoredTroopsFortMacomb.jpeg*. 1863. Engraving. <https://commons.wikimedia.org/wiki/File:OurColoredTroopsFortMacomb.jpeg>.

Artist, Unknown. *Aerial Photograph of Flood, Unidentified Stretch of Lower Mississippi River (ARC No. 285959)*. National Archives and Records Administration, Washington DC. Photograph. <https://commons.wikimedia.org/wiki/File:Aerial_photograph_of_flood,_unidentified_stretch_of_lower_Mississippi_River._-_NARA_-_285959.jpg>.

Artist, Unknown. *American Civil War Scene - Our colored troops at work - the 1st Louisiana Guard Disembarking at Ft. McComb, Louisiana*. <https://commons.wikimedia.org/wiki/File:OurColoredTroopsFortMacomb.jpeg>.

Artist, Unknown. *Co. E, 4th US Infantry, Ft. Lincoln, Defense of Washington*. Library of Congress. *Images of War, Vol. 3, p 235*. Washington, DC, n.d.

Artist, Unknown. *The Atlantic Slave Trade and Slave Life in America: A Visual Record*. University of Virginia Library. *Slaves Baptized in a Monrovian Congregation*. n.d. Image ID: NW0174.

Artist, Unnown. *Aerial Photograph of Flood, Unidentified Stretch of Lower Mississippi River (ARC No. 285959)*. National Archives and Records Administration, Washington DC. Photograph. <https://commons.wikimedia.org/wiki/File:Aerial_photograph_of_flood,_unidentified_stretch_of_lower_Mississippi_River._-_NARA_-_285959.jpg>.

Artist, Unnown. *Funeral of Andre Cailloux in New Orleans, July 29, 1863. Harper's Weekly*. New York: Harper's Weekly, 1863.

Artst, Commercial. *Broadside advertsing sale of slave with 10 individuals listed*. New Orleans, LA, 1835.

ArvSamJosPie1880. *U.S. Federal Census, Avoyelles Parish, LA, Marksville, Dist. 003, Family No. 50*. Census Report. Washington DC: U.S. Census Bureau, 1880.

Ashur772. "Sullivan Family Tree." 2011. *Ancestry.com*.

AugCleJam1910. *U.S. Federal Census, Avoyelles Parish, LA, Ward 3, Dist 0016, Family No. 12*. Census Report. Washington DC: U.S. Census Bureau, 1910.

AugCleJamesMarriage. *Avoyelles Parish Louisiana Marriages: "H - J" Surnames*. 2016. <http://laghn.usghn.org/avoyelles/index.html>.

AugCleoJam1900. *U.S. Federal Census, Avoyelles Parish LA., Ward 3, Dist. 0014, Family No. 49*. Census Report. Washington DC: U.S. Census Bureau, 1900.

AugCleoJam1920. *U.S. Federal Census, Avoyelles Parish, LA, Ward 3, Dist 005, Family No. 136*. Census Report. Washington DC: U.S. Census Bureau, 1920.

AugJamDeath1925. *Ancestry.com. Louisiana, Statewide Death Index, 1900-1949 [database on-line]*. . 14 October 1925. <http://search.ancestry.com/search/db.aspx?dbid=6697>.

Augustine, Laura. Interview. D.G. Prier. Mansura, 1990.

AurPryDeath. "Aurelian Pryor Death Record." *Louisiana Statewide Death Index*. Marksville, LA: Avoyelles Parish Coroner's Office, 19 April 1926.

AurPryErnMagMarriage. "Marriage of Aurelian Pryor and Ernestine Magloire." *Avoyelles Parish Marriage Records*. Marksville, LA: Avoyelles Parish Clerk of Court, 8 December 1887.

AusSusSam1880. *U.S. Federal Census, Avoyelles Parish, Ward 003, Family No. 484*. Census Report. Washington DC: U.S. Census Burteau, 1880.

AusSuSSam1900. *U.S. Federal Census, Avoyelles Parish, Marksville, 0014, Family No. 259*. Census Report. Washinton DC: U.S. Census Bureau, 1900.

Author, T-P Unknown. "A Lynching in Mansura, LA." *New Orleans Times-Picayune* `4 N9vember 1892: 9. Newspaper.

—. "The Lynching at Mansura, Louisiana, September 2, 1892." *New Orleans Times-Picayune* 11 September 1892: 7. Newspaper.

AvitClaraMarr. "Avoyelles Parish Marriages, Book F, p. 542." *Marriage of Avit Augustin and Clara Dupas*. Marksville, LA: Avoyelles Parish Clerk of Court, 1 January 1893. <http://laghn.usghn.org/avoyelles/marriages.html>.

AvitJaneMarr. "Marriage of Avit Augustine and Jane Lavalais." *Avoyelles Parish Marriages, Book 7, p. 336*. Marksville, LA: Avoyelles Parish Clerk Of Court, 2 October 1923.

AvitLadyMarr. "Marriage of Avit Augustin and Lady Johnson." *Avoyelles Parish Marriages, Book B-3, p. 295*. Marksville, LA: Avoyelles Parish Clerk of Court, 10 May 1866.

AvitLilySS. "U.S. Social Security Claims Index for Lilly Drummer." *U.S., Social Security Applications and Claims Index, 1936-2007*. Provo, UT: Ancestry.com, 2015.

AvitSusanMarr. "Marriage of Avit Augustine and Susan Alison." *Avoyelles Parish Marriages, Book H, p. 514*. Marksville, LA: Avoyelles Parish Clerk of Court, 13 December 1905.

Avoyelles, La Commission des. *Avoyelles: Crossroads of Louisiana Where All Cultures Meet*. Ed. Sue Eakins. Gretna: Pelican Publishing Company, 1999.

AziaFran1910. "1910 United States Federal Census for Isaiah Francisco ." *Thirteenth Census of the United States for Avoyelles Parish,LA*. Mansura, LA : Ancestry.com, 1910.

Ballard, Dave. "Death of Oliver Rabalais, a.k.a. Oliver Oliver." *Oliver Olivier in Dave Ballard III Family Tree on Ancestry.com*. Ancestry.com, n.d.

Barry, John M. *Rising Tide: The Great Mississippi Flood of 1927 and How It Changed America*. Touchstone, 1997.

BasHonMarr. "Marriage of Basil Olivier and Honorine Francois." *Ancestry Member Tree: Avoyelles Parish to the Twin Territories*. Marksville, LA: Ancestry.com, 1877.

BasHonOli1880. "Basil Olivier in the 1880 U.S. Census for Avoyelles Parish, LA, , page 395A." Marksville, LA: Ancestry.com, 1880.

BasHonOliv1870. "Basil Olivier in the 1870 U.S. Federal Census, Subdivision 6, Avoyelles, Louisiana." Ancestry.com, 1870.

BasOlivDeath. "Bazile Olivier, in the New Orleans, Louisiana, Death Records Index, 1804-1949." Ancestry.com, n.d.

bazarts1900. "1900 United States Federal Census, Louisiana Avoyelles Police Jury Ward 01 District 0012." *Twelfthe Census of the United States: Schedule No. 1 - Population*. Avoyelles Parish, LA, 1900. Ancestry.com.

BazOlivProb. "Probate Sale of Possessions of the late Lucien Joffrion, Vol. B, p. 18." *Avoyelles Parish Probate Sales*. Marksville, LA: Ancestry.com, 18 April 1855.

Bellis, Mary. "A History of American Agriculture 1776-1990." 2015. *About.com*.

BenBla1910. "1910 United States Federal Census for Benjamin Blackman, Louisiana Avoyelles Police Jury Ward 8 District 0023, Family 467." *Thirteenth Census of the United States:1910 - Population*. Moreauville, LA: Ancestry.com, 1910.

BenBla1920. "1920 United States Federal Census for Ben Blackman, Louisiana Avoyelles Police Jury Ward 8 District 0011, Family192." *Fourteenth Census of the United States: 1920 - Population*. Moreauville, LA: Ancestry.com, 1920.

BenBla1930. "1930 United States Federal Census for Ben Blackman, Louisiana Avoyelles Police Jury Ward 8 District 0019, Family 182." *Fifteenth Census of the United States: 1930 - Population*. Moreauville, LA: Ancestry.com, 1930.

BenBla1940. "1940 United States Federal Census for Ben Blackman, Louisiana Avoyelles Other Places 5-20 , Family 86." *Sixteenth Census of the United States: 1940 - Population*. Moreauville, LA: Ancestry.com, 1940.

BenBlaWWI. " U.S., World War I Draft Registration Cards, 1917-1918 for Benjamin Blackman, Louisiana Avoyelles County Draft Card B ." *World War I Draft Registration Cards, 1917-1918*. Marksville, LA: Ancestry.com, 5 June 1917.

BenMelSam1880. "Ben and Melice Sampson in 1880 Census." *1880 U.S. Federal Census, Avoyelles Parish, Marksville, LA, Ward 003, Familu No. 74*. Washington DC: U.S. Census Office, 1880.

BenRacSamp1870. "Ben and Rachal Sampson in 1870 U.S. Census." *U.S. Federal Census, Avoyelles Parish, LA, Subdivsion 6, Family No. 766*. Washington, DC: U.S. Census Bureau, 1870.

BenSam1830. "1830 United States Federal Census for Benjamin Sampson , Virginia Sussex Not Stated ." Sussex County, VA: Ancestry.com, n.d.

BenSamDeath. "Benjamin Sampson Death Record." *St. Paul the Apostle Catholic Church Burial Records, Book V (1886-1905)*. Mansura, LA: Diocese of Alexandria, 4 June 1881.

BenSamp1840. "1840 United States Federal Census for Ben Sampon, Virginia Sussex Not Stated ." Ancestry.com, 1840.

BenSamSale. "Probate Sale of Property Belonging to David Orr, ." *Avoyelles Probate Sale, Vol. A-B, p. 97*. Marksville, LA: Ancestry.com, 10 January 1849.

BerMarBerMarr. "Marriage of Berzat Berzat and Marie Rebecca Augustin." *Hunting For Bears, comp.. Louisiana, Marriages, 1718-1925*. Marksville, Louisiana: Ancestry.Com, 3 November 1890.

Berry, Mary F. "Negro Troops in Blue and Gray: The Louisiana Native Guard, 1861-1863." *The Louisiana Purchase Bicentennial Series in Louisiana History - The African American Experience in Louisiana*. Ed. Charles Vincent. Vol. XI. Lafayette: Center for Louisiana Studies, University of Louisiana at Lafayetter, 2000. 21-38. Book.

Berz1870. "1870 United States Federal Census." *U.S. Federal Census for Avoyelles Parish, Louisiana, Subdivision 6, page 67, 99*. Marksville, Louisiana: Ancestry.com, 6 July 1870.

Berzat. *1930 United States Federal Census*. Census. Washington, DC: United States Government, 1930.

Biard, Francois Auguste. *The Slave Trade (Slaves on the West Coast of Africa)*. Wilberforce House Museum. Oil Painting.

billieking943. "Marceline Dufour." *Ancestry Family Tree*. Ancestry.com, n.d.

Blackman, Pilger Nathan. "90 Year Old Recalls Highlights of His Life." *The Greater Avoyelles Journal* 5 AUGUST 1990: 1. Newspaper.

Blake, Tom. "Avoyelles Parish. Louisiana: Largest Slaveholders from 1860 Census and Surname Matches for African Americans on 1870 Census." 2001. *Rootsweb.com*. 2015. <http.//freepages.genealogy.rootsweb.com>.

Bolton, Charles C. "Farmers Without Land: The Plight of White Tenant Farmers and Sharecroppers." 2004. *Mississippi History Now*. Mississippi Historical Society. 15 May 2015. <http://mshistory.k12.ms.us/index.php?s=extra&id=228>.

Bordelon, Jerry. "Dominique Coco II (1785-1864)." *Find A Grave*. Find A Grave Memorial# 32782056. Ancestry.com Operations, 9 January 2009. <http://www.findagrave.com/cgi-bin/fg.cgi?page=gr&GRid=32782056>.

—. "Dominique Coco II (1785-1864) - Find A Grave Memorial # 32782056." 9 January 2009. *Find A Grave*. Ancestry.com . <http://www.findagrave.com/cgi-bin/fg.cgi?page=gr&GRid=32782056&ref=acom>.

—. "Edward Batiste ." *FindaGrave*. Mansura, LA: Ancestry.com, 10 February 2015.

—. "Leandre François Roy in the U.S., Find A Grave Index, 1600s-Current, Grave Memorial Number 58410445." *Find A Grave Index*. Ancestry.com Oerations Inc., 9 September 2010. <http://www.findagrave.com/cgi-bin/fg.cgi?page=gr&GRid=58410445&ref=acom>.

—. "Lucien Dominique Coco, III." *U.S., Find A Grave Index, 1600s-Current*. Comp. Find A Grave. Find A Grave. http://www.findagrave.com/cgi-bin/fg.cgi. Find A Grave.com. Provo: Ancestry.com, 10 August 2010.

—. "Valery Coco." 7 August 2010. *Find A Grave.com.* Ancestry.com Operations Inc. <http://www.findagrave.com/cgi-bin/fg.cgi?page=gr&GRid=57244032&ref=acom>.

—. "Valery Coco." 17 August 2010. *Find A Grave.com.* Ancestry.com Operations inc. <http://www.findagrave.com/cgi-bin/fg.cgi?page=gr&GRid=57244032&ref=acom>.

Bordelon, L. *1850 US Census for Avoyelles Parish, Louisiana.* Census Record. United States Census Bureau. Washington, DC: Ancestry.com, 1850.

Bordelon, L. *Joseph Laurent in 1850 US Census.* Census Report. US Government. Avoyelles Parish, LA: Ancestry.com, 1850.

Bordelon, M. *Rosalie Gustin James, St. Paul Burial Records, Book V, p. 31.* Mansura, LA: Diocese of Alexandria, LA, 1998.

Bordelon, Mildred. *Death of Sylvain Francisco.* Vol. V. Mansura: Diocese of Alexandria, Louisiana, 1998.

—. "Ursin Augustine, Sr." *St. Paul the Apostle Catholic Church Burial Register, 1886-1905, p.27.* Vol. Book V27. Mansura, LA: Diocese of Alexandria, LA, 5 October 1901.

Boucher, Jack E. *Magnolia Plantation, Slave Quarters.* Cane River National Heritage Area Commission; National Parks Service, Natchitoches, Louisiana.

Boyd, John Jr. "High Price of Monopoly: Why American Farmers Must Buy From Just One Seed." *National Black Farmers Association* 2012.

Bradley, Michelle Cadoree. "Paul Oliver in Cadoree of Avoyelles Family Tree by Michelle Cadoree Bradley." *Ancestry Family Tree.* Mansura, LA: Ancestry.com, n.d.

Bradshaw, Jim. *Great Flood of 1927.* Ed. David Johnson. 13 May 2013. 9 May 2015. <http://www.knowla.org/entry/763/>.

Britannica, Encyclopedia. "African Religions." 4 February 2016. *Encyclopedia Britannica On-Line.* On-Line Document. <http://www.britannica.com/topic/African-religions>.

Brown, Yvonne U. "Trahan Darrin Keone Family Tree." *Ancestry Family Tree.* Ancestry.com, n.d.

Bureau, 1920 U.S. Census. "1920 U.S. Census for Avoyelles Parish, Ward 3." *1920 U.S. Federal Census.* Washngton DC, n.d.

Bureau, Census. *1830 United States Census for Avoyelles Parish, Louisiana.* Census Records. Washington, DC: United States Government, 1830.

—. *1900 U.S. Federal Census, Avoyelles Parish, LA, Ward 3, District 0014.* Census Report. Washington DC: U.S. Census Bureau, 1900.

Bureau, U.S. Census. *1810 United States Census for Avoyelles Parish, Louisiana.* Washington, DC: U.S. Government, 1810.

—. *1810 United States Federal Census.* Provo, UT: Ancestry.com, n.d. Microfilm - Record Group 29; NARA microfilm publication M252, 71 rolls.

—. *1810 US Census for Avoyelles Parish Louisiana.* Census Report. Washington, DC: US Census Bureau, 1810.

—. *1820 United States Census for Avoyelles Parish, Louisiana.* Washington, DC: U.S. Government, 1820.

—. *1830 United States Federal Census for Avoyelles Parish, LA.* Provo, UT: Ancestry.com Operations, Inc, 1830. <http://search.ancestry.com/cgi-bin/sse.dll?indiv=1&db=1830usfedcenancestry&gss=angs-d&new=1&rank=1&msT=1&gsfn=p&gsln=normand%2c+norman&msrpn__ftp=Avoyelles+Parish

%2c+Louisiana%2c+USA&msrpn=213&msrpn_PInfo=7-
%7c0%7c1652393%7c0%7c2%7c3246%7c21%7c0%7c213%7c0>).

Bureau, U.S. Census 1850. *1810 US Census for Avoyelles Parish Louisiana*. Census Report. Washington, DC: US Census Bureau, 1810.

Bureau, U.S. Census. "1850 U.S. Census for Avoyelles Parish, Louisiana." *1850 U.S. Census*. Washington, DC: U.S. Government, 1850.

Bureau, U.S. Census 1860. "1860 United States Federal Census for Avoyelles Parish, Louisiana." 1860.

Bureau, U.S. Census. *1860 U.S. Federal Census - Slave Schedules*. Provo, UT: Ancestry.com Operations Inc., 2010.

—. "1860 United States Federal Census for Avoyelles Parish, Louisiana." 1860.

—. *1870 United Census for Avoyelles Parish, LA Division 5, Family No. 631*. Census Report. Provo, UT: Ancestry.com Operations, Inc., n.d. <http://interactive.ancestry.com/7163/4269407_00216/30550307?backurl=http%3a%2f%2fsearch.ancestry.com%2f%2fcgi-bin%2fsse.dll%3fdb%3d1870usfedcen%26indiv%3dtry%26h%3d30550307&ssrc=&backlabel=ReturnRecord#?imageId=4269407_00215>.

—. "1910 United Federal Census for Avoyelles Parish, LA, Ward 3." Ancestry.com Operations, Inc., n.d.

Bureau, United States Census. "1850 U.S. Federal Census - Slave Schedules ." *Bureau of the Census. Seventh Census of the United States, 1850*. Ancestry.com. Washington, DC: Ancestry.com Operations Inc., 1850. <http://search.ancestry.com/cgi-bin/sse.dll?gss=angs-c&new=1&rank=1&msT=1&gsfn=lucien+dominique&gsln=coco&mswpn__ftp=Avoyelles+Parish%2c+Louisiana%2c+USA&mswpn=213&mswpn_PInfo=7-%7c0%7c1652393%7c0%7c2%7c3246%7c21%7c0%7c213%7c0%7c0%7c&MSAV=1&msbdy=1812&cpxt>.

Bureau, US Census. "1840 U.S. Census for Pointe Coupee Parish, Louisiana." *U.S. Census*. U.S. Government, 1840.

—. *1840 U.S. for Avoyelles Parish, LA*. Provo, UT: Ancestry.com, n.d. <http://interactive.ancestry.com/8057/4409529_00572/1310161?backurl=http%3a%2f%2fsearch.ancestry.com%2f%2fcgi-bin%2fsse.dll%3fgss%3dangs-g%26new%3d1%26rank%3d1%26msT%3d1%26gsfn%3dlaurent%2bsr.%26gsln%3dnormand%26mswpn__ftp%3dAvoyelles%2bParish%252c%2bLouis>.

Calvin Peter Thampson. Dir. Tom Whitehead. Prod. W. Belton. Townsend Foundation, 1979.

Calvin Peter Thampson. Dir. Tom Whitehead. Prod. W. Belton. Townsend Foundation, 1979. Movie.

Calvin Peter Thompson. Dir. Tom Whitehead. Prod. W Belmont. 1979.

Calvin Peter Thompson. Dir. Tom Whitehead. Prod. W. Belmont. 1979. Movie.

Car, The Little Black. *Slave cabins at the Audubon State Historic Site in Louisiana*. Audubon State Historic Site. <http://www.flickr.com/photos/littleblackcar/4815714757/>.

CarBatDeath. "Carrie M Batiste." *Find A Grave, Memorial# 119676657*. Marksville, LA: Ancestry.com, 2 November 2013.

—. "Carrie T. Batiste Death." *FindaGrave Memorial# 64259059, By Jerry Bordelon*. Mansura, LA: Ancestry.com, 16 January 2011.

Cargo. *Description of a slave ship*. British Museum, London. Wood Engraving. <https://commons.wikimedia.org/wiki/File:Description_of_a_slave_slip_by_anonymous_wood_engraving_1789.jpg>.

CelAntPic. *Celestine Antoine. Antoine & Washington Family Tree*. Ancestry.com, n.d.

CelGab1900. *U.S. Federal Census, Avoyelles Parish, LA, Ward 04, Dist. 0015*. Census Report. Washington DC: U.S. Census Bureau, 1900.

CelGabJoMag1871. *Marriage Certificate of Jacque Dupas and Celestine Gabriel*. Marriage Certificate. Mansura, LA: St. Paul the Apostle Catholic Church, 1871.

Census, 1900 U.S. "1900 U.S. Census for Avoyelles Parish." *1900 U.S. Federal Census*. Washington, DC: U.S.Census Bureau, n.d.

—. "1900 United States Federal Census, Avoyelles Parish, Ward 3." *Clara Normand Coco*. Police Jury Ward 3, Avoyelles; Enumeration District 0014: US Census Bureau, 1900. Roll: 558; Page: 1B.

Census, US. *1860 US Census*. Census. Washington DC: US Department of the Census, 1860.

CerGrem1850. "Ceran Gremillion." *1850 United States Federal Census for Ciran Gremillion*. Marksville, LA: Ancestry.com, 22 August 1850. Ancestry.com.

CerGrem1870. "1870 United States Federal Census for Ceran Gremillion." *U.S. Census for Avoyelles Parish*. Marksville, LA, 1870.

CharVicMarr. "Marriage of Charles Dupas and Victorine Davis." *Charles Dupas in the Louisiana Marriages, 1718-1925*. Marksville: Ancestry.com, 23 December 1884.

ChDupMarr1. "Marriage of Charles Dupas and Eupheme Day." *Brides Book of Avoyelles Parish, LA, 1856-1880, Vol. Vol. 2*. Marksville, LA: Ancestry.com, 27 December 1877.

Church, Priests of St. Paul the Apostle Catholic. *St. Paul the Apostle Baptism Records*. Church Records. Mansura, LA: Diocese of Alexandria, Louisiana, n.d.

CJ. "Jean Pierre Normand." 10 September 2012. *Find A Grave Memorial*. Ancestry.com. <http://www.findagrave.com/cgi-bin/fg.cgi?page=gr&GRid=96846810&ref=acom>.

ClaFisDeath. "Clara Fisher Death Certificate." *Louisiana Certificate of Death, Register No. 14679*. Opelousas, LA: St. Landry Coroner's Office, 24 October 1924.

ClaPrySale. "Marie Mayeaux Probate Sale." *Avoyelles Parish Probate Sale*. Marksville, LA: Ancestry.com, 21 May 1856.

ClarBat1940. "1940 United States Federal Census for Clara Batiste, Louisiana Avoyelles Other Places 5-4, Family 310." *Sixteenth Census of the United States: 1940 - Population Schedule*. Marksville, LA: Ancestry.com, n.d.

ClarBatCar1930. *1930 United States Federal Census, Louisiana Avoyelles Police Jury Ward 3 District 0007 , Family 103*. Mansura, LA: Ancestry.com, 1930.

ClarBatDeath. "Clarice Gaspard Batiste Louisiana Death Index, 1819-1964." Mansura, LA: Ancestry.com, 6 November 1940.

ClarJBte. "clarisse gaspard jean baptiste." *Ancestry Posting*. Mansura, LA: Ancestry.com, 6 December 2010.

clarpri1910. "1910 United States Federal Census for Claira Pette, Louisiana Avoyelles Police Jury Ward 6 District 0020 , Family 379." *Thirteenth Census of the United States:1910 - Population*. Ancestry.com, 1910.

ClarPryDeath. "Clarice Prier in the Louisiana, Statewide Death Index, 1819-1964." Marksville: Ancestry.com, 2002.

ClaTelSteFisMarr. "Marriage of Clara Pryor and Stephen Fisher." *Marriage Certificate, State of Louisiana, Parish of St. Landry*. Opelousas: St. Landry Parish Clerk of Court, 18 November 1896.

ClebBat1940. "1940 United States Federal Census for Clebert Batiste, Louisiana Avoyelles Mansura 5-6 , Family 53." Mansura, LA: Ancestry.com, 1940.

ClebBatdeath. "Clebert Batiste." *Louisiana, Statewide Death Index, 1819-1964*. Mansura, LA: Ancestry.com, 1948.

ClebRos1920. "1920 United States Federal Census for Clebert Batiste, Louisiana Avoyelles Police Jury Ward 4 District 0007 , Family 283." Avoyelles Parish, LA: Ancestry.com, 1920.

ClemFran1900. *U.S. Federal Census, A voyelles Parish, LA., Ward 3, Dist. 0014, Family No. 270*. Census Report. Washington DC: U.S. Census Bureau, 1900.

Cline, Isaac M. "SPECIAL REPORT ON THE GALVESTON HURRICANE." 4 February 2004. *NOAA History - A Science Odyssey*. 6 March 2016. <http://www.history.noaa.gov/stories_tales/cline2.html>.

Cockrone, E.E. *Joseph Laurent in 1860 US Census for Avoyelles Parish, LA*. Census Report. Census Bureau. Provo, UT: Ancestry.com Operations, 1860. <http://interactive.ancestry.com/7667/4231218_00425?pid=38462247&backurl=http%3a%2f%2fsearch.ancestry.com%2f%2fcgi-bin%2fsse.dll%3findiv%3d1%26db%3d1860usfedcenancestry%26h%3d38462247%26tid%3d%26pid%3d%26usePUB%3dtrue%26rhSource%3d7163&treeid=&personid=&hi>.

Committee, Avoyellean of the Year. "Dominique Coco I, Avoyellean of 1786." n.d. *Avoyelles.com*. Ed. Randy Decuir. <http://avoyelles.com/Avoyelleans/1786-DominiqueCoco/bio.html>.

Congress, Library of. *Map of Avoyelles Parish Louisiana*. Washington DC, 1879. Library of Congress Document.

ConsDes1837. *Early Baptism Records: St. Paul the Apostle Catholic Church 1824-1844*. Ed. Alberta Rousseau G.R.S Ducote. Mansura, LA: St. Paul the Apostle Catholic Church, n.d.

Contributors, H-Net. "African Muslim Slaves in America." 5 February 2016. *H-Net.org*. <http://www.h-net.org/~africa/threads/muslimslaves.html>.

contributors, Wikipedia. "Battle of Fort De Russy." 28 July 2015. *Wikipedia, The Free Encyclopedia*. <https://en.wikipedia.org/w/index.php?title=Special:CiteThisPage&page=Battle_of_Fort_De_Russy&id=673440145>.

—. "Battle of Mansura." 10 September 2013. *Wikipedia, The Free Encyclopedia*. <https://en.wikipedia.org/w/index.php?title=Special:CiteThisPage&page=Battle_of_Mansura&id=572272371>.

Contributors, Wikipedia Staff and. "Siege of Port Hudson." n.d. *Wiipedia.com*. <https://en.wikipedia.org/wiki/Siege_of_Port_Hudson>.

Coroner, Avoyelles Parish. "Claris Pryor, Certificate of Death." Marksville, LA: Avoyelles Parish Clerk of Court, 17 November 1917.

Coronor, Avoyelles Parish. "Joseph Laurent." *Louisiana Death Records*. Louisiana Vital Records, 11 September 1870.

Cotes1930. *U.S. Federal Census, Avoyelles Parish, LA, Ward 3, Dist 8*. Census Report. Washington DC: U.S. Census Bureau, 1930.

CurDem1920. "1920 United States Federal Census for Curtis Demouy, Louisiana Avoyelles Police Jury Ward 3 District 0005, Family 150." *Fourteenth Census of the United States: 1920 - Population*. Mansura, LA: Ancestry.com, 1920.

cyrang1910. "1910 United States Federal Census for Cyrias Francisco, Louisiana Avoyelles Police Jury Ward 3 District 0016, Family 274." *Thirteenth Census of thr United States:1910-Population*. Mansura, LA: Ancestry.com, 1910.

Daggett, US Army Copyist. *US Colored Troops Military Service Records, 1863-1865*. Provo, UT: Ancestry.com/National Archives and Records Administration, 1864. On-line Database.

Database, US Government. "U.S., Civil War Pension Index: General Index to Pension Files, 1861-1934 for Jean B Berzat." 1901.

Dauphine, James G. "The Knights of the White Camelia and the Election of 1868: Louisiana's White Terrorists; a Benighting Legacy." Vincent, Charles. *The African American Experience in Louisiana; Part B: From the Civil War to Jim Crow*. Lafayette, Louisiana: Center for Louisiana Studies, University of Louisiana at Lafayette, 2000. 223-238. Hardcover Book.

Davis, Burke. "The Civil War, Strange and Fascinating Facts." 1 Nvember 2004. *CivilWarHome.com*. <http://civilwarhome.com/casualties.htm>.

Davis, Theodore R. *The riot in New Orleans – murdering negroes in the rear of Mechanics' Institute. Harper's Weekly*. New Yor, 1866. Engraving.

De Mouy, Michael. "Arthur Demouy ." *Arthur Demouy in De Mouy as of 2013 Family Tree*. Ancestry.com, n.d.

Decuir, Randy. "Avoyelles Almanac." *The Bunkie Record, The Marksville Weekly News* 20 March 2014.

Delano, Jack. *Sharecroppers chopping cotton on rented land near White Plains, Greene County, Ga*. Library of Congress Prints and Photographs Division, Farm Security Administration, Washington DC. Photograph.

DelpDeath. "Death Record of Delphine Francisco." *St. Paul's Mansura, Louisiana Burial Records, 1886-1905*. Mansura, LA: Diocese of Alexandria, LA, n.d.

delphsale1848. "Probate Sale of Property Belonging to Marguerite Lacour." *Avoyelles Parish Probate Sales*. Hydropolis, Louisiana: Ancestry.com, 29 January 1848.

Dethloff, Henry C. and Jones, Robert R. "Race Relations in Louisiana, 1877-98." Vincent, Charles. *The African American Experience in Louisiana, Part B: From the Civil War to Jim Crow*. Lafayette, Louisiana: Center for Louisiana Studies, University of Louisiana Studies, 2000. 501. Hardcover Book.

Dobak, William A. "Buffalo Soldiers." 2015. *HistoryNet*. <http://www.historynet.com/buffalo-soldiers>.

Dodd, Jordan R and et. al.. *Early American Marriages: Louisiana to 1850*. Bountiful, UT: Precision Indexing Publishers, 1824.

Dodd, Jordan R. and et al. "Early American Marriages: Louisiana to 1850." *Elza Bordelon*. Bountiful: Precision Indexing Publishers, 30 July 1829.

Dodd, Jordan R. et al. *Joseph Laurent in Louisiana Marriages to 1850*. Database. Provo, UT: Ancestry.com Operations, n.d. <http://search.ancestry.com/cgi-bin/sse.dll?indiv=1&db=eamla&h=101346&tid=&pid=&usePUB=true&rhSource=8054>.

Dodd, Jordan R., et al. "Clara Normand." n.d. *Louisiana Marriages to 1850*. Ancestry.com Operations Inc. <http://search.ancestry.com/cgi-bin/sse.dll?gss=angs-

g&new=1&rank=1&msT=1&gsfn=clara&gsln=normand&mswpn__ftp=Avoyelles+Parish%2c+Loui
siana%2c+USA&mswpn=213&mswpn_PInfo=7-
%7c0%7c1652393%7c0%7c2%7c3246%7c21%7c0%7c213%7c0%7c0%7c&MSAV=1&msbdy=183
4&cpxt=1&cp=12>.

—. "Joseph Dominique Coco." 1997. *Early American Marriages: Louisiana to 1850*. Ancestry.com
Operations inc. <http://search.ancestry.com/cgi-bin/sse.dll?gss=angs-
c&new=1&rank=1&msT=1&gsfn=joseph+dominique&gsln=coco&mswpn__ftp=Avoyelles+Parish
%2c+Louisiana%2c+USA&mswpn=213&mswpn_PInfo=7-
%7c0%7c1652393%7c0%7c2%7c3246%7c21%7c0%7c213%7c0%7c0%7c&MSAV=1&msbdy=182
7&cpxt>.

Dollarhide, William. *The Census Book: A Genealogist's Guide to Federal Census Facts, Schedules and Indexes*. Bountiful, UT: Heritage Quest, 2000.

DorArm1850. "1850 United States Federal Census for Doesin Armand, Louisiana Avoyelles Not Stated , Family 53." *1850 U.S. Census for Avoyelles Parish, LA*. Marksville, LA: Ancestry.com, 1850.

DorArmII. "Dorsineau "Dorsin" Armand II." *Lemoine Family Tree, "Pollysteapot"*. Ancestry.com, n.d.

DorArmLand. "Dorcineau Armand." *Louisiana, Homestead and Cash Entry Patents, Pre-1908; Document 519; 1 N½SE LOUISIANA No 1 N 4 E 13*. Opelousas, LA: Ancestry.com, 1 October 1852.

DorArmMarr. "Dorsin Armand." *Louisiana, Compiled Marriages, 1728-1850*. Marksville, LA: Ancestry.com, 16 February 1847.

DorArmSlaves. "1860 U.S. Federal Census - Slave Schedules , Avoyelles Parish, LA." Marksville, LA: Ancestry.com, n.d.

DorArmWar. "Dorsin Armand." *U.S. Civil War Soldiers, 1861-1865*. Ancestry.com, n.d.

DorAugLife. "Dorsin Augustin in Sherpatrick washington Famiy Tree." *Ancestry Family Trees*. Ancestry,com, n.d.

douetk. "Lemoine Family Tree." *Ancestry.com*. Ancestry.com Operations Inc., n.d. <http://trees.ancestry.com/tree/50013383/person/28206360913>.

Du Bois, W.E.B. *Black Reconstruction in America: 1860-1880*. New York, NY: Atheneum, 1972. Paperback.

Du Bois, W.E.Burghardt. *The Souls of Black Folks*. Chicago, IL: A.C. McClung & Co., 1903.

Du Bois, William Edward Burghardt. *The story of the Niagara Movement and the N. A. A. C. P*. Amherst, MA: University of Massachusetts Amherst ; Special Collections & University Archives : University Libraries, 1945.

Dubose, William E. B. *The Georgia Negro*. African American Photographs Assembled for 1900 Paris Exposition. *Negro Exhibit of the American Section at the Paris Exposition Universelle in 1900*. Paris: U.S. Library of Congress, 1900. <Image download: http://lcweb2.loc.gov/master/pnp/ppmsca/33800/33863a.tif>.

Ducote, Alberta Rousseau. "Baptism of Slave Baby Delphine." *Early Baptism Records, St. Paul the Apostle Catholic Church, 1824-1844, Page 169*. Mansura, LA: Diocese of Aexandria, LA, n.d.

—. *Early Baptism Records, St. Paul the Apostle Catholic Church, 1824-1831, 1832-1844, 1845-1850*. Mansura, LA: St. Paul the Apostle Catholic Church, n.d. Book.

Ducote, Willie J. *Avoyelles Parish- St. Paul, Mansura, Louisiana Burial Register*. Trans. Willie J Ducote. Vols. 4, 5. Mansura, LA: St. Paul the Apostle Catholic Church, 1998. 5 vols.

Dufour. "Birth and Baptism of Mary Jane Augustin." *Avoyelleans of Yesteryear, No. 5, p 63*. Marksville, 28 November 1878.

Eakin, Sue. *Sue Eakin Papers*. University Archives and Central Louisiana Collection, James C. Baldwin Library, Alexandria . Photograph.

Eakins, Sue. *Calvin Peter Thompson*. James C. Bolton Library, Louisiana State University, Alexandria. Sue Eakins Papers Collection, Central Louisiana Collection.

EdAli1920. "1920 United States Federal Census for Edward Batiste, Louisiana Avoyelles Marksville District 0002 , Family 821." Marksville, LA: Ancestry.com, 1920.

EdBatDraft. "U.S., World War I Draft Registration Cards, 1917-1918 for Edward Batiste, ." Marksville, LA: Ancestry.com, 12 September 1918.

EdEmCoco1910. *U.S. Federal Census, Avoyelles Parish, LA, Ward 3, Dist. 0016, Family No. 436*. Census Report. Washington DC: U.S. Census Bureau, 1910.

Editor, Obit. "Lucien Dominique Coco, III." *Marksville Bulletin* 12 September 1879: 3.

EdMar1910. "1910 United States Federal Census for Edward S Oliver , Louisiana Avoyelles Police Jury Ward 3 District 0016 ." Ancestry.com, 1910.

EdOlDeath. "Edward Louis Oliver, in the Louisiana, Statewide Death Index, 1819-1964." Ancestry.com, n.d.

EdvBerz1860. "1860 United States Federal Census for Edvin Berzat." *United States Federal Census for Avoyelles Parish, Louisiana, Page 138*. Marksville, LA: Ancestry.com, 28 November 1860.

Edwards, Everett Eugene. *Bibliography of the History of Agriculture in the United States*. University of Michigan, 1930. Book.

Ehret, Christopher. *The Civilizations of Africa: A History to 1800*. Richmond, VA: University of Virginia Press, 2002.

ElArBer1920. "1920 United States Federal Census for Ella Berger." *Fourteenth United States Census: 1920 - Population*. New Orleans, LA: Ancestry.com, 1920.

ElBerDeath. "Ella Berger in U.S., Find A Grave Index, 1600s-Current, Find A Grave Memorial# 90803007." *Find A Grave*. New Orleans, LA: Ancestry.com, n.d.

EliJulRic1900. "1900 United States Federal Census for Julie Ricard, Louisiana Avoyelles Police Jury Ward 08 District 0021, Family No. 270." *Twelfth Census of the United States: Schedule No. 1 - Population*. Mansura, LA: Ancestry.com, 1900.

ElizAugMarr. "Marriage of Elizabeth Augustin and Pierre Francisco." *Avoyelles Parish Bride's Book*. Marksville, LA: Avoyelles Parish, LA Clerk of Court, 26 January 1898.

ElizAugMarr2. "Marriage of Elizabert Augustin and Hippolite Ravare." *Avoyelles Parish Brides Book*. Marksville, LA: Avoyelles Parish Clerk of Court, 23 January 1902.

ElizCo. "1910 United States Federal Census for Elizene Coco, Louisiana Avoyelles Police Jury Ward 3 District 0016, Family 70." *Thirteenth Census of the United States: 1910 - Population*. Mansura, LA: Ancestry.com, n.d.

ElizCoc1920. "1920 United States Federal Census for Elizene Coco, Louisiana Avoyelles Police Jury Ward 3 District 0005 , Family 156." *Fourteenth Census of the United States: 1920 - Population*. Mansura, LA: Ancestry.com, 1920.

ElizCocDeath. "Marie Elizene Coco." *U.S. Find A Grave Index, Reference Number 95521666*. Ancestry.com, n.d.

ElJam1910. "1910 United States Federal Census for Elouis Augustin , Louisiana Avoyelles Police Jury Ward 3 District 0016 , Family 45." *Thirteenth Census of the United States: 1910 Poulation*. Mansura: Ancestry.com, 1910.

ElJam1930. "1930 United States Federal Census for Heloise Augustine, Louisiana Avoyelles Police Jury Ward 3 District 0007 , Family 7." *Fifteenth Census of the United States: 1930 Population Schedule*. Mansura, LA: Ancestry.com, 1930.

ElJamWilWalMarriage1895. "Marriage of Elizabeth James and Willie Walton." *St. Paul the Apostle Marriage Record*. Mansura: Diocese of Alexandria, 10 January 1895.

ElJulRic. "1880 United States Federal Census for J. Ricar, Louisiana Avoyelles Not Stated 004 ." *1880 U.S. census for Avoyelles Parish, LA*. Mansura, LA: Ancestry.com, 1880.

Ellis, David and Martin Halbert. "The Trans-Atlantic Slave Trade Databaseoyages: The Trans-Atlantic Slave Trade Database." 2015. *Slave Voyages.org*. Emory University. <http://www.slavevoyages.org/tast/about/team.faces>.

Emelie. "Baptism of Emelie." *Early Baptism Records 1824-1844*. Mansura, Louisiana: St. Paul the Apostle Catholic Church, 1844.

EmJulPryMarriage. *Marriage of Emile Pryor and Julienne Francisco*. Marriage Record, Book F, p. 563. Marksville, LA: Avoyelles Parish Clerk of Court, February 4, 1894.

EmPryDeath. *Emile Pryor Death Certificate*. Louisiana Statewide Death Index, Avoyelles Parish, Certificate 11820, Vol. 28. Marksville, LA: Avoyelles Parish Coroner, October 12, 1931.

ErnOli1900. "1900 United States Federal Census for Estelle Olivier , Louisiana Avoyelles Police Jury Ward 03 District 0014 ." Mansura, LA: Ancestry.com, n.d.

ErnOzeMar. "1930 United States Federal Census for Ernestine Fontenot , Louisiana Avoyelles Police Jury Ward 3 District 0007 ." Mansura, LA: Ancestry.com, n.d.

EugJam1910. "1910 United States Federal Census for Forest Titus, Louisiana Avoyelles Police Jury Ward 3 District 0016 , Family 430." *Twelfth Census of the United States: 1910 Population*. Mansura, LA: Ancestry.com, 1910.

EvarJamBur. "Burial of Evariste James, January 18, 1903." *St. Paul's Burial Records, Book V 1886-1905, p. 29*. Diocese of Alexandria, , October 1998. Booklet.

Faber, Lo and Charles Chamberlain. "Spanish Colonial Louisiana (1763 - 1802)." 7 February 2014. *KnowLa: Encyclopedia of Louisiana*. Ed. David Jihnson. Louisiana Endowment for the Humanities. 30 May 2015. <http://knowla.org/entry/773/>.

Faragher, John Mack. *A Great and Noble Scheme: The Tragic Story of the Expulsion of the French Acadians from Their American Homeland*. New York, NY: WW Norton & Company, 2005.

Fatal Flood, The American Experience. By Chana Gazit. Dir. Chana Gazit. Prod. Chana Gazit. n.d.

Fauburg Treme - The Untold Story of Black New Orleans. By Lolis Eric Elie. Dir. Dawn Logsdon. Prod. Dawn Logsdon & Lolis Eric Elie Lucie Faulknor. PBS.org, HBO, n.d. Television. <http://www.tremedoc.com/>.

FelAug1870. "1870 United States Federal Census for Ursin Augustin, Louisiana Avoyelles Subdivision 5, Family 14." *1870 U.S Census for Avoyelles Parish, LA*. Marksville, LA: Ancestry.com, 1870.

FelMag1870. "1870 United States Federal Census for F Magloire, p. 76, Family No. 652, Louisiana Avoyelles Subdivision 6 ." *U.S. Census for 1870*. Ancestry.com, 1870.

FelMag1880. "Felicien Magluire, 1880 United States Federal Census, Louisiana Avoyelles Marksville 003 , p. 45." *1880 U.S. Census.* Marksville, LA: Ancestry.com, 1880.

FelSylv1838. *St. Paul's Baptismal Records.* Baptismal Record. Mansura, LA: St. Paul the Apostle Catholic Church, 1838. Paper.

FerlrRegard1900. *U.S. Federal Census, Avoyelles Parish, LA, Ward 3, Dist. 0014, Family No. 2.* Census Report. Washington DC: U.S. Federal Census, 1900.

FilCocDeath. "Emile Filmore Coco." *U.S. Find A Grave Index, Memoril No. 95521643.* Ancestry.com, n.d.

Finley, Keith. "Lynchings." 21 December 2012. *KnowLa Encyclopedia of Louisiana.* Ed. David Johnson. Louisiana Endowment for the Humanities. 8 February 2016.

—. "Lynchings (ca. 1860 - 1940s)." *KnowLa Encyclopedia of Louisiana* (2012).

FloPryMatBouMarriage. "Marriage of Florestine Pryor and Mathew Bourgs." *Marriage Certificate.* Marksville, LA: Avoyelles Parish Clerk of Court, 31 December 1894.

FlorPryThomFoxMarriage. "Marriage of Florida Pryor and Thomas Fox." *Avoyelles Parish Marriage Record.* Marsville, LA: Avoyelles Parish Clerk of Court, 15 December 1887.

Fort, Bruce. 10 August 1996. *American Slave Narratives - An Online Anthology.* American Hypertext Workshop at the University of Virginia, Summer 1996. <http://xroads.virginia.edu/~hyper/wpa/wpahome.html>.

Fortier, Alcee and James McLoughlin. "Louisiana." *The Catholic Encyclopedia* 1910. <http://www.newadvent.org/cathen/09378a.htm>.

ForTit1920. "1920 United States Federal Census for Forrest Titus, Louisiana Avoyelles Police Jury Ward 3 District 0004 , Family 375." *Fourteenth Census of the United States: 1920 Population.* Mansura, LA: Ancestry.com, 1920.

ForTitDeath. "Forest Titus Certificate 31818." *Texas Death Index, 1903-2000, .* Port Arthur, TX: Ancestry.com, n.d.

Foundation, Constitutional Rights. "A Brief History of Jim Crow." 2014. *CRF-USA.org.* 11 February 2016. <http://www.crf-usa.org/black-history-month/a-brief-history-of-jim-crow>.

Francisco, Robena. *Booklet of Francisco History.* Bakersfield, CA: Unpublished, 1975. Private Booklet.

FranciscoProbSale. "Probate Sale in Avoyelles Parish." *Public Court Record.* Vols. Vol. C-D. Mansura, LA: Ancestry.com, 13 October 1863. 422.

FranClemFran1880. *U.S. Federal Census, Marksville, Avoyelles Parish, LA, Dist. 003, Family No. 500.* Census Report. Washington DC: U.S. Census Bureau, 1880.

FranClemMarr. "Marriage of Francois Francisco and Clementine Steven Kemper." *Avoyelles Parish Marriage Records, Book D, p. 220.* Marksville, LA: Avoyelles Parish Clerk of Court, 13 February 1877.

FranDelFran1870. *U.S. Federal Census, Avoyelles Parish, Subdivision 6, Family No. 774.* Census Report. Washington DC: U.S. Census Bureau, 1870.

FranFran1870. *U.S. Federal Census, Avoyelles Parish, LA. Sibdivision 6, Family No. 774.* Census Report. Washington DC: U.S. Census Bureau, 1870.

FranFranDeath. "Death of Francois Francisco." *St. Paul's Mansura, Louisiana Burial Regster, 1886-1905.* Vol. V. Trans. Mildred Bordelon. Mansura, October 1998. 24.

FranFranll1880. *U.S. Federal Census, Avoyelles Parish, Marksville, LA, Dist. 003, Family No. 459*. Census Report. Washington DC: U.S. Census Biureau, 1880.

Frankel, Neil. *THE ATLANTIC SLAVE TRADE AND SLAVERY IN AMERICA*. 2007. <http://slaverysite.com/Body/maps.htm#map5>.

Frankenfeld, A. L. *The Floods of 1927 in the Mississippi Basin*. NOAA - Historic NWS Collection. *1927 Monthly Weather Review*. Silver Spring, and Suitland: Wikimedia Commons, n.d. 13 March 2016. <http://www.photolib.noaa.gov/htmls/wea00733.htm>.

Frankenfeld, H.C. *The Floods of 1927 in the Mississippi Basin*. Vol. Supplement No. 29. 1927 Monthly Weather Review, 1927.

FranLuc1900. "1900 United States Federal Census for Francois Luke." *Twelfth Census of the United States for Avoyelles Parish, Ward 3, District 0014*. Mansura, Louisiana: Ancestry.com, 4 June 1900.

FranLuk1900. "1900 United States Federal Census for Francois Luke." *U.S. Census for Avoyelles Parish, LA Ward 03, District 0014, Family 53*. Mansura, LA: Ancestry.com, 4 June 1900. Internet.

FredAug1900. "1900 United States Federal Census for Frederick Augustin, Louisiana Avoyelles Police Jury Ward 03 District 0014, Family 380." *Twelfth Census of the United States: Schedule No. 1 - Population*. Mansura, LA: Ancestry.com, 1900.

French, B. F. "Louisiana's Code Noir (1724)." 1851. *BlackPast.org*. <http://www.blackpast.org/primary/louisianas-code-noir-1724>.

FulFranDeath. "Death of Fulgence Francisco." *Louisiana, Statewide Death Index, 1819-1964*. Mansura, LA: Ancestry.com, 23 December 1929.

FulFranMarriage. "Marriage of Fulgence Francisco and Marie Reason." *the Louisiana, Marriages, 1718-1925*. Marksville: Ancestry.com, 1 May 1873.

Gaba, Eric. *Africa Slave Regions. The Atlantic World: Europeans, Africans, Indians and Their Shared History, 1400 - 1900*. Cambridge, England: Cambridge University Press, n.d. 340. <https://commons.wikimedia.org/wiki/File%3AAfrica_slave_Regions.svg>.

GabBerz1850. "1850 United States Federal Census for Gabriel Berza, Louisiana Avoyelles Not Stated , Family 199." *1850 U.S. Census for Avoyelles Parish, Louisiana*. Marksville, LA: Ancestry.com, n.d.

GabBerz1870. "1860 United States Federal Census for Edwin Berzat (nee AdviseBerzat)." *U.S. Federal Census for Avoyelles Parish, Louisiana, page 138*. Marksville, LA: Ancestry.com, 28 November 1860.

GabMag1870. "1870 United States Federal Census for Gabriel Maylone, Louisiana Avoyelles Subdivision 6 , Family 532." Marksville: Ancestry.com, 1870.

—. *Gabriel Magloire*. Census Report for Avoyelles Parish, Louisiana. Washington, DC: Ancestry.com, 1870. <http://interactive.ancestry.com/7163/4269407_00062?pid=30544824&backurl=//search.ances try.com//cgi-bin/sse.dll?indiv%3D1%26db%3D1870usfedcen%26h%3D30544824%26tid%3D%26pid%3D%26u sePUB%3Dtrue%26_phsrc%3Dvyn60%26_phstart%3DsuccessSource%26usePUBJs%3Dtrue%26r >.

GabSale. "Sale of Slave Gabriel." *Avoyelles Parish Probate Sales, Vol.A-B, p. 154*. Mansura, Louisiana: Ancestry.com, 6 May 1848.

GadMag1880. *Gabriel Magloire*. Census Report for Avoyelles Parish, ED 3. Washington, DC: Ancestry.com, 1880. <http://interactive.ancestry.com/6742/4241285-00166?pid=8533955&backurl=//search.ancestry.com//cgi-bin/sse.dll?indiv%3D1%26db%3D1880usfedcen%26h%3D8533955%26tid%3D%26pid%3D%26usePUB%3Dtrue%26_phsrc%3Dvyn60%26_phstart%3DsuccessSource%26usePUBJs%3Dtrue%26rhS>.

Galveston. *History of Galveston, Texas*. Wikipedia, 1915.

Gates, Henry Louis Jr. "Did Black People Own Slaves?" 4 March 2013. *The Root*. 30 May 2015. <http://www.theroot.com/articles/history/2013/03/black_slave_owners_did_they_exist.html>.

Gates, Henry Louis, Jr. "Did African-American Slaves Rebel?" 2013. *The African Americans, Many Rivers to Cross*. PBS.

General view looking from the north along west row of cabins - Magnolia Plantation, Slave Quarters, LA Route 119, Natchitoches, Natchitoches Parish, LA .

GenevaSwis. "Notes on Joseph Joffrion II." 7 November 2007. *Ancestry.com*. <http://trees.ancestry.com/tree/3454724/person/-1613111471/story/bbdd9def-2996-471f-999b-ecfbed30d84a?src=search>.

GeoBer1860. "1860 U.S. Federal Census - Slave Schedules ." *1860 U.S. Census for Avoyelles Parish, LA*. Marksville, LA: Ancestry.com, 1860.

George, Octavia. *Former Slave* OWP Interviewer. Oklahoma Writer's Project, 1938.

GerMc1900. *U.S. Federal Census, Jefferson County, MS, Beat 5, Dist. 0090, Family No. 239*. Census Report. Washington DC: U.S. Census Bureau, 1900.

GertBatDeath. "Gertrude Batiste." *U.S., Find A Grave Index, 1600s-Current*. Mansura, LA: Ancestry.com, 1972.

Gibson, James F. *Cumberland Landing, Va. Group of "contrabands" at Foller's house*. US Army. *Photograph from the main eastern theater of war, The Peninsular Campaign, May-August 1862*. . Library of Congress, n.d. <http://hdl.loc.gov/loc.pnp/pp.print>.

Gilbert, Charlene. *Homecoming: The Story of African-American Farmers*. 2002.

Gilbert, J et al. *The Decline (and Revival?) of Black farmers and Rural Landowners. A Review of the Research Literature"*. . Land Tech Center, University of Wisconsin, 2001.

gipierson. "Marie Chevalier Berzat." *Ancestry Family Trees*. Ancestry.com, n.d.

Gladstone, William A. *United States Colored Troops, 1863-1867*. Gettysburg, PA: Thomas Publications, 1996.

glaure49. "Sale of Slave Record #10344." *Avoyelles Parish Clerk of Court Conveyence Record*. Marksville: Ancestry.com, 10 July 1859.

Government, US. "US Census." 1880, 1900, 1930.

Great Migration. By History.com Staff. History Channel, 2010. <http://www.history.com/topics/black-history/great-migration>.

Great Migration. By History.com Staff. A&E Network. History Channel, 2010. Television. 6 June 2016. <http://www.history.com/topics/black-history/great-migration>.

Gremillion, L.V. "Estate of Julien Goudeau, deceased." Trans. PeteNormand1949. Bayou Rouge Prairie, Avoyelles Parish: Ancestry.com, 16 January 1858. <http://mv.ancestry.com/viewer/742266b3-285f-47f4-80f9-8e8c574ccdb5/7048077/-1175110605?_phsrc=opB2&usePUBJs=true>.

—. "Inventory of the Estate of Julien Jules Goudeau I." Trans. PeteNormand1949. Bayou Rouge Priarie, Avoyelles Parish: Ancestry.com, 12 January 1858. <http://mv.ancestry.com/viewer/1e4aa80e-591d-4ac4-810e-2bd637ccd51a/7048077/-1175110605?_phsrc=opB2&usePUBJs=true>.

Gremillion, Paulin M., Avoyelles Parish Deputy-Recorder. "Avit Augustin To His natural Children." *Act of Acknowledgement*. Marksville. Louisiana: Avoyelles Parish Clerk of Court, 16 February 1872.

Guillory, Reverend Charles. *St. John Community Church-Baptist is on Facebook*. n.d.

—. *St. John Community Church-Baptist is on Facebook*. n.d. Social Media.

GusAug1880. "1880 United States Federal Census for Gustin Augustin, Louisiana Avoyelles Marksville 003, Family 70." *1880 U.S. Census*. Marksville, LA: Ancstry.com, n.d.

GusAugMarr. "Gustin Augustin." *Hunting For Bears, comp.. Louisiana, Marriages, 1718-1925*. Marksville, LA: Ancestry.com, 2004.

—. "Marriage of Gustave Augustin and Fannie Patton." *Avoyelles Parish, LA Bride's Book, E-449*. Marksville, LA: Avoyelles Parish Clerk of Court, 1885.

GusOli1900. "U.S. Census for Gustave L Oliver, ." Ancestry.com, 1900.

GusOli1920. "1920 United States Federal Census for Gust L Oliver , Oklahoma Lincoln Wellston District 0138 ." Ancestry.com, 1920.

GusOli1930. "1930 United States Federal Census for Gustave Oliver , Oklahoma Lincoln Wellston District 0049 ." Ancestry.com, 1930.

GusOliv1940. "1940 United States Federal Census for Gustave L Olwer, Oklahoma Lincoln Wellston 41-44 ." Ancestry.com, n.d.

Haley, Alex. *Roots: the Saga of an American Family*. New York, NY: Vanguard Books, 1974. Book.

Hall, Gwendolyn Midlo. *Africans in Colonial Louisiana: The Development of Afro-Creole Culture in the Eighteenth Century*. Baton Rouge, LA: Louisiana State University Press, 1995.

—. "Berri in the Louisiana, Slave Records, 1719-1820." n.d. *Ancestry.com*. <http://search.ancestry.com/cgi-bin/sse.dll?gss=angs-g&new=1&rank=1&gsfn=joseph&gsln=joffrion&mswpn__ftp=Avoyelles+Parish%2c+Louisiana%2c+USA&mswpn=213&mswpn_PInfo=7-%7c0%7c1652393%7c0%7c2%7c3246%7c21%7c0%7c213%7c0%7c0%7c&MSAV=1&msbdy=1755&_83004003-n_xcl=>.

—. "Louisiana Freed Slave Records, 1719-1820." *Afro Louisiana History and Genealogy, 1719-1820*. Ancestry.com Operations Inc., 2003. <http://www.ibiblio.org/laslave/>.

—. "Louisiana, Slave Records, 1719-1820." 2009. *Ancestry.com Operations*. <http://search.ancestry.com/cgi-bin/sse.dll?gss=angs-g&new=1&rank=1&msT=1&gsfn=joseph&gsln=joffrion&mswpn__ftp=Avoyelles+Parish%2c+Louisiana%2c+USA&mswpn=213&mswpn_PInfo=7-%7c0%7c1652393%7c0%7c2%7c3246%7c21%7c0%7c213%7c0%7c0%7c&MSAV=1&msbdy=1775&cpxt=1&cp=>.

—. *Louisiana, Slave Records, 1719-1820*. Ancestry.com, Inc. Operations Inc. Provo, 2003. On-Line Database. <http://search.ancestry.com/cgi-bin/sse.dll?gss=angs-g&new=1&rank=1&msT=1&gsfn=magloire&mswpn__ftp=Avoyelles+Parish%2c+Louisiana%2c+USA&mswpn=213&mswpn_PInfo=7-%7c0%7c1652393%7c0%7c2%7c3246%7c21%7c0%7c213%7c0%7c0%7c&msbdy_x=1&msbdp=5&MSAV=1&msbdy=1794&_830>.

—. "Louisiana, Slave Records, 1719-1820." Ancestry.com, 2009.

HamBat1910. "1910 United States Federal Census for Hamilton Jeanbattis." Mansura, LA: Ancestry.com, 1910.

HamBat1930. "1930 United States Federal Census for Hamilton Batiste, Louisiana Avoyelles Mansura District 0006 , Family 33." Mansura, LA: Ancestry.com, 1930.

HamBat1940. "1940 United States Federal Census for Hamilton Batiste, Louisiana Avoyelles Mansura 5-6 , Family 59." Mansura, LA: Ancestry.com, 1940.

HamBatDeath. "Hamilton Batiste." *U.S., Social Security Death Index, 1935-2014*. Mansura. LA: Ancestry.com, 1969.

HamBatSSI. "Gertrude Barbin." *U.S., Social Security Applications and Claims Index, 1936-2007*. Mansura, LA: Ancestry.com, n.d.

HamBatWWI. "U.S., World War I Draft Registration Cards, 1917-1918 for Hamilton John Baptiste ." Marksville, LA: Ancestry.com, 5 June 1917.

Hamilton. Harper's Weekly Newspaper, April 18, 1863 Edition . *Contemporary Newspaper view of theUnion fleet passing Port Hudson published by "Harper's Weekly Newspaper" April 18, 1863*. New York: Harper's Weekly, 1863. Wiipedia.com. <https://en.wikipedia.org/wiki/Siege_of_Port_Hudson#/media/File:Port_Hudson_Navy_Harpers .jpg>.

Harlan, Louis R. *Booker T. Washington: The Wizard of Tuskegee, 1901-1915*. Oxford, U.K.: Oxford University Press, 1986.

—. *The Booker T. Washington Papers*. Ed. Louis R. Harlan. Vol. 3. Urbana: University of Illinois Press, 1974.

—. *The Booker T. Washington Papers*. Vol. 3. Urbana: University of Illinois Press, 1974.

Harper, Douglas. "American Colonialization Society." 2003. *Slavery in The North*. <http://slavenorth.com/colonize.htm>.

Harper's Weekly Newspaper, April 18, 1863 Edition. *Photograph of black soldiers of the Native Guard regiments of the Union army at Port Hudson, Louisiana, 1862-1864*. National Archives, Archival Research Catalog, Washington, DC. Archival Research Catalog, digital images, National Archives, ARC identifier 594179, Local Identifier 165-JT-433B. <https://commons.wikimedia.org/wiki/File:Port_Hudson_Native_Guard.gif#filehistory>.

Harper's Weekly Staff. "The Louisiana Murders—Gathering The Dead And Wounded." *Harper's Weekly* 10 May 1873: 397. <http://blackhistory.harpweek.com/7Illustrations/Reconstruction/Illustrations/0397w500.jpg>.

HarRozDem1920. "1920 United States Federal Census for Henry Demouy, Louisiana Avoyelles Police Jury Ward 3 District 0005, Family 72 ." *Fourteenth Census of the United States: 1920 - Population*. Marksville, LA: Ancestry.com, n.d.

HarryDemDeath. "Death of Harry T, Demouy, Sr." *Louisiana Statewide Death Index, 1819-1964*. Alexandria, LA: Ancestry.com, 10 June 1934.

Hathorn, Billy. *Sharecropper's Cabin, Lake Providence, LA*. Louisiana State Cotton Museum in Lake Providence, LA, Lake Providence, LA. Photograph.

Heinnemann, R.L. "Robert Russa Moton (1867-1940)." *Encyclopedia Virginia*. Virginia Foundation for the Humanities, 2014.

HelPolGuil1920. "Helel and Poland Guillory in 1920 Census." *14th Census of the United States: 1920 Population*. Louisiana , Avoyelles , Police Jury Ward 3, District 0004 : Ancestry.com, 17 January 1920.

HenAug1870. "1870 United States Federal Census for Henry Augustin, Louisiana Avoyelles Subdivision 5 , Family 347." *1870 U.S. Census*. Marksville, LA: Ancestry.com, 1870.

HenAug1880. "1880 United States Federal Census for Robert Rogers, Louisiana Avoyelles Marksville 003, Family 17." *1880 U.S. Census for Avoyelles Parish, LA*. Marksville, LA: Ancestry.com, n.d.

HenAug1900. "1900 U.S. Census for Henry Augustin, Louisiana Avoyelles Police Jury Ward 06 District 0017, Family 217." *Twelfth Census of the United States: 1900 - Population*. Moreauville, LA: Ancestry.com, 1900.

HenBlkmn1900. *U.S. Federal Census, Avoyellesw Parish, Ward 8, Dist. 0021, Family No. 341*. Census Report. Washington DC: Census Bureau, 1900.

HenBlkmn1910. *1910 U.S. Federal Census, Avoyelles Parish, .* Census Report. Washington DC: Census Bureau, 1910.

HenBlkmn1920. *1920 U.S. Federal Census, Mansura, LA, Dist 0005, Family No. 38*. Census Reort. Washinjgton DC: Census Bureau, 1920.

HenBlkmn1930. *1930 U.S. Federal Census, Avoyelles Parish, Ward 3, Dist. 8, Family No. 18*. Census Report. Washington DC: Census Bureau, 1930.

HenLetMcG1920. *U.S. Federal Census, Spring Hill, Rapides Parish, LA, Ward 4, Dist. 0065, Family No. 807*. Census Report. Washington DC: U.S. Census Bureau, 1920.

HenRozDem1930. "1930 United States Federal Census for Henry Demouy, Louisiana Rapides Police Jury Ward 1 District 0015 , Family 457." *Fifteenth Census of the United States: 1930 - Population*. Marksville, LA: Ancestry.com, 1030.

Henry, Ashley. *Medal of Honor recognition long overdue*. 9 May 2008. 9 May 2015. <http://www.army.mil/article/9075/medal-of-honor-recognition-long-overdue/>.

Herbert_Holmes_1. "Oliver Normand and Lucinda Sampson." 2015. *Ancestry.com*. <http://trees.ancestry.com/tree/75282541/person/32316540762/story/e664b873-9e94-479e-9965-e385cb5f4898?src=search>.

Hewitt, Lawrence E. *Port Hudson, Confederate Bastion on the Mississippi*. Baton Rouge, LA: Lousiana State University Press, 1987.

Hollandsworth, James G. *An Absolute Massacre: The New Orleans Race Riot of July 30, 1866*. Baton Rouge, Louisiana: Louisiana State University Press, 2004.

Holmes, Jack D. L. "The Abortive Slave Revolt at Pointe Coupée, Louisiana, 1795." *Louisiana History: The Journal of the Louisiana Historical Association* 11.4 (1970): 341-362. <http://www.jstor.org/stable/4231151?seq=1#page_scan_tab_contents>.

Holt, Thomas C. *The Second Great Migration, 1940-1970*. Ed. Molly Hodgens. Chicago: University of Chicago, n.d.

HorAug1910. "1910 United States Federal Census for Aurace Augustine, Louisiana Avoyelles Police Jury Ward 3 District 0016, Family 561." *Thirteenth Census of the United States: 1910 - Population*. Mansura, LA: Ancestry.com, 1910.

HorAug1920. "1920 United States Federal Census for Horace Augustine, Louisiana Avoyelles Police Jury Ward 3 District 0005, Family 142." *Fourteenth Census of the United States: 1920 - Population*. Mansura, LA: Ancestry.com, 1920.

HTDemRos1910. "1910 United States Federal Census for Henry T Demouy, Louisiana Avoyelles Police Jury Ward 3 District 0016 , Family 82." *Thirteenth Census of the United States: 1910 - Population*. Marksville, LA: Ancestry.com, 1910.

Hunter, Clementine and Cammie G Henry. *Melrose Plantation, African House, State Highway 119, Melrose, Natchitoches Parish, LA*. Library of Congress Prints and Photographs Division, Washington, D.C. 20540 USA. < http://hdl.loc.gov/loc.pnp/pp.print>.

Hyacinth, Mother Mary. "The Murder of Laurent Normand." McCants, Sister Dorothy. *They Came To Louisiana; Letters of a Catholic Mission 1854-1882*. Trans. Daughter of the Cross Sister Dorothea McCants. LSU Press, 1970. 90-91.

InDem1910. "1910 United States Federal Census for Eunice Normand, Louisiana Avoyelles Police Jury Ward 3 District 0016, Family 83." *Thirteenth Census of the United States: 1910 - Population*. Mansura, LA: Ancestry.com, 1910.

IrDupMarr2. "Marriage of Irma Dupas and Louis Berzat." *Avoyelles Parish Louisiana Marriages*. Marksville, LA: LAGHN, 30 July 1889.

IreDemDeath. "Irene Marie Prevot Demouy." *Louisiana, Statewide Death Index, 1819-1964*. Mansura, LA: Ancestry.com, n.d.

IrLuc1880. "1880 United States Federal Census for Irma Luc , Louisiana Avoyelles Marksville 003 , Family 88." *United States Federal Census for Avoyelles*. Marksville: Ancestry.com, 188.

IrmDup1910. "1910 United States Federal Census for Irma Dupas , Louisiana Avoyelles Police Jury Ward 8 0022 , Family 117." *Thirteenth Census of the United States: 1910 - Population*. Moreauville, LA: Ancestry.com, 1910.

IrmDupMarr. "Marriage of Irma Dupas to Jean Baptiste Luke." *Avoyelles Parish Louisiana Marriages*. Marksville, LA: Avoyelles Parish LAGHN, 15 February 1872.

IrwJosSam1900. *U.S. Federal Census, Avoyelles Parish, LA, Marksville, Dist 0014, Family No. 60*. Census Report. Washington DC: U.S. Census Bureau, 1900.

IsaiFran1930. "Isiah Francisco." *1930 United States Federal Census*. Mansura, LA: Ancestry.com, 1930.

jacdup1880. *1880 U.S. Federal Census, Avoyelles Parish, Subdivision 6, Family 755*. Census Report. Washington DC: U.S. Census Bureau, 1880.

JacDup1880. *St. Paul Burial Register, 1870-1885, Book IV, P.20*. Mansura, LA: St. Paul the Apostle Catholic Church, 1880.

JacDupRosGab1870. *Avoyelles Parish LAGHN*. 5 1 2016. Internet. 2016. <http://laghn.usghn.org/avoyelles/marriagesd.html>.

JacqAug1870. "1870 United States Federal Census for Avoyelles Parish, Louisiana, Subdivision 6." *1870 U.S. Federal Census*. Provo: Ancestry.com Operations Inc., 1870. <http://search.ancestry.com/cgi-bin/sse.dll?gss=angs-g&new=1&rank=1&msT=1&gsfn=celeste&gsln=normand&mswpn__ftp=Avoyelles+Parish%2c+Louisiana%2c+USA&mswpn=213&mswpn_PInfo=7-%7c0%7c1652393%7c0%7c2%7c3246%7c21%7c0%7c213%7c0%7c0%7c&msbdy_x=1&msbdp=10&MSAV=1&ms>.

JacqAug1880. "1880 U.S. Federal Census for Avoyelles Parish, Ward 8." *1880 U.S. Federal Census.* Washington DC, n.d.

JacRosDup1870. *1870 U.S. Federal Census, Avoyelles Parish LA., Subdivision 6, Family No. 756.* Census Report. Washington DC: Census Bureau, 1870.

JacRosDup1880. *1880 U.S. Federal Census, Avoyelles Parish, Marksville, LA, Dist. 003, Family No. 89.* Census Report. Washington DC: Census Bureau, 1880.

James, Ola. Interview. D.G. Prier. 2014.

JamMarRan1930. "1930 United States Federal Census for Mary S Randall, Louisiana Avoyelles Police Jury Ward 8 District 0019, Family 26." *Fifteenth Census of the United States: 1930 - Population.* Moreauville, LA: Ancestry.com, 1930.

JamMayRan1910. "1910 United States Federal Census for May S Rundol, Louisiana Avoyelles Police Jury Ward 8 District 0022, Family 68." *Twelfth Census of the United States: 1910 - Population.* Moreauville, LA: Ancestry.com, 1910.

JamMayRan1920. "1920 United States Federal Census for Mary Randell , Louisiana Avoyelles Police Jury Ward 8 District 0011, Family 322." *Fourteenth Census of the United States: 1920 - Population.* Moreauville, LA: Ancestry.com, 1920.

JBAugDeath. "U.S. Federal Census Mortality Schedules, 1850-1885 for Jean Augustin, 1870 Louisiana Avoyelles Line 5." *U.S. Federal Census Mortality Schedules, 1850-1885,.* Moreauville, LA: Ancestry.com, 1870.

jbbarnette153. "Inez (Eunice) Demouy in Reynaud Family Tree." *Ancestry Family Trees.* Ancestry.com, n.d.

JBBerz1880. "U.S. Federal Census." *U.S. Federal Census for Avoyelles Parish, Louisiana.* Marsville, Louisiana: Ancestry.com, 29 June 1880.

JBBerzat1870. *U.S. Federal Census, Avoyelles Parish, Subdivision 6, Family No. 751.* Census Record. Washington DC: Census Bureau, 1870.

JBBerzat1880. "1880 U.S. Federal Census for Jean Bte Berzat." *U.S. Census for Avoyelles Parish, Louisiana, Marksville, Ward 3, Page 54.* Marksville, LA: Ancestry.com, 29 June 1880.

JBBPension. *Civil War Pension Index, Application No. 748130.* Washington DC: National Archives and Records Administration, 1901.

JBLem. "Pinerocousar (1) Family Tree ." *Ancestry Family Trees.* Mansura, LA: Ancestry.com, n.d.

"JBLemSale." *Avoyelles Parish Probate Sale, November 9, 1860, Vol. C-D, p. 200.* Mansura, LA: Ancestry.com, 9 November 1860.

JBTE_JosMarriage. "St. Paul Marriage Certificate for Jean Baptiste Berzat & Josephine Luc." Mansura, LA: St. Paul the Apostle Catholic Church, 5 December 1869.

JeanBirth. "Birth of the Slave Child, Jean." *Early Baptism Records, St. Paul the Apostle Catholic Church, 1832-1844.* Mansura, Louisiana: Diocese of Alexandria, LA, n.d.

JeanBteIrmaDupMarr. "Jean Bte . Luke in Louisiana Marriages." *Hunting For Bears, comp.. Louisiana, Marriages, 1718-1925.* Marksville, LA: Ancestry.com, 15 February 1872.

JeanGab1870. *1870 U.S. Federal Census, Avoyelles Parish, LA, Subdivision 6, Family 754.* Census Report. Washington DC: U.S. Census Bureau, 1870.

JeanPSale. "Avoyelles Parish Court Probate Sale, Vol. C-D, p.126." *Probate Sale of Property Belonging to Laurent Normand.* Mansura, LA: Ancestry.com, 20 March 1860.

JLMag1870. "1870 United States Federal Census for Josephine Maylone [Magloire], Louisiana Avoyelles Subdivision 6 , Family No. 291." *1870 United States Federal Census*. Marksville: Ancestry.com, 2009.

JLMagMarr. "Marriage of Josephene Augustin, Louisiana, Marriages, 1718-1925." *Hunting For Bears*. Mansura, LA: Ancestry.com, 2004.

JM1880. "J . Magloire, ." *1880 United States Federal Census, Louisiana, Avoyelles, Not Stated, E.D. 004* . Marksville, LA: Ancestry.com, n.d.

JoeHel1900. "1900 United States Federal Census for Joseph Barker." *Twelfth Census of the United States for Avoyelles Parish, LA Ward 3, Sheet 8*. Mansura, LA: Ancestry.com, 8 June 1900.

JoeHel1910. "1910 United States Federal Census for Joseph V Barker ." *Thirteenth Census of the United States: 1910 Population for Avoyelles Parish, LA, Ward 3, Sheet 30*. Mansura, Louisiana: Ancestry.com, 11 May 1910.

JoeMag1900. "1900 United States Federal Census for Joe Mcglory, Louisiana Rapides Alexandria District 0123 , Family 69." *Twelfth Census of the United States - Schedule No. 1 - Population*. Alexandria, LA: Ancestry.com, n.d.

JoffJamBirth. "1930 US Federal Census." Mansura, Avoyelles, Louisiana, Roll 784, p. 6A, ED 0006: Ancestry.com, 1930.

Joffrion, Lucien. "Probate Sale of Property of Late Lucien Joffrion." *Avoyelles Parish Probate Sale, Vol. B, p.18*. Marsville, LA: Ancestry.com, 18 April 1855.

JohnPriDeath. "Death of John Prier." *Certificate of Death*. Moreauville, LA: Louisiana State Board of Health, 1 January 1930.

JoJBte1880. "1880 United States Federal Census for Bte Joseph Jean, Louisiana Avoyelles Marksville 003 ." Marksville: Ancestry.com, 1880.

JoMagMarr. "Marriage of Joseph Magloire and Celestine Gabriel." *Hunting For Bears, comp.. Louisiana, Marriages, 1718-1925* . Marksville, LA: Ancestry.com, 23 February 1871.

Jones, Amara. "Outflow of Africans to the Americas and Europe." 2015. *SlaveryBlog*. <http://slaveryblog.tumblr.com/AboutAdministrator>.

Jones, Terry L. "The Free Men of Color Go to War." *New Yor Times Opinionator* 19 October 2012. <http://opinionator.blogs.nytimes.com/2012/10/19/the-free-men-of-color-go-to-war/?_r=0>.

JoPri1920. *U.S. Federal Census, Avoyelles Parish, LA, Ward 3, Dist. 004, Family No. 386*. Census Report. Washngto DC: U.S. Census Bureau, 1920.

JoPri1930. *U.S. Federal Census, Avoyelles Parish, LA, Ward 3, Dist. 8, Family No. 196*. Census Report. Washington DC: U.S. Census Bureau, 1930.

JoPrRoGauMarr. "Marriage of John Pryor and Rosa Gauthier." *Avoyelles Parish Marriage Records*. Marksville, LA: Avoyelles Parish Clerk of Court office, 30 September 1880.

JoPryDeath. "John Pryor Death Record." *Avoyelles Parish Death Certificate*. Marsville, LA: Avoyelles Parish Coroners Office, 1 January 1930.

JoPryLucOwMarriage. "Marriage of John Pryor and Lucy Owings." *Avoyelles Parish Marriage Records*. Marksville, LA: Avoyelles Parish Clerk of Court Office, 13 February 1872.

JoRoPry1880. *U.S. Federal Census, Avoyelles Parish, Marksville, LA. Dist. 003, Family No. 95*. Census Report. Wasshington DC: U.S. Census Bureau, 1880.

JosAg1930. "1930 United States Federal Census for Joe Barker ." *Fifteenth Cemsus of the United States for Ellis, Texas, Precinct 3, Sheet 4B*. Ellis, Texas: Ancestry.com, 5 April 1930.

JosAgnMarr. "Joseph Barker in the Texas, County Marriages, 1817-1965." *Ancestry.com. Texas, County Marriages, 1817-1965* . Ellis, TX: Ancestry.com, 27 November 1927.

JosAMag1870. *U.S. Federal Census, Avoyelles Parish, Subdivision 6, Family No. 691*. Census Report. Washington DC: U.S. Census Bureau, 1870.

JosAug1900. "1900 United States Federal Census for Joseph Augustin, Louisiana Avoyelles Police Jury Ward 08 District 0021, Family 141." *Twelfth Census of the United States: 1900 - Population*. Moreauville, LA: Ancestry.com, 1900.

JosBarDeath. "Joe V T Barker in the Texas, Death Certificates, 1903-1982." *Ancestry.com. Texas, Death Certificates, 1903-1982 Provo, UT, USA: Ancestry.com Operations, Inc., 2013*. . Ellis, TX: Ancestry.com, 10 May 1930.

JosBerDeath. "Death of Josephine Berzat." *Findagrave.com*. Mansura, Louisiana: Ancestry.com, 30 October 1941.

JosBerz1940. *1940 U.S. Census Record, Avoyelles Parish, LA, District 6, Family No. 251*. Census Report. Washington DC: Census Bureau, 1940.

JosCelMc1880. *U.S. Federal Census, Avoyelles Parish, Marksville, LA, Dist. 003, Family No. 428*. Census Report. Washington DC: U.S. Census Bureau, 1880.

JosClar1900. "1900 United States Federal Census for John Bte Joseph , Louisiana Avoyelles Police Jury Ward 03 District 0014 , Family No. 77." Mansura, LA: Ancestry.com, 1900.

JosClar1910. " 1910 United States Federal Census for Joseph Jeanbattis, Louisiana Avoyelles Police Jury Ward 3 District 0016 , Family 422." Mansura, LA: Ancestry.com, 1910.

JosClarMarr. "Marriage Record of Joseph Jean Baptiste and Clarisse Gasard." Marksville, LA: Ancestry.com, 14 December 1878.

JosJBteDeath. "Joseph Jean Baptiste , Louisiana, Statewide Death Index, 1819-1964, Certificate Number:." Mansura, LA: Ancestry.com, 12 September 1911.

JosJBteWar. "Jean Baptiste Joseph in the U.S. Civil War Soldiers, 1861-1865, M589 roll 50." *U.S. Civil War Soldiers*. Ancestry.com, 207.

JosLuc1900. "1900 U.S. Federal Census, Avoyelles Parish, Marksville, LA , District 003, Family No. 82." *U.S. Federal Census*. Washington, DC: Ancestry.com, 1990.

JosLucJBBerzMarriage. "Hunting For Bears, comp.. Louisiana, Marriages, 1718-1925]. ." Provo, UT, USA: Ancestry.com Operations Inc, 2004.

JosLucSale1. "Justine Normand Probate Sale ." *Avoyelles Parish Probate Sales, Vol.B, page 8*. Marksville, LA: Ancestry.com, 4 June 1865.

JosLucSale2. "David L. Orr Probate Sale." *Avoyelles Parish Probate Sales, Vol. B, page 8*. Marksville, LA: Ancestry.com, 10 January 1849.

JosMag1870. *U.S. Federal Census, Avoyelles Parish, Subdivision 6, Family*. Census Report. Washington DC: U.S. Census Bureau, 1870.

JosMag1910. "1910 United States Federal Census." *13th Census of the United States*. Beat 5: Ancestry.com, 5 May 1910. Beat 5, District 0008.

JosMagPen. *U.S., Civil War Pension Index: General Index to Pension Files, 1861-1934; U.S. Civil War Soldier Records and Profiles, 1861-1865*. 2000.

JosMar19010. "1910 United States Federal Census for Joseph Jeenbattis, Louisiana Avoyelles Police Jury Ward 3 0016 , Family 175." Mansura, LA: Ancestry.com, 1910.

JosMar1930. "1930 United States Federal Census for Joseph Baptiste, Louisiana Avoyelles Police Jury Ward 3 District 0007 , Family 84." Mansura, LA: Ancestry.com, 1930.

JosMarJBte. "Marie Jacob, Louisiana, Marriages, 1718-1925." Mansura, LA: Ancestry.com, 1898.

JosMarJr1920. "1920 United States Federal Census for Joseph Jeabatiste, Louisiana Avoyelles Mansura District 0004 , Family 166." Mansura, LA: Ancestry.com, 1920.

JosMarr1970. "Marriage of Joseph Magloire and Marguerite Baker." *Hunting for Bears, St. Paul Marriages, page 196, sheet 48*. Mansura, LA: Diocese of Louisiana, n.d.

JosMcG1900Census. "1900 U.S. Census." *12th Census of the United States*. Rodney: U.S. Census Bureau, 19 June 1900. Sheet 11.

JosOliv1900. "1900 U.S. Census for Josephine Olivier." Mansura, LA: Ancestry.com, n.d.

JosOlivMarr. "Ancestry Family Tree Matching for Josephine Oliver." Ancestry.com, n.d.

JosPauSampdeath. "Pauin Sampson." *Find A Grave Memorial# 142525239*. Mansura, LA: Ancestry.com, 12 February 2015.

JosRab1785Census. n.d.

JosRabAncestry. "Rabalais Family Document." n.d. *Ancestry*.

JPASucc. "Succession of Jean Pierre Augustine." *Oaths and Bonds of Tutor Admnistration, Vol. C, 1872-1889*. Marksville, LA: Ancestry.com, 1878.

JPAug1870. *1870 U.S. Federal Census, Avoyelles Parish, LA, Subdivision 6, Family No. 1031*. Washington DC: Census Bureau, 1870.

—. "1870 United States Federal Census for Jesse Augustin, Louisiana Avoyelles Subdivision 6, Family 1031." *1870 U.S. Census for Avoyelles Parish*. Marksville, LA: Ancestry.com, n.d.

JPAugCourt. "Ursin Augustin, fils et al. versus A.L. Boyer." *District Court, Parish of Avoyelles*. Marksville, LA: Avoyelles Parish Clerk of Court, 19 December 1881.

JPAugDeath. "U.S. Federal Census Mortality Schedules, 1850-1885 for Jean Augustin, 1870 Louisiana Avoyelles ." Avoyelles Parish, LA: Ancestry.com, 1870.

JPAugJrDeath. "Jean Pierre Augustine." *Louisiana, Statewide Death Index, 1819-1964*. Mansura, LA: Ancestry.com, 1923.

JPAugMarr. "Marriage of Jean Gustin and Felicite." *Brides Book of Avoyelles Parish, B3-314*. Marksville, LA: Avoyelles Parish Clerk of Court, 15 August 1866.

JPAugTut. "Louisiana, Wills and Probate Records, 1756-1984 for Jean Pierre Augustin ." *Louisiana Oaths and Bonds of Tutor Administration, Vol C, 1872-1889*. Marksville, LA: Ancestry.com, 6 April 1878.

JPJamDeath1927. *Louisiana State Death Index*. Death Record. New Orleans: State of Louisiana, Bureau of Vital Records, 1927.

JPLorJam1900. *U.S. Federal Census, Avoyelles Parish, LA, Ward 3, Dist. 0014, Family No. 69*. Census Report. Washington DC: U.S. Census Bureau, 1900.

JPLorJam1910. *U.S. Federal Census, Avoyelles Parish, LA, Ward 3, Dist 0016, Family No. 42*. Census Report. Washington DC: U.S. Census Bureau, 1910.

JsAugDeath. "Certificate of Death for Josephine Augustine, Registered No. 71." *Louisiana Certificate of Death*. Mansura, LA: Louisiana State Bureau of Vital Records, 7 February 1934.

JulBerz1850. "1850 United States Federal Census for Julien Berza." *U.S. Census for Avoyelles Parish, Lousisana, page 235*. Marksville, LA: Ancestry.com, 5 September 1850.

—. "Julien Berza in the 1850 U.S. Census ." *U.S. Census for Avoyelles Parish, Louisiana, Page 235*. Marksville, LA: Ancestry.com, 5 September 1850.

JulDup1880. "1880 United States Federal Census for Julien Dupas, Louisiana Avoyelles Marksville 003, Family 92." *1880 U.S. Census for Avoyelles Parish, LA*. Mansura, LA: Ancestry.com, 1880.

JulDupDeath. "Louisiana, Statewide Death Index, 1819-1964 for Julian Dupas." Mansura: Ancestry.com, 14 August 1937.

JulDupMarFranMarr. "Marriage of Julian Dupas and Mary Francsco." *Avoyelles Parish Louisiana Marriages - LAGHN*. Marksville, LA: LAGHN, 22 December 1885.

JulDuPRosGabMarr. "Marriage of Julian Dupas and Roseline Gabriel." *Avoyelles Parish Louisiana Marriages - LAGHN*. Marksville, LA: LAGHN, 15 December 1870.

JulFran1880. *U.S. Federal Census, Avoyelles Parish, LA, Marksville, Dist. 003, Family No. 337*. Census Report. Washington DC: U.S. Census Bureau, 1880.

JulFran1900. *U.S. Federal Census, Avoyelles Parish, LA, Ward 3, Dist. 0014, Famly No. 138*. Census Report. Washington DC: U.S. Census Bureau, 1900.

JulFran1910. *U.S. Federal Census, Avoyelles Parish, LA, Ward 2, Dist. 0016, Family No. 176*. Census Report. Washington DC: U.S. Census Bureau, 1910.

JulFranSamPry1880. *1880 U.S. Federal Census, Marksville, Avoyelles Parish, LA, Dist. 003, Family No. 504* . Washington DC: Census Bureau, 1880.

JulJacLife. "Julie Jacques." *Leonard Kimble Family Tree on Ancestry.com*. Ancestry.com, n.d.

JulJacMarr. "Marriage of Julie Jacques and Elie Ricard." *Sacred Heart Catholic Church Marriage Index, 1917-1952*. Moreauville, LA: Sacred Heart Catholic Church, n.d.

JulJosDup1900. "1900 United States Federal Census for Julian Dupas, Louisiana Avoyelles Police Jury Ward 03 District 0014, Family 235." *Twelfth Census of the United States: Schedule No. 1 - Population*. Mansura, LA: Ancestry.com, 1900.

JulJosDup1910. "1910 United States Federal Census for Julien Dupas, Louisiana Avoyelles Police Jury Ward 3 District 0016, Family 33." *Thirteenth Census of the United States: 1910 - Population*. Mansura, LA: Ancestry.com, 1910.

JulJosDup1930. "1930 United States Federal Census for Wilson Francisco, Louisiana Avoyelles Police Jury Ward 3 District 0007, Family 247." *Fifteenth Census of the United States: 1930 - Population*. Mansura, LA: Ancestry.com, 1930.

JulLen1940. "Jules Batiste." *1940 United States Federal Census for Lena Batiste, Louisiana Avoyelles Mansura 5-6 , Family 55*. Mansura, LA: Ancestry.com, 1940.

JulLena1930. "Jules Batiste." *1930 United States Federal Census for Lena Batiste, Louisiana Avoyelles Mansura District 0006, Family 38* . Mansura, LA: Ancestry.com, 1930.

JulLena1954. "Jules Batiste." *U.S. City Directories, 1822-1995 for Jules Batiste , Louisiana Alexandria 1954 Alexandria, Louisiana, City Directory, 1954, page 18*. Alexandria, LA: Ancestry.com, 1954.

JulLenBapMarr. "Lena Lavalais." *U.S., Social Security Applications and Claims Index, 1936-2007*. Mansura, LA: Ancestry.com, n.d.

JulPauBat1930. "Julius Batiste." *1930 United States Federal Census for Pauline Batiste , Louisiana Avoyelles Mansura District 0006 , Family 30*. Mansura, LA: Ancestry.com, 1930.

JulPaulBat1940. "Paul "Jess" Batiste." *1940 United States Federal Census for Jess Batiste, Louisiana Avoyelles Mansura 5-6 , House 54*. Mansura, LA: Ancestry.com, 1940.

JulPry1900. *U.S. Federal Census, Avoyelles Parish, LA, Ward 3, Dist.0014, Family Number 337*. Census Report. Washington DC: Census Bureau, 1900.

—. *U.S. Federal Census, Avoyelles Parish, Ward 3, Dist. 0014, Family No. 337*. Census Report. Washington DC: U.S. Census Bureau, 1900.

JulPryor1900. "1900 US Census for Julienne Pryor." *Twelfth Census of the United States, Ward 3, Avoyelles Parish, LA Family 337*. Marksville: Ancestry.com, 21 June 1900.

JulRic1910. "1910 United States Federal Census for Julia Ricord, Louisiana Avoyelles Police Jury Ward 8 0022, Family 123." *Thirteenth Census of the United States: 1910 - Population*. Mansura, LA: Ancestry.com, 1910.

Katz, William Loren. *Black Indians: A Hidden Heritage*. New York: Atheneum Books, 1986.

Kendall, John Smith. *History of New Orleans*. Chicago: Lewis Publishing Co., 1922.

Kenmayer. *ites of first operations by African Americans in the American Civil War, 1862-1863*. National Park Service. <https://commons.wikimedia.org/wiki/File:AfricanAmericanCivlWarMap1.jpg>.

Kimball. *Wilson Chinn, a branded slave from Louisiana--Also exhibiting instruments of torture used to punish slaves*. Library of Congress Prints and Photographs Division Washington, D.C. 20540 USA, New York, NY.

Kimble, Leonard. "Leonard Kimble Family Tree on Ancestry." *Ancestry Family Trees*. Ancestry.com, n.d.

King & Baird, engravers. *Emancipation*. S. Bott, Philadelphia. 1 print on wove paper : wood engraving printed in black and rose ; image 36 x 52.1 cm. <http://cdn.loc.gov/service/pnp/pga/03800/03898r.jpg>.

La Cour, Jeraldine Dufour. *Brides' book of Avoyelles Parish, Louisiana*. 3 vols. Bunkie, LA, 1979.

LaCour, Geraldine Dufour. *Brides' book of Avoyelles Parish, Louisiana*. Bunkie, LA: Open Library, 1979. Book.

Laird, Father Martin. "Our Lady of Prompt Succor, Mansura." n.d. *The Diocese of Alexandria*. 2 May 2016. <http://www.diocesealex.org/churches/our-lady-prompt-succor-mansura-mansura>.

—. "Our Lady of Prompt Succor, Mansura." n.d. *The Diocese of Alexandria*. Church Website. 2 May 2016. <http://www.diocesealex.org/churches/our-lady-prompt-succor-mansura-mansura>.

Lakwete, Angela. *Inventing the Cotton Gin: Machine and Myth in Antebellum America*. JHU Press, 2003.

lanie1956. "Joseph Emile Jean Baptiste." *McGlory Family Tree*. Ancestry.com, 2017.

—. "Mildred Mae Carmouche Family Tree ." *Ancestry Family Trees*. Ancestry.com, n.d.

LanMag1910. "1910 United States Federal Census for Landry Magloire , Family No. 149." *Thirteenth Census of the United States - 1910 Population Schedule*. Grand Cotes, LA: Ancestry.com, 2006.

LanMagMarr. "Landry Magloire Marriage." *Louisiana, Marriages, 1718-1925*. Marksville, LA: Ancestry.com, 2004.

Laughlin, S.H. "US Land Office Certificate No. 4685." *Land Office Land Purchase*. Opelousas, LA: US Land Office, January 1849.

—. "US Land Office Certificate No. 4721." *United States Land Office Records, 1796-1907 for Francois Roy*. Opelousas: United States Land Office, 1 January 1849.

Laver, Tara Zachary (Curator of Manuscripts). "Free People of Color in Louisiana - Revealing an Unknown Past." n.d. *LSU Libraries.* <http://www.lib.lsu.edu/sites/all/files/sc/fpoc/index.html>.

L'Eglise1900. *U.S. Federal Census, Avoyelles Parish, Ward 3, Dist. 0014.* Census Report. Washington DC: U.S. Census Bureau, 1900.

Lemoine, Sidney J. "1910 United States Federal Census for Ward 3, District 0016 of Avoyelles Parish, Louisiana." UNited States Census Bureau, 1910.

LeonMag1900. "1900 United States Federal Census for Leon Magloise, Louisiana Avoyelles Police Jury Ward 02 District 0013 , Family No. 436." *Twelfth Census of the United States, Schedule No. 1 - Population.* Ancestry.com, 2004.

LeonMag1910. "1910 United States Federal Census for Leon Magloire, Louisiana Avoyelles Marksville District 0014 , Family No. 317." *Thirteenth Census of the United States, 1910 = Population.* Marksville, LA: Ancestry.com, n.d.

Leslie, Frank. *Bailey's Dam in Alexandria, Louisiana During the Red River Campaign, 1864.* Wikimedia Commons. *Frank Leslie's Scenes and Portraits of the Civil War (1894.* 1894. Engraving. <https://commons.wikimedia.org/wiki/File:Frank_Leslie%27s_Scenes_and_Portraits_-_Bailey%27s_Dam.jpg>.

Levin, Jeff et al. *Religion in the Lives of African Americans.* Thousand Oaks, CA: Sage Publications, Inc., 2010. Amazon.

Levtzion, Nehemia. *History Of Islam In Africa.* Athens, OH: Ohio University Press, 2012. Project Muse; https://muse.jhu.edu/.

Lewis-Jones, Huw. "The Royal Navy and the Battle to End Slavery." 2011. *History.* BBC. <http://www.bbc.co.uk/history/british/abolition/royal_navy_article_01.shtml>.

LeyMarSam1870. *U.S. Federal Census, Avoyelles Parish, Subdivision 6, Family No. 760.* Census Report. Washington DC: U.S. Census Office, 1870.

LindaNall66. "Haydel Family Tree." n.d. *Ancestry.com.* <http://trees.ancestry.com/tree/79180024/person/38393521580>.

LorJam1930. *U.S. Federal Census, Avoyelles Parish, LA, Ward 3, Dist 7, Family No. 12.* Census Report. Washington DC: U.S. Census Bureau, 1930.

LouAug190. "1900 United States Federal Census for Eli Johnson, Louisiana Avoyelles Police Jury Ward 08 District 0021, Family 418." *Twelfth Census of the United States: Schedule No. 1 - Population.* Moreauville, LA: Ancestry.com, 1900.

LouAug1910. "1910 United States Federal Census for Louisa Augustin, Louisiana Avoyelles Police Jury Ward 8 District 0022 , Fa,ily 124." *Thirteenth Census of the United Statesn 1910 - Population.* Moreauville, LA: Ancestry.com, 1910.

LouAugMarr. "Marriage of Marie Louise Augustin and Ei Johnson." *Avoyelles Parish, LA Bride's Book, D-210.* Marksville, LA: Avoyelles Parish Clerk of Courts, 6 February 1877.

LouBat1920. "1920 United States Federal Census for Louis Batiste, Louisiana Avoyelles Marksville District 0002, Family 799." *Fourteenth Census of the United States: 1920 - Population.* Ancestry.com, 1920.

LouBat1930. "1930 United States Federal Census for Louis Batiste, Louisiana Avoyelles Police Jury Ward 3 District 0007, Family 244." *Fifteenth Census of the United States: 1930 - Population.* Ancestry.com, 1930.

LouBer1870. "1870 United States Federal Census for Louise Berzat, Louisiana Avoyelles Subdivision 6, Famiy 837." *1870 U.S. Census for Avoyelles Parish, LA*. Marksville, LA: Ancestry.com, 1870.

LouDemDeath. "Louis E. Demouy." *U.S., Social Security Death Index, 1935-2014*. Mansura, Louisiana: Ancestry.com, 1969.

LouFran1910. "1910 United States Federal Census for Louis Francisco." *US Census for Avoyelles Parish, LA, Ward 3, District 00016, Family 216*. Marksville, LA: Ancestry.com, 29 April 1910.

LouIreDem1920. "1920 United States Federal Census for Louis Demouy, Louisiana Avoyelles Police Jury Ward 3 District 0005, Family 149." *Fourteenth Census of the United States: 1920 - Population*. Mansura, LA: Ancestry.com, 1920.

LouIreDem1930. "1930 United States Federal Census for Louis Demouy, Louisiana Avoyelles Police Jury Ward 3 District 0007, Famiy 44." *Fifteenth Census of the United States: 1930 - Population*. Mansura, LA: Ancestry.com, 1930.

LouIreDem1940. "1940 United States Federal Census for Louis Demoury, Louisiana Avoyelles Other Places 5-7, Family 107." *Sixteeenth United States Census: 1940 - Population*. Mansura LA: Ancestry.com, n.d.

Louisiana, State of. "Poste Des Avoyelles." Waymarker.com, n.d.

LouMar1880. "1880 United States Federal Census for Marie Olivier, Louisiana Avoyelles Marksville 003 ." Ancestry.com, n.d.

LouMarMarr. "Louis Olivier in Louisiana, Marriages, 1718-1925." *Hunting For Bears*. Ancestry.com, 2004.

LouOli1870. "1870 U.S. Census for Louis Olivier." *U.S. Census for Avoyelles Parish Louisiana, Subdivision 6*. Marksville, LA: Ancestry.com, 1870.

LouOlideath. "Succession on the Matter of Louis Oliver." Marksville, LA: Ancestry.com, 9 August 1886.

LouOliMil. "U.S., Colored Troops Military Service Records, 1863-1865 for Lewis Oliver , Artillery 02nd Regiment U.S. Colored Light Artillery Moffet, John - Pattiller, Alfred ." Ancestry.com, n.d.

Luc 1870 - Takers, 1870 Census. *1870 U.S. Federal Census, Avoyelles Parish, Ward 3, District 0014, Family 369*. Washington DC: U.S. Census Bureau, 1870.

Luc 1880 - Census Takers, 1880 Census. *1880 U.S. Federal Census, Avoyelles, Marksville, LA, District 003, Family No. 82*. Washington, DC: U.S. Census Bureau, 1880.

LucAug1910. *1910 U.S. Federal Census*. Washington DC: Census Bureau, 1910.

LucFran1910. *U.S. Federal Census, Avoyelles Parish, Ward 3, Dist. 0016, Family No. 176*. Census Report. Washington DC: U.S. Census Bureau, 1910.

LucFran1920. *U.S. Federal Census, Avoyelles Parish, LA, Ward 3, Dist.008, Family No. 272*. Census Report. Washington DC: U.S. Census Bireau, 1920.

LucFranDeath. "Death of Lucille Francisco Augustine." *Louisiana Statewide Death Index, 1819-1964*. Moreauville, Louisiana: Ancestry.com, 13 August 1928.

LucJamDeath. "Death of Lucille James." *Sacred Heart Burial Records 1908-1974*. Diocese of Alexandria, LA, n.d.

LucSamp. "1880 United States Federal Census for Lucenda Sampson, Louisiana Avoyelles Marksville 001, Family 160." *1880 U.S. Census for Avoyelles Parish, LA*. Marksville, LA: Ancestry.com, n.d.

LudAliMag1900. *U.S. Federal Census, Avoyelles Parish, LA, Ward 4, Dist. 0015, Family No. 137*. Census Report. Washington DC: U.S. Census Bureau, 1900.

Lugo, Luis. *Tolerance and Tension: Islam and Christianity in Sub-Saharan Africa*. Study. Washington DC: Pew Forum on Religion & Public Lif, 2010. <http://www.voltairenet.org/IMG/pdf/Islam_and_Christianity.pdf>.

LukAgBer1910. "Thirteenth Census of the United States." *U.S. Census for the Parish of Avoyelles Parish, Louisiana*. Mansura, Louisiana: Ancestry.com, 4 May 1910. Sheet 27.

LukBerzDeath. "Luke Joseph Berzat in the Louisiana, Statewide Death Index, 1819-1964." *Louisiana, Statewide Death Index, 1819-1964*. Provo, UT, USA: Ancestry.com Operations, Inc., 2002. . Mansura, LA: Ancestry.com, 12 October 1961.

Luttrell, Natalie. "Guthrey Family Tree." n.d. *Ancestry.com*. <http://trees.ancestry.com/tree/72283831/person/32347080106/facts/facts>.

Maffly-Kipp, Laurie F. *The Church in the Southern Black Community, Documenting the American South*. Chapel Hill: University Library, The University of North Carolina at Chapel Hill, 2004.

MagMarr. "Marriages of Several Magloire Men at St. Paul." *St. Paul the Apostle Marriage Records*. Louisianalineage.com, n.d.

MagSlave. *Louisiana Slave Records, 1719-1820, Avoyelles, Document Number 267, Alienation Book A*. 7 May 1812.

Management, Office of Land. "U.S. General Land Office Records, 1796-1907." Provo, UT: Ancestry.com Operations, Inc., 2008. <http://search.ancestry.com/cgi-bin/sse.dll?db=BLMlandpatents&h=836402&indiv=try&o_vc=Record:OtherRecord&rhSource=8058>.

Mansura1900. *U.S. Federal Census, Avoyelles Parish, LA, Ward 3, District 0014*. Census Records. Washinggton DC: U.S. Census Bureau, 1900.

Mansura1930. *U.S. Federal Census, Avoyelles Parish, LA, Ward 3, Dist 7*. Census Report. Washington DC: U.S. Census Bureau, 1930.

MarAug1920. "1920 United States Federal Census for Marcelin Augustine, Louisiana Avoyelles Police Jury Ward 8 District 0011, Family 289." *Fourtenth Census of the United States: 1920 - Population*. Moreauville, LA: Ancestry.com, 1920.

MarBatDraft. "U.S., World War I Draft Registration Cards, 1917-1918 for Martin Jean Baptiste, ." Mansura, LA: Ancestry.com, 12 September 1918.

MarBer1910. "1910 United States Federal Census for Oliver Augustine, Louisiana Avoyelles Police Jury Ward 3 District 0016 , Family 441." *Thirteenth Census of the United States: 1910 - Population*. Mansura, LA: Ancestry.com, 1910.

MarBer1920. "1920 United States Federal Census for Olivier Augustine, Louisiana Avoyelles Police Jury Ward 3 District 0005, Family 65." *Fourteenth Census of the United States: 1920 - Population*. Mansura, LA: Ancestry.com, 1920.

MarBer1930. "1930 United States Federal Census for Oliver Augustine, Louisiana Avoyelles Police Jury Ward 3 District 0008, Family 19." *Fifteenth Census of the United States: 1930 - Population*. Mansura, LA: Ancestry.com, 1930.

MarcAug1910. "1910 United States Federal Census for Marcelin Augustin, Louisiana Avoyelles Police Jury Ward 8 0022 , Family 181." *Thirteenth Census of the United States: 1910 - Population*. Moreauville, LA: Ancestry.com, 1910.

MarCel. "Mary Celestine." *U.S., Find A Grave Index, 1600s-Current, Find A Grave Memorial# 136318549*. Cottonport, LA: Ancestry.com, 23 September 2014.

MarElCel1870. "1870 United States Federal Census for Marie Celestin, Louisiana Avoyelles Subdivision 5, Family 1166." *1870 U.S. Census for Avoyelles Parish, LA*. Marksville, LA: Ancestry.com, n.d.

MarElCel1880. "1880 United States Federal Census for Mary Celestin, Louisiana Avoyelles Not Stated 004 ." *1880 U.S. Census for Avoyelles Parish, LA*. Marksville, LA: Ancestry.com, 1880.

MarEun1920. "1920 United States Federal Census for Martin Jean Baptist , Louisiana Avoyelles Police Jury Ward 3 District 0005 , Family 152." Mansura, LA: Ancestry.com, 1920.

MarEun1930. "1930 United States Federal Census for Martin J Baptiste , Louisiana Avoyelles Police Jury Ward 3 District 0007 ." Ward 3, Avoyelles Parish: Ancestry.com, 16 April 1930.

MarFer1910. "1910 United States Federal Census for Ferrier St. Romain, Louisiana Avoyelles Police Jury Ward 3 0016 , Family 174." Mansura, LA: Ancestry.com, 1910.

MarFer1920. "1920 United States Federal Census for Maria Stroman , Louisiana Avoyelles Police Jury Ward 3 District 0004 , Family 168." Mansura, LA: Ancestry.com, 7 January 1920.

MarFerStR1930. "1930 United States Federal Census for Maria St Romain, Louisiana Avoyelles Police Jury Ward 3 District 0007 , Family 91." Mansura, LA: Ancestry.com, 1930.

MarFran1930. " Mary Francisco in the 1930 United States Federal Census." *1930 United States Federal Census for Mary Francisco*. Ancestry.com, 1930.

MarFranDeath. "Death of Mrs. Fulgence Francisco." *Louisiana, Statewide Death Index, 1819-1964*. Mansura: Ancestry.com, 20 October 1936.

MarieAug1895. "Marriage of Mary Augustine and Shelby Francisco." *Avoyelles Parish Bride's Book, G-14*. Marksville, LA: Avoyelles Parish Clerk of Court, n.d.

MarJosClarPryMrriage. "Marriage of Claris Pryor and Marceline Joseph." *Avoyelles Parish Marriage Records*. Marksville, LA: Avoyelles Parish Clerk of Court Office, 5 September 1889.

MarOlDeath. "Martha P. Oliver, Find A Grave Memorial# 95522583." *Findagrave*. Ancestry.com, 2012.

MarOliDeath. "Death of Marie Oliver, ." *Louisiana Statewide Death Index, 1819-1964*. Ancestry.com, n.d.

MarSam1900. *U.S. Federal Census, Avoyelles Parish, Ward 003, Family No. 74*. Census Report. Washington DC: U.S. Census Bureau, 1900.

Martin-Quiatte, Stephenie K. "LOUISIANA SLAVES SALES: 1800-1832." n.d. <http://files.usgwarchives.net/la/state/history/afriamer/slaves/sale.txt>.

MatBapDeath. "Martin Jean Baptiste, Louisiana, Statewide Death Index, 1819-1964." Mansura, LA: Ancestry.com, 26 December 1961.

MayBlaMarr. "Mary S. Blackman Marriage to James Randall." *Hunting For Bears, comp.. Louisiana, Marriages, 1718-1925*. Moreauville, LA: Ancestry.com, 17 July 1897.

Mayeux, Carlos and Randy Decuir. *Mansura: Prairie des Avoyelles*. Mansura: Avoyelles Publications, 2010.

mbag80. *Baggett family Tree with Tombstones - Zenon Lemoine. Ancestry.com*. 2015.

McAllenR14. *Carbo/Jeansonne Family Tree*. Comp. McAllenR14. Ancestry.com . Ancestry.com , n.d. <http://trees.ancestry.com/tree/34736916/person/18689167600>.

McGough, Michael R. *The 1889 Flood in Johnstown, Pennsylvania*. 2002.

McKellar, Ian. *Slave cabin at Destrehan Plantation in Louisiana*.

McMickle, Marvin Andrew. *"The Black Church", A Brief History. An Encyclopedia of African American Christian Heritage*. The Center for African American Ministries and Black Church Studies. Chicago: Judson Press, 2002.

Meeler, Brenda. "Bowman's/Meeler's Family Tree." n.d. *Ancestry.com*. Ed. Ancestry.com Operations Inc. <http://trees.ancestry.com/tree/9645101/family?fpid=6068121037>.

Mertins, J.L. *Henry Smith's lynching in 1893*. Wikimedia Commons, Paris, TX. Photograph. <https://commons.wikimedia.org/wiki/Category:1893_photographs>.

MerTit1930. " Merlin Titus. 1930 United States Federal Census, Louisiana Avoyelles Police Jury Ward 3 District 0008 , Family 20." *Fifteenth Census of the United States: 1930 Population Schedule*. Mansura, LA: Ancestry.com, 1930.

Messner, William F. "Black Violence and White Response: Louisiana, 1862." *The African American Experience in Louisiana*. Ed. Charles Vincent. Vol. 11. Lafayette: Centers for Louisiana Studies, University of Louisiana at Lafayetter, 2000. 18 vols. 39-55.

michaeldemouy1. "Arthur Demouy, 1852-1930." 2013. *Ancestry.com*. <http://person.ancestry.com/tree/51843730/person/13262880485/facts>.

Midlo Hall, Gwendolyn. *Africans in Colonial Louisiana: The Development of Afro-Creole Culture in the Eighteenth Century*. Baton Rouge, LA: Louisiana State University Press, 1992.

Mitchner, Patsy. "Black Codes (United States)." 1937. *Wikipedia.Com*. Ed. Slave Narrative Collection. Federal Writer's Project of the WPA. <https://en.wikipedia.org/wiki/Black_Codes_(United_States)>.

Mizelle, Richard M. *Backwater Blues: The Mississippi Flood of 1927 in the African American Imagination*. Mineapolis, MN: University of Minneasota Press, 2014. Book.

Moi/PrySale. "Probate Sale of Slaves Held by Laurent Normand, Jr." *Avoyelles Parish Probate Sale, Vol. C-D, p.126*. Marksville. LA: Avoyelles Parish Clerk of Court, 20 March 1860.

MoiMarPryMarriage. "Marriage of Moise Pryor and Mary Smith." *Avoyelles Parish Marriage Records*. Marksville: Avoyelles Parish Clerk of Court, 6 June 1867.

MoisePry. "Birth of Moise Pryor." *Wright Family Tree, Owner:Sharepetra*. Ancestry.com, November 2003.

MoisPryMarr. "Marriage of Moise Pryor and Mary Smith." *Avoyelles Parish Marriage records, Book B-3, p.397*. Marksville, LA: Avoyelles Parish Clerk of Courts, 6 June 1864.

Moissennet, F. *Well dressed mulatto woman*. New Orleans, LA. 6-Plate Daguerreotype.

Moissennet, F. *Well dressed mulatto woman*. Wikipedia Commons, New Orleans, LA. 6-Plate Daguerreotype.

Moore, John Hebron. *The Emergence of the Cotton Kingdom in the Old Southwest: Mississippi, 1770-1860*. LSU Press, 1988.

Moore, Sam. *U.S. Farmers During the Great Depression*. Ogden Publications, Inc., 2015.

Moreau, Harry James. *Dr. Edmé Goudeau and his American Descendants*. 2 vols. Baton Rouge, LA: Self, 2006.

Moton, Robert R. *The Final Report of the Colored Advisory Commission Appointed to Cooperate with The American National Red Cross and the Presi-dent's Committee on Relief Work in the Mississippi Valley Flood Disaster of 1927*. Washington, DC, 1927.

Mouy, Michael De. "Demouy as of 2013 Family Tree on Ancestry." *Ancestry Family Trees*. Ancestry.com, n.d.

Mrsbethbarton. *Slave Cabin Interior*. Booker T. Washington National Monument.

msrae65. "SHERIFF PIERRE McGLOIRE - 2nd black sheriff of Avoyelles." Ancestry.com, 2013.

mulattoes. *Mulatoes, Creoles & Mixed Race*. n.d. 2015.

Museum, Franklin D. Roosevelt Presidential Library and. Franklin D. Roosevelt Presidential Library and Museum, Portland, Oregon.

nacu, Andre. *Red River campaign March-May 1864*. Wikipedia. <https://commons.wikimedia.org/wiki/File:Red_River_campaign.svg>.

NatBlaMarriage. "Lousisiana Marriages, 1718-1925." *Hunting for Bears*. Marksville, LA: Ancestry.com Operations Inc., 23 April 1850. <http://search.ancestry.com/cgi-bin/sse.dll?gss=angs-c&new=1&rank=1&msT=1&gsfn=Edgar&gsln=Francisco&mswpn__ftp=Avoyelles+Parish%2c+Louisiana%2c+USA&mswpn=213&mswpn_PInfo=7-%7c0%7c1652393%7c0%7c2%7c3246%7c21%7c0%7c213%7c0%7c0%7c&MSAV=1&msfng=Francois&msfns=>.

NBlkmn1900. *1900 U.S. Federal Census, Avoyelles Parish, LA, Ward 8, Dist. 0021, Family No. 341*. Census Record. Washington DC: Census Bureau, 1900.

NBlkmn1910. *1910 U.S. Federal Census, Avoyelles Parish, LA, Ward 3, Dist. 0016, Family No. 152*. Census Report. Washington DC: Census Bureau, 1910.

NHC-NOAA. *Hurricanes in History*. n.d. 6 March 2016. <http://www.nhc.noaa.gov/outreach/history/>.

Normand, Mark J. "The Murder of Laurent Normand." 2012. *Ancestry.com*. Ed. NancyLawrence1217.

Normand, Mark. *The Normand Book*. Mark Normand, 2011.

—. "The Normand Family of Avoyelles Parish." 3 July 2012. *Ancestry.com*. <http://trees.ancestry.com/tree/7048077/person/-1175429613/story/569db023-a892-43d2-b3d3-66563a859aa5?src=search>.

NorOl1900. "1900 United States Federal Census for Nora Oliver , Oklahoma Lincoln Wellston District 0130 ." Ancestry.com, 1900.

Northrup, Solomon. *12 Years a Slave*. Ed. David Wilson. Auburn, NY: DERBY AND MILLER, 1853.

Notary, LA. "Louisiana, Slave Records, 1719-1820." n.d.

OctAur1880. "1880 United States Federal Census for Octavie George , Louisiana Avoyelles Marksville 003 ." Mansura, LA: Ancestry.com, 1880.

OctCamMarr. "Marriage of Octavie Oliver and Camile Normand." *Louisiana, Marriages, 1718-1925*. Marsville, LA: Ancestry.com, 22 January 1896.

O'Dell, Larry. "FEDERAL WRITERS' PROJECT." 2009. *Oklahoma Historical Society*. Oklahoma History Center. <http://www.okhistory.org/publications/enc/entry.php?entry=FE005>.

Office, Avoyelles Parish Clerk of Court. "Lawsuit of Auguste Augustin and Others versus Carmouche." Marksville, LA: Avoyelles Parish Clerk of Court Office, n.d. Court Records.

Office, US Land. "Laurent Normand." *United States Land Office Records, 1796-1907*. Marksville, 1 May 1849.

Oldershaw, J. *Black soldier in Union Army Sergeant uniform 1864*. Beinecke Rare Book & Manuscript Library, Yale University, New Haven, CN.

OliNero1920. "1920 United States Federal Census for Oliver Nero, Oklahoma Lincoln Wellston District 0138 , Family 117." *Fourteenth Census of the United States: 1920 - Population* . Wellston, OK: Ancestry.com, 1920.

OlivAug1910. "U.S. Federal Census for Oliver Augustine." *1910 U.S. Federal Census for Avoyelles Parish, Louisiana, Ward 3, District 0016, Page 30*. Ward 3: Ancestry.com, 11 May 1910.

OlivNero1910. "1910 United States Federal Census for Oliver Nero, Oklahoma Lincoln Wellston District 0115, Family 152." *Thirteenth Census of the United States1910- Populatio*. Wellston, OK: Ancestry.com, 1910.

OlivRab1910. "1910 United States Federal Census for Olivert Oliver , Louisiana Avoyelles Police Jury Ward 3 District 0016 ." Ancestry.com, n.d.

OneMarSam1900. *U.S. Federal Census, Avoyelles Parish, LA, Marksville, Dist. 0014, Family No. 61*. Census Report. Washington DC: U.S. Census Bureau, 1900.

OneSamDeath. *Death of Onezeme Sampson*. Certificate of Death. Mansura, LA: Avoyelles Parish Coroner's Office, 1923. Louisiana Statewide Death Index, 1900-1949, Certificate No. 3574, Vol. 9; On Ancestry,com.

OnMarPryMarriage. *Marriage of Oneal Pryor and Maria Francisco*. Marriage Records, Book F, p. 571. Marksville, LA: Avoyelles Parish Clerk of Court, February 6, 1894.

OnPryDeath. "Oneal Pryor Death Certificate." *Louisiana Statewide Death Index, Avoyelles Parish*. Marksville, LA: Avoyelles Parish Coroner's Office, 15 April 1925.

OnzMarSam1880. *U.S. Federal Census, Avoyelles Parish, Marksville, LA, Dist. 003, Family No. 72*. Census Report. Washington DC: U.S. Census Bureau, 1880.

OnzSamMarMarMarriage. "Marriage of Onzimie Sampson and Marie Louise Martin." *Louisiana Marriages, 1718-1925 on Ancestry,com*. 22 September 1885.

Operations, Ancestry.com. *U.S. General Land Office Records, 1796-1907*. Land Office Record. Provo, UT: Ancestry.com, 2008.

Original, New York Public Library Scan of. *Sweet angel, whisper low*. New York Public Library, New York. <https://commons.wikimedia.org/wiki/File:Sweet_angel,_whisper_low_(NYPL_Hades-609036-1257198).jpg>.

Ott, Thomas O. "The Haitian Revolution (1791-1804)." 1973. *BlackPast.org*. PBS.org. <http://www.blackpast.org/gah/haitian-revolution-1791-1804>.

OziMarSam1910. *U.S. Federal Census, Avoyelles Parish, Ward 3, Dist, 0016, Family No. 239*. Census Report. Washington DC: U.S. Census Bureau, 1910.

Painter, Nell. "Modern Voices - Nell Irvan Painter on soul murder and slavery." n.d. *Africans in America*. PBS.org. <http://www.pbs.org/wgbh/aia/part4/4i3084.htm>.

Pastor, Church. "Our Lady of Prompt Succor, Mansura." n.d. *The Diocese of Alexandria*. 5 February 2016. <http://www.diocesealex.org/churches/our-lady-prompt-succor-mansura-mansura>.

patsybaker19. "Our Family Through the Years." n.d. *Ancestry.com*. <http://trees.ancestry.com/tree/6657845/family/familygroup>.

PaulBatDeath. "Pauline Batiste." *Louisiana, Statewide Death Index, 1819-1964*. Mansura, LA: Ancestry.com, 23 July 1950.

PaulCecMarr. "Marriage of Paul Olivier and Cecelia Holmes." *Avoyelles Parish,LA Marriage Records, Book D, p. 396*. Marksville, LA: Avoyelles Parish Clerk of Court, 4 July 1878.

PaulFran1900. *U.S. Federal Census, Avoyelles Parish, LA, Ward 3, Dist. 0014, Family No. 391*. Census Report. Washington DC: U.S> Census Bureau, 1900.

PaulFran1910. *U.S. Federal Census, Ofuskee County, OK, Creek, District 7, Family No. 155*. Census Report. Washington DC: U.S. Census Bureau, 1910.

PaulOl1900. "Paul Oliver, in the 1900 United States Federal Census." Ancestry.com, n.d.

PaulOlDeath. "Death of Paul Oliver." *Ancestry family Tree: From Avoyelles to the Twin Territories*. Ancestry.com, n.d.

PaulOli1880. "1880 United States Federal Census for Paul Oliver, Louisiana Avoyelles 2nd Ward 002 ." Marksville, LA: Ancestry.com, 1880.

PaulOliv1910. "Paul Olivar, in the 1910 United States Federal Census." Ancestry.com, n.d.

PaulOliv1930. "Paul Oliver in the 1930 United States Federal Census." Deep Fork, Ok: Ancestry, n.d.

Percy, William Alexander. *Lanterns on the Levee: Recollections of a Planter's Son*. Louisiana State University Press, Baton Rouge. 1998, 1941.

PhilDemWWI. "U.S., World War I Draft Registration Cards, 1917-1918 for Phillip Demouy , Oklahoma Okmulgee County Draft Card D ." *U.S., World War I Draft Registration Cards, 1917-1918 on Ancestry.com*. Okmulgee, OK: Ancestry.com, 12 September 1918.

PhilJosDem1910. "1910 United States Federal Census for Philip Demony, Oklahoma Okmulgee Schulter District 0155, Family 168." *Thirteenth Census of the United States: 1910 - Population*. Okmulgee, OK: Ancestry.com, 1910.

Photographer, Our Lady of Prompt Succor Church. *Our Lady of Prompt Succor*. Mansura, LA. Church Bulletin.

Photographer, Unknown Army. *Soldiers of the 369th (15th N.Y.) who won the Croix de Guerre for gallantry in action, 1919*. U.S. National Archives, Washington DC. Photograph.

Photographer, Unknown Government. *Sharecropper plowing. Montgomery County, Alabama*. United States Library of Congress's Prints and Photographs division under the digital ID fsa.8b36026., Washngton DC. Photograph. <https://commons.wikimedia.org/wiki/File:Sharecropper_plowing_loc.jpg>.

Photographer, Unknown. *Refugees at Hamburg*. National Archives, Washington DC. Photograph.

Photographer, Unknown USGS. *Refugees at Hamburg*. U.S. Geologic Survey, Washington DC. Photograph.

Photographer, Unknown. *Workmen repair levees near Geismar during the Mississippi River flood of 1927*. Baton Rouge Advocate, Baton Rouge. Photograph. 7 March 2016. <https://www.facebook.com/theadvocatebr/photos/br.AbrH03lSq9Zr0gcGce-SQR070EOCskS4q3jQ_yqRZQN2a_u_IJ3wC_c8hjwx76kifqRUSYH282pfsXp86MWp0YdqYcEmP4G pukN6LROGlzn-A-oA2R806SELygUU7v0_oil/10153247145322524/?type=1&opaqueCursor=AbqGEVFDZTjrjZkMPvh jfPqWXXeO-cZghAI>.

Photographer, Unnown Government. *Sharecropper plowing. Montgomery County, Alabama*. United States Library of Congress's Prints and Photographs division under the digital ID fsa.8b36026., Washngton DC. Photograph. <https://commons.wikimedia.org/wiki/File:Sharecropper_plowing_loc.jpg>.

Photographer, Unnown. *Refugees at Hamburg*. National Archives, Washington DC. Photograph.

Photographer, USDA. *Cotton Plant, Texas*. USDA Natural Resources Conservation Service, Washington DC. Photograph. <http://photogallery.nrcs.usda.gov/Index.asp ==Licensing== {{PD-USGov-USDA}}>.

Photographer, USGS. *Refugees Receiving Water*. U.S. Geologic Survey, Washington DC. Photograph.

PieMar1880. *Pierre and Marie Sampson in U.S. Federal Census, Avoyelles Parish, Marksville, Dist. 003, Family No. 97*. Census Report. Washington DC: U.S. Census Bureau, 1880.

PieMar1900. *Pierre and Marie Sampson in U.S. Federal Census, Avoyelles Parish, Marksville, Ward 3, Dist. 0014, Family No. 195*. Census Report. Washington DC: U.S. Census Bureau, 1900.

PieMarSam1880. *U.S. Federal Census, Avoyelles Parish, Ward 3, Dist. 0014, Family No. 239*. Census Report. Washington DC: U.S. Census Bureau, 1880.

PieMarSam1920. *Pierre and Marie Sampson: U.S. Federal Census, Avoyelles Parish, LA, Marksville, Ward 3, Dist. 0005, Family No. 145*. Census Report. Washington DC: U.S. Census Bureau, 1920.

PierrFran1900. "1900 United States Federal Census for Pierre Francisco ." *Twelfth Census of the United States, for Avoyelles Parish, LA , Ward 3, District 0014*. Mansura, LA: Ancestry.com, 1900.

PierrJamDeath. "Pierre James." *U.S., Social Security Death Index, 1935-2014*. Mansura, LA: Ancestry.com, 15 December 1967.

PieSamDeath. "Pierre Sampson Death Record." 8 April 1927. *Louisiana Statewide Death Indices 1900-1929, Certificate Number 3574, Vol: 9*. Ancestry.com.

PieSampVet. *Veteran's Schedule, Avoyelles, Marksville, Family No. 9 for Pierre Sampson*. List of Union Veterans. Washington DC: Ancestry.com, 1890.

pinkladyrider59. "Coco Family Tree." n.d. *Ancestry.com*. <http://trees.ancestry.com/tree/58787125/family/familygroup>.

PolHelG1920. *U.S. Federal Census, Avoyelles Parish, LA, Ward 3, Dist. 0004, Family No. 355*. Census Report. Washington DC: U.S. Census Bureau, 1920.

Pope, John. "Huff Post Religion." 11 October 2012. *Huffington Post*. 6 May 2015. <http://www.huffingtonpost.com/2012/10/11/vatican-ii-catholic-church-changes_n_1956641.html>.

PresBat. "Preston Batiste." *Chris Batiste Family Tree*. Marksville, LA: Ancestry.com, 2013.

Press, Columbia University. "Abolishionists." 2012. *Infoplease: The Columbia Electronic Encyclopedia, 6th ed.* Columbia University Press.

Prier, Donald G. *Back Through the Veil*. Katy, TX: CreativeSpace, 2016. Paperback Book.

Prier, Donald G. *Cooking Cracklings at Home of Benjamin Jean's Residence*. Rosharon, Texas. Photograph.

Prier, Donald G. *Desfosse' House*. Mansura.

Prier, Donald G. *Down Town Mansura, LA*. Katy, TX. Photograph.

Project, WPA Writers. "American Life Histories: Manuscripts from the Federal Writers' Project, 1936-1940." n.d. *Library of Congress*. <http://www.loc.gov/collection/federal-writers-project/about-this-collection/>.

Psycheward. "M&M G Family Tree." n.d. *Ancestry.com*. <http://trees.ancestry.com/tree/54919270/person/13741681740>.

Purdy, James E. *W.E.B. Du Bois*. United States Library of Congress's Prints and Photographs division under the digital ID cph.3a29260, Washington DC. Photograph.

Raper, A.F. *The Tragedy of Lynching*. Chapel Hill, NC: University of North Carolina Press, 1933. Book.

Recorder, Marriage. "US and International Marriage Records." 1851. *Ancestry.com*. <http://search.ancestry.com/cgi-bin/sse.dll?db=WorldMarr_ga&h=251958&indiv=try&o_vc=Record:OtherRecord&rhSource=7163>.

Recorders, Land Office. "U.S. General Land Office Records, 1796-1907." Accession Numbers: LA1290_.292; LA1330_.161; LA1350_.324; LA1350_.331. Ancestry.com Operations, 2008.

Reed, Karl V. "Karl V. Reed Family Tree." Ancestry.com, 2016.

RegBat1930. "1930 United States Federal Census for Regina Sampson, Louisiana Avoyelles Police Jury Ward 3 District 0007, Family 107." Mansura, LA: Ancestry.com, 1930.

RegBat1940. "1940 United States Federal Census for Ragina Sampson , Louisiana Avoyelles Other Places 5-7 , family 178." Mansura, LA: Ancestry.com, 1940.

RegBatSamDeath. "Regina Baptiste Sampson." *Find A Grave Memorial# 142525346*. Mansura, LA: Ancestry.com, 12 February 2015.

Ripley, C. Peter. "Confederate Slavery." *The Louisiana Purchase Bicentennial Series in Louisiana History - The African American Experience in Louisiana*. Vol. XI. Lafayette: Center for Louisiana Studies, University of Louisiana at Lafayettr, 2000. XVIII vols. 7-20.

Robertson, S. B. "Map of Avoyelles Parish, Louisiana." 1879. *Library of Congress*. 1 map on 2 sheets : col. ; 107 x 101 cm., each sheet 58 x 103 cm. <http://www.loc.gov/item/2012592318/>.

Robertson, S.B. "Map of Avoyelles Parish, Louisiana." *https://lccn.loc.gov/2012592318* . Mansura, LA: Library of Congress, 1879.

RobRog1900. "1900 United States Federal Census for Robert Rogers, Louisiana Avoyelles Police Jury Ward 03 District 0014, Family 64." *Twelfth Census of the united States: Schedule No. 1 - Population*. Mansura: Ancestry.com, 1900.

Rodriguez, Junius P. ""We'll Hang Jeff Davis on the Sour Apple Tree" - Civil War Resistance in Louisiana." *The Louisiana Purchase Bicentennial Series in Louisiana History - The African American Experience*. Ed. Charles Vincent. Vol. XI. Lafayette: Center for Louisiana Studies, University of Louisiana at Lafayette, 2000. XVIII vols. 95-106.

RosaBatDeath. "Rosa L. Batiste." *Louisiana, Statewide Death Index, 1819-1964*. Mansura, LA: Ancestry.com, 28 January 1934.

Rosenberg, Jennifer. *1918 Spanish Flu Pandemic*. 2015. 9 May 2015. <http://history1900s.about.com/od/1910s/p/spanishflu.htm>.

—. *World War I*. 2015. 9 May 2015. <http://history1900s.about.com/od/worldwari/p/World-War-I.htm>.

RosGab1880. *1880 U.S. Federal Census, Avoyelles Parish, Marsville, LA, District 003, Family 89*. Census Report. WAshington DC: U.S. Census Bureau, 1880.

RosGab1900. *1900 U.S. Federal Census, Avoyelles Parish, LA, Ward 3, Dist. 0014, Family 234*. Census Report. Washington DC: U.S. Census Bureau, 1900.

—. *1900 U.S. Federal Census, Avoyelles Parish, Ward 003, District 0014, Family No. 234*. Washngton DC: Census Bureau, 1900.

RosGabDup1900. *St. Paul the Apostle Catholic Church Burial Records, Book IV, Page 20*. Mansura: St. Paul the Apostle Catholic, November 5, 1900.

RosJam2burial. "Burial of Rosalie James 2, 14 February 1882." *St Paul's Bural Register 1870-1885, Book IV, p. 24,* . Mansura, LA: Willie Ducote, 1998.

RosRog1870. "1870 United States Federal Census for Rosette Rogers, Louisiana Avoyelles Subdivision 5 Family 347." *1870 United States Census*. Mansura, LA: Ancestry.com, 1870.

rscott4003. "Philip Demouy in Renaud Plus2016 Family Tree." *Ancestry Family Trees*. Ancestry.com, n.d.

Sacher, John M. "Civil War Louisiana." 6 January 2011. *KnowLA Encyclopedia of Louisiana*. Ed. David Johnson. Louisiana Endowment for the Humanities. 10 September 2015. <http://www.knowla.org/entry/536/>.

SamPrideath. "Certificate of Death for Emile Prier." *Louisiana State Board of Health Certificate of Death No. 11820*. Mansura, LA: La. State Bureau of Vital Records, 13 October 1931.

SamPry1880. *U.S. Federal Census, Avoyelles Parish, Marksville, LA, Dist. 003, Family No. 503*. Census Report. Washington DC: U.S. Census Bureau, 1880.

SamPryJulFranMarr. "Samuel Pryor and Julienne Francisco Marriage ." *Avoyelles Parish Marriage Certificate*. Marksville, LA: Avoyelles Parish Clerk of Court, 25 April 1881.

SamPrySale. "Zenon Lemoine Probate Sale, Vol. A-B, p. 208." *Avoyelles Parish Probate Sale*. Marksville, LA: Ancestry.com, 12 December 1850.

Saucier, Corinne L. *A History of Avoyelles*. Louisiana State Normal College. Natchitouches, LA, 1943.

Shellystafford. "FGW's Family Tree." n.d. *Ancestry.com.* Ancestry.com Operations inc.

Slavery and the Making of America. By M.S., Jennifer Hallam, Ph.D., Kimberly Sambol-Tosco, M.A. Nicholas Boston. Prod. David McCarty Brian Brunius. PBS.org, 2004. <http://www.pbs.org/wnet/slavery/about/credits.html>.

Slavery and the Making of America. By M.S., Jennifer Hallam, Ph.D., Kimberly Sambol-Tosco, M.A. Nicholas Boston. Prod. David McCarty Brian Brunius. PBS.org, 2004. Television. <http://www.pbs.org/wnet/slavery/about/credits.html>.

Slavery and the Making of America: Education, Arts & Culture. By Kimberly Sambol-Tosco. Thirteen/WNET New York. PBS, 2004. Television.

Slavery in America. Prod. History.com. 2009. <http://www.history.com/topics/black-history/slavery>.

SMCALLISTER505. "Family Tree: Octavia Joseph, 1852-1939." *Avoyelles Parish to the Twin Territories* . Ancestry.com, n.d. <http://person.ancestry.com/tree/18989044/person/745173921/story>.

Sorrels, D.G. "Where the Family Came From." 10 August 2012. *Ancestry.com.* <http://trees.ancestry.com/tree/2229227/person/823733837/story/23c6e271-7e2b-4162-b311-240b91f1ccc4?src=search>.

SosAugMarr. "Marriage of Sosthene Augustin to Joseph Andre'." *Avoyelles Parish Louisiana Marriages: "A - Be" Surnames*. Marksville, LA: USGHN.org, 2 February 1887.

Sotrbook. "Aimee the Slave Mistress." 1 October 2011. *Ancestry.com.*

Staff, Ancestry.com. "Hunting For Bears, comp.. Louisiana, Marriages, 1718-1925." 2004. *Ancestry.com.* Ancestry.com Operations. <http://search.ancestry.com/cgi-bin/sse.dll?indiv=1&db=LAmarriages_ga&h=383780&tid=&pid=&usePUB=true&rhSource=8667>
.

Staff, Biography. "William Lloyd Garrison, Biography." n.d. *Biography.com*. A+E Television Network. <http://www.biography.com/people/william-lloyd-garrison-9307251>.

Staff, Black History in America. *Black History*. 2010. <http://myblackhistory.net/Jim_crow.htm>.

Staff, Catholic Church. "Pierre Normand's Date of Birth." *Sacramental Records of the Roman Catholic Church of the Archdiocese of New Orleans*. Vol. 3. Ancestry.com, n.d. 224.

Staff, Civil War Trust. "United States Colored Troops (USCT)." 2014. *Civil War Trust - Saving America's Civil War Battlefields*. <http://www.civilwar.org/education/history/usct/usct-united-states-colored.html>.

Staff, Civil-War.net. "The Civil War Home Page." n.d. *Civil-War.net*. 10 September 2015. <http://www.civil-war.net/>.

Staff, Harper's Weekly. "The Louisiana Murders—Gathering The Dead And Wounded." *Harper's Weekly* 10 May 1873: 397. <http://blackhistory.harpweek.com/7Illustrations/Reconstruction/Illustrations/0397w500.jpg>.

Staff, History Channel. "Slave Rebellions." 2009. *History.com*. 2 September 2015. <http://www.history.com/topics/black-history/slavery-iv-slave-rebellions>.

Staff, History.com. "Abolishionist Movement." 2009. *History.com*. A+E Networks. <http://www.history.com/topics/black-history/abolitionist-movement>.

—. *Black Codes*. 2010. A+E Networks. <http://www.history.com/topics/black-history/black-codes>.

—. "Brown versus Board of Education." 2009. *History.com*. A&E Networks. 18 February 2016.

—. "Dust Bowl." 2009. *History.com*. A+E Networks. 15 May 2015. <http://www.history.com/topics/dust-bowl>.

—. "Freedmen's Bureau." 2010. *History.com*. A+E Network. <http://www.history.com/topics/black-history/freedmens-bureau>.

—. "Sharecropping." 2010. *History.com*. A&E Network. <http://www.history.com/topics/black-history/sharecropping>.

—. "Sharecropping." 210. *History.com*. A&E Networks. 18 February 2016. <http://www.history.com/topics/black-history/sharecropping#section_1>.

Staff, Hunting for Bears. "Louis Olivier in Louisiana Marriages, 1718-1925." 2004. *Ancestry.com*.

Staff, Louisiana Freedmen's Bureau. "Miscellaneous Reports and Lists Relating to Murders and Outrages" Mar. 1867 - Nov. 1868." 1868. *Freedmen's Bureau On-Line*. <http://freedmensbureau.com/louisiana/outrages/outrages4.htm>.

Staff, S&R. *Slavery and Remembrance*. n.d. The Colonial Williamsburg Foundation . <http://slaveryandremembrance.org/articles/article/?id=A0117>.

Staff, Slave Rebellion Website. "The 1795 Conspiracy in Pointe Coupee." n.d. *Slaverebellion.org*. <http://slaverebellion.org/index.php?page=the-1795-conspiracy-in-pointe-coupee>.

Staff, St. Paul. *Burial Register of St. Paul's Church*. Trans. Willie J. Ducote. Vol. 1. Mansura, 1997.

Staff, U.S. Census. *Slave Inhsbitants in the Parish of Avoyelles, Louisiana*. Washington: U.S. Government, 1860.

Staff, Whitney Plantation. *Slavery in Louisiana*. 2015. <http://www.whitneyplantation.com/slavery-in-louisiana.html>.

Staff, Wikimedia Commons. *Slave bill of sale for Nancy 1816-6-27.* n.d. 2015.
<http://commons.wikimedia.org/wiki/File:Slave_bill_of_sale_for_Nancy_1816-6-27.jpg>.

Staff, Wikipedia. *Corpus Christi, Texas.* Wikipedia, n.d.

—. "Louisiana in the American Civil War." 2015. *Wikipedia, the free encyclopedia.* 2 October 2015.
<https://en.wikipedia.org/wiki/Louisiana_in_the_American_Civil_War>.

—. "Red River Campaign." 2015. *Wikipedia.Com.* <https://en.wikipedia.org/wiki/Red_River_Campaign>.

—. *War Industries Board.* 2015. 9 May 2015. <http://en.wikipedia.org/wiki/War_Industries_Board>.

Staff, WMS. *Avoyelles Parish Education, Geography, and History.* 2004-2016. (WMSI) Web Marketing
Services LLC.

Staff-About.News. "The Great Depression of 1929." 2015. *About.com.* AboutNews.
<http://useconomy.about.com/od/grossdomesticproduct/p/1929_Depression.htm>.

Staff-WIkipedia. *Great Mississippi Flood of 1927.* 2015.
<http://en.wikipedia.org/wiki/Great_Mississippi_Flood_of_1927>.

Staff-Wikipedia. *Hurricane Katrina.* 2015.

—. *World War 1.* 2015. 9 May 2015.

Stolp-Smith, Michael. "The Colfax Massacre (1873)." n.d. *BlackPast.org, Remembered & Reclaimec.*
University of Washington, Seattle. <http://www.blackpast.org/aah/colfax-massacre-1873>.

StPaulBurIV. *St. Paul the Apostle Catholic Church Burial Register: 1870-1885, Book IV.* Trans. Willie D.
Ducote. Mansura, Louisiana: Diocese of Alexandria, Louisiana, 1998.

StPaulBurV. *St. Paul the Apostle Catholic Church Burial Register: 1886-1905.* Trans. Mildred Bordelon.
Vol. V. Mansura: Diocese of Alexandria, Louisiana, 1888.

Sturgell, Cathy Lemoine. "Joseph D. Coco." 25 December 2013. *Find A Grave.com.* Ancestry.com
Operations Inc. <http://www.findagrave.com/cgi-
bin/fg.cgi?page=gr&GRid=122137827&ref=acom>.

—. "Pierre Lemoine Land Claim." *Ancestry - Public Member Photos & Scanned Documents.* Marksvlle, LA:
Ancestry.com, 12 December 2016.

Survey, Coast and Geodetic. "1927 LA Flood Map." 1927. <http://www.archives.gov/global-pages/larger-
image.html?i=/publications/prologue/2007/spring/images/coast-miss-flood-
l.jpg&c=/publications/prologue/2007/spring/images/coast-miss-flood.caption.html>.

—. "MIssissippi River Flood of 1927 Showing Flooded Areas and Field of Operations." 1927. *Wikimedia
Commons.* <http://www.archives.gov/global-pages/larger-
image.html?i=/publications/prologue/2007/spring/images/coast-miss-flood-
l.jpg&c=/publications/prologue/2007/spring/images/coast-miss-flood.caption.html>.

SylFran1900. "1900 U.S. Census for Avoyelles Parish Louisiana, Ward 3, District 0014." *Twelfth Census of
the United States.* Mansura: Ancestry.com, 26 June 1900. Family No.379.

SylFranDeath. "Mose Francisco Social Security Application." *U.S., Social Security Applications and Claims
Index, 1936-2007.* Marksville, LA: Ancestry.com, 2015.

SylFranSS. "Sylvar Francisco Social Security Application." *U.S., Social Security Applications and Claims
Index, 1936-2007.* Mansura, LA: Ancestry.com, 2015.

Taker, 1850 Census. "1850 U.S. Federal Census - Slave Schedules." 2004. *Ancestry.com.* Ancestry.com
Operations Inc. <http://search.ancestry.com/cgi-bin/sse.dll?gss=angs-

g&new=1&rank=1&msT=1&gsfn=valery&gsln=coco&mswpn__ftp=Avoyelles+Parish%2c+Louisia
na%2c+USA&mswpn=213&mswpn_PInfo=7-
%7c0%7c1652393%7c0%7c2%7c3246%7c21%7c0%7c213%7c0%7c0%7c&MSAV=1&msbdy=182
7&cpxt=1&cp=12&c>.

Taker, 1880 Avoyelles Parish Census. "1880 United States Federal Census for Louis Olivier; Family
Number 96." *10 United States Census*. Avoyelles Parish, Louisiana: Ancestry.com/The Church of
Jesus Christ of Latter-day Saints, 1880.

Takers, 1880 Census. "Valery Coco." *1880 US Census*. Vol. Roll 448 ; Image: 0124. Marksville, Avoyelles,
Louisiana: US Government, 1880. 389B.

Takers, 1910 Census. "Clara Normand Coco." *1910 US Federal Census*. Police Jury Ward 3, Avoyelles;
Enumeration District: 0016: Ancestry.com, 1910. Roll: T624_508; Page: 23A.
<http://search.ancestry.com/cgi-bin/sse.dll?gss=angs-
g&new=1&rank=1&gsfn=clara+normand&gsln=coco&mswpn__ftp=Avoyelles+Parish%2c+Louisia
na%2c+USA&mswpn=213&mswpn_PInfo=7-
%7c0%7c1652393%7c0%7c2%7c3246%7c21%7c0%7c213%7c0%7c0%7c&MSAV=1&msbdy=183
7&mssng0=valery>.

Takers, 1920 Census. "Edward Coco." *1920 US Federal Census*. Mansura, Avoyelles Parish; Enumeration
District: 4; Image: 175: Ancestry.com Operations Inc., 1920. T625_605; Page: 1A.

Takers, Census. "Valery Coco." Subdivision 5. Avoyelles Parish, LA, 1870. 420B; Image 216. Family History
Library Film: 552005.

Takers, US Census. "1870 United States Federal Census." 2009. *Ancestry.com.* Ancestry.com Operations,
Inc., Provo, UT.
<http://search.ancestry.com/search/db.aspx?htx=List&dbid=7163&offerid=0%3a7858%3a0>.

Talbott, William F. "$1200 to 1250 Dollars for Negroes." 1853.
<http://www.nytimes.com/2014/03/30/books/review/the-problem-of-slavery-in-the-age-of-
emancipation-by-david-brion-davis.html>.

Tarver, A.B. *Mansura, LA*. Library of Congress on Facebook. *Flood of 1927-Avoyelles Parish Tarver
Photos*. Mansura, LA, 1927. Phitograph.
<https://www.facebook.com/photo.php?fbid=10205582294850818&set=a.1020558229405079
8.1073741869.1056279623&type=3&theater>.

Tate, Albert Jr. and W.N. Sr. Gremillion. "1785 Census of Avoyelles Post, Avoyelles Parish, Louisiana."
Louisiana Genealogical Register (1981): 121-125.

Taylor, James E. *African American Students in Classroom with Teachers*. Freedman's Bureau. *The Misses
Cooks School*. Richmond, VA: Library of Congress, Illustration in AP2.L52, 1866. Sketch.

Terry, E.S. "US Land Office Certificate No. 4668." *U.S. General Land Office Records, 1796-1907*.
Opelousas: US Government Land Office, 15 May 1852.

TheoBat1920. "Theophile Batiste." *1920 United States Federal Census for Theopl Batiste, Louisiana
Avoyelles Mansura District 0004, Family 122*. Mansura, LA: Ancestry.com, 1920.

TheoBatDeath. "Theophile Batiste." *Find A Grave Memorial# 119676641*. Marksville, LA: Ancestry.com, 2
November 2013.

TheoBatWW1. "Theophile Batiste." *U.S., World War I Draft Registration Cards, 1917-1918 for Theophile
Batiste*. Mansura, LA: Ancestry.com, 12 September 1918.

TheoCarBat1930. "Theophile Batiste." *1930 United States Federal Census for Theophile Batiste, Louisiana Avoyelles Police Jury Ward 2 District 0005 , Family 94.* Marksville, LA: Ancestry.com, 1930.

TheoCarr1940. "Theophile Batiste." *1940 United States Federal Census for Theophile Batiste, Louisiana Avoyelles Other Places 5-4, Family 56.* Marksville, LA: Ancestry.com, 1940.

TheoCarrMarr. "Carrie Mayeux Batiste." *Find A Grave Memorial# 119676657.* Marksville, LA: Ancestry.com, n.d.

TheoMagMarr. "Marriage of Theophile Magloire." *Louisiana, Marriages, 1718-1925.* Marksville, LA: Ancestry.com, 2004.

Thomas, J. D. "Law of Slavery in the State of Louisiana." 24 August 2011. *Accesible-Archives.com.* 3 September 2015. <http://www.accessible-archives.com/2011/08/law-of-slavery-in-the-state-of-louisiana/>.

ThomElRoy1900. *U.S. Federal Census, Avoyelles Parish, Ward 3, Dist. 0014, Family No. 4.* Census Report. Washington DC: U.S.Census Bureau, 1900.

ThomElRoy1910. *U.S. Federal Census, Aviyelles Parish, LA, Ward 3, Dist 0016.* Census Report. Washington DC: U.S. Census Bureau, 1910.

topalicia. "Adolph Joseph Demouy." *Ancestry Family Trees.* Ancestry.com, n.d.

Topalicia. "Ancestry.com." 3 February 2016. *Jacob Family Tree.* <http://person.ancestry.com/tree/28776384/person/12549805991/facts>.

—. "Clebert Batiste." *2 Jacob Family Tree.* Ancestry.com, n.d.

topalicia. "Louis Demouy in 2 Jacob Family Tree." *Ancestry family Trees.* Ancestry.com, n.d.

Topalicia. "Rose Lavalais." *2 Jacob Family Tree.* Marksville, LA: Ancestry.com, n.d.

Topicicia. "Onezeme Olysim Sampson." *2 Jacobs Family Tree.* Mansura, LA: Ancestry.com, n.d.

Turner, Patricia A. *Ceramic Uncles & Celluloid mammies: Black Images and Their Influence on Culture.* University of Virginia Press, 2002.

Tyrr, Tanith. "Processing a Pig for Meat." 1 January 2001. *The Pig Site.* 5M Publishing. Internet. 30 March 2016. <http://www.thepigsite.com/articles/600/processing-a-pig-for-meat/>.

U.S. and International Marriage Records, 1560-1900. "Marriage of Jean Pierre Normand and Marguerite Vicknair." Yates Publishing - Ancestry.com Operations Inc. 2004, n.d.

U.S. Census Bureau. "1870 U.S. Federal Census, Avoyelles Parish, Subdivision 6." *1870 U.S. Census.* U.S. Census Bureau, 1870.

Underwood, Underwood &. *Cabins where slaves were raised for market--The famous Hermitage, Savannah, Georgia.* Library of Congress Prints and Photographs Division Washington, D.C. 20540 USA , New York. 1 photographic print on stereo card : stereograph.

Unknown. "1785 Census Pointe Coupee." Census Record. 1785. <http://usgwarchives.net/copyright.htm http://usgwarchives.net/la/lafiles.htm >.

—. "Anti-Slavery Movement in the United States." n.d. *National Library of Australia.* Lost Cause Press. Collecrtion. <http://www.nla.gov.au/selected-library-collections/anti-slavery-movement-in-the-united-states>.

Unknown. *Booker T. Washington in a poster in 1911.* <https://commons.wikimedia.org/wiki/File%3ABooker_T_Washington_-_1911.jpg>.

Unknown. *Common Street Slave Market*. 1850s drawing from New Orleans Notorial Archives. *Lost New Orleans*. American Legacy Press, 1980.

Unknown. *English: The Church at Eala (Bongandanga district), Congo, ca. 1900-1915*. *International Mission Photography Archive, ca.1860-ca.1960*. University of Edinburgh, U.K: University of Southern California. Libraries, ca.1900-ca.1940s. lantern slides 8.2 x 8.2cm.

Unknown. *Freedmen Voting in New Orleans 1867*. New York Public Library Digital Collection, New York. This is a faithful photographic reproduction of a two-dimensional, public domain work of art. <https://commons.wikimedia.org/wiki/File:FreedmenVotingInNewOrleans1867.jpeg>.

Unknown. *Horrid massacre in Virginia*. Library of Congress, Southampton County, Virginia. Wood Cut. <http://www.loc.gov/resource/cph.3a39248/>.

Unknown. *Liberators of Cuba, soldiers of the 10th Cavalry after the Spanish-American War*. Wikimedia.com.

Unknown. *Map Showing the Route of the Army During the Red River Campaign in the Spring of 1864*. U.S. National Archives and Records Administration. *Map Showing the Route of the Army During the Red River Campaign*. Washington DC, 1864. Map.

Unknown. *Mississippi River Flood of 1927*. Library of Congress, Washington DC. <https://www.loc.gov/item/2002707619/>.

Unknown. *Slave Market, Common Street*. New Orleans Notorial Archives. *Lost New Orleans by Mary Cable*. American Legacy Press, 1980.

Unknown, ASA. *View of a section of Alexandria, with a slave ship receiving her cargo of slaves*. American Antislavery Society. <http://www.loc.gov/pictures/item/2008661294/>.

UrsAug1900. *U.S. Census Report for the Town of Mansura, LA*. Census Report. Washington: U.S. Census Bureau, 1900.

UrsAugAck. "Ursin Augustine to His Children." *Act of Acknowledgement*. Marksville, LA: Avoyelles Parish Clerk of Court, 16 February 1872.

UrsAugJr1870. *1870 U.S. Federal Census, Avoyelles Parish, LA, Subdivision 6, Family No. 1032*. Washngton DC: Census Bureau, 1870.

UrsAugProb. "Probate Sale of Property belonging to Zenon Lemoine." *Avoyelles Parish Probate Records, Vol. A-B, p. 208*. Marksville, LA: Ancestry.com, 12 December 1850.

UrsJrMarr. "Marriage of Ursin Augustine and Fany Harris." *Marriages - St. Paul the Apostle Catholic Church: 1830-1871*. Mansura, LA: Diocese of Alexandra, 22 August 1867.

USDA, Staff. "Civil Rights Action Team." 1997.

USGHN-LAGHN.com. *Marriage of Samuel Pryor and Julienne Francisco*. Marksville, Avoyelles Parish, Louisiana, 25 April 1881. Marriage Certificate.

USGS. "The Great 1906 San Francisco Earthquake." n.d. *USGS Science for a Changing World*. 6 March 2016.

ValAugdeath. "Death of Valentine Augustine." *Louisiana Statewide Death Indices 1900-1929*. Moreauville: Ancestry.com, 18 June 1924.

Vanitah. "Sanders - Swain Family Tree on Ancestry." *Ancestry Family Treed*. Ancestry.com, n.d.

Vedhapudi, Nadia. "Vedhapudi Family Tree." *Ancestry Family Trees*. Ancestry.com, n.d.

VicBatSSN. "Victoria Batiste, U.S., Social Security Applications and Claims Index, 1936-2007."
Ancestry.com, n.d.

VicBerMarMarriage. "Marriage of Victor Berzat and Mary Barker." *Hunting For Bears, comp.. Louisiana,
Marriages, 1718-1925*. Marksville, Louisiana: Ancestry.com, 29 November 1888.

VicBerzMag1870. "1870 United States Federal Census for Victoria Berzat." *U.S. Federal Census for
Avoyelles Parish*. Marksville: Ancestry.com, 14 July 1870. 359.

VicEdHol1940. *U.S Federal Census, Avoyelles Parish, LA., Mansura, District 5-6, Family No. 133*. Census
Report. Washington DC: U.S. Census Bureau, 1940.

VicHolDeath. "Voctoria Hollis Death." *Findagrave.com*. Mansura: Ancestry.com, 23 June 1964.

VicJBTe1930. "1930 United States Federal Census for Victoria Guillory, Louisiana Avoyelles Police Jury
Ward 4 District 0010 , Family 37." Hessmer, LA: Ancestry.com, 1930.

VicMag1910. "Thirteenth Census of the United States: 1910 Population." *1910 Census of Avoyelles
Parish, Louisiana for Beulah Maglaire*. Marksville: Ancestry.com, 17 May 1910. 31.

Vincent, Charles. "Black Louisianians During the Civil War and Reconstruction: Aspects of Their Struggles
and Achievements." Vincent, Charles. *The African American Experience in Louisiana; Part B:
From the Civil War to Jim Crow*. Lafayette, Louisiana: Center for Louisiana Studies, University of
Louisiana at Lafayette, 2000. 120-141.

Voltz, Noah Mellick. "'It's no disgrace to a colored girl to placer': Sexual Commodification and
Negotiation among Louisiana's "Quadroons," 1805-1860." 2014. *Mixed Race Studies*. Ohio State
University. Dissertation. <http://www.mixedracestudies.org/wordpress/?tag=quadroon-balls>.

W.E.B.Dubois. *Black Reconstruction in America, 1860 - 1880*. 1935.

Walker, Evans 1903-1975. *Lucille Burroughs, daughter of a cotton sharecropper. Hale County, Alabama*.
Library of Congress Prints and Photographs Division Washington, DC 20540 USA, Washington
DC. Photograph. <http://hdl.loc.gov/loc.pnp/fsa.8c52249>.

wanda_j1956. "Ozilia Ricard in the Johnson Family Tree." *Ancestry Family Trees*. Ancestry.com, n.d.

Warren, Kim. "Seeking the Promised Land: African American Migrations to Kansas." 2015. *Civil War on
the Western Border*. The Kansas City Public Library.
<http://www.civilwaronthewesternborder.org/essay/seeking-promised-land-african-american-
migrations-kansas>.

Wattenberg, Ben J. *Statistical History of the United States from Colonial Times to the Present*. New York:
Basic Books, Inc., 1970.

Waud, Alfred R. *The Freedman's Bureau*. Harper's Weekly, New York, NY.
<https://commons.wikimedia.org/wiki/File:Freedman_bureau_harpers_cartoon.jpg>.

Weekly, Harper's. *The Slave Deck of the Bark "Wildfire. Harper's Weekly*. New York, NY, 1860.
Newspaper. <http://www.pbs.org/wgbh/aia/part1/1h300.html>.

WGBH. *The African Slave Trade and the Middle Passage*. n.d. PBS Online. TV Series.
<http://www.pbs.org/wgbh/aia/part1/1narr4.html>.

Wikipedia, Staff -. *Great Mississippi Flood of 1927*. 2015.
<http://en.wikipedia.org/wiki/Great_Mississippi_Flood_of_1927>.

Wikipedia, Staff-. *Flood Control Act*. 2015.

Wikipedia-Staff. "Mansura, Louisiana." 2015. *Wikipedia, The Free Encyclopedia*.
<http://en.wikipedia.org/wiki/Mansura,_Louisiana>.

wilCat1930. "1930 United States Federal Census for Edward Oliver , Louisiana Avoyelles Police Jury Ward 3 District 0007 ." Ancestry.com, n.d.

WilJamRosAugMarr1866. "Marriage Record of William James and Rosalie Gustin." *St. Paul the Apostle Catholic Church Marriage Record*. Mansura, LA: Diocese of Alexandria, LA, 30 September 1866.

Williams, Alex. "Alex Williams Family Tree on Ancestry." *Ancestry Family Trees*. Ancestry.com, n.d.

Williams, Chad. *African Americans and World War I*. 2015. Schomberg Center for Reseacrh in black Culture - New York Public Library. 9 May 2015.

Williams, Heather Andrea. *Help Me to Find My People*. University of North Carolina Press, 2012.

WillJam1800. "1880 United States Federal Census for William James , Avoyelles Parish, LA, Ward 2, Dist. 003, Family No. 32." Marksville: Ancestry.com, 4 June 1880.

WilMag1870. "Wm Magloire, 1870 United States Federal Census, Louisiana Avoyelles Subdivision 6 ." *1870 United States Federal Census for Wm Magloire*. Ancestry.com, 1870.

Wilmag1910. "1910 United States Federal Census for William Magloine, Louisiana Avoyelles Police Jury Ward 8 0022 ." *Thirteenth Census of the United States, 1910 - Population*. Ancestry.com, n.d.

WilMarMcG1920. *U.S. Federal Census, Avoyelles Parish, LA, Ward 8, Dist. 0011, Family No. 313*. Census Report. Washington DC: U.S. Census Bureau, 1920.

WilMarMcG1930. *U.S. Federal Census, Glenmora, Rapides Parish, LA, Ward 4, Dist. 0025, Family No. 436*. Census Report. Washington DC: U.S. Census Bureau, 1930.

WilMarMcg1940. *U.S. Federal Census, Glenmora, Rapides Parish, LA, Ward 4, Dist 40-32, Family No. 220*. Census Report. Washington DC: U.S. Census Bureau, 1930.

WilRosJam1900. *U.S. Federal Census, Avoyelles Parish, LA., Ward 3, Dist. 0014, Family 32*. Census Report. Washington DC: U.S. Census Bureau, 1900.

—. *U.S. Federal Census, Avoyelles Parish, LA., Ward 3. Dist. 0014, Family No. 340*. Census Report. Washington DC: U.S. Census Bureau, 1900.

WLBlkmn1910. *1910 U.S. Federal Census, Avoyelles Parish, LA., Ward 3, Dist 0016, Family No. 151*. Census Report. Washington DC: Census Bureau, 1910.

WLBlmn1920. *1920 U.S. Federal Census, Avoyelles Parish, LA, Ward 3, Dist. 0005, Family No. 77*. Census Record. Washington DC: Census Bureau, 1920.

"WIMag1900." *1900 United States Federal Census for William Magloire , Louisiana Avoyelles Police Jury Ward 08 District 0021* . Ancestry.com, n.d.

Writers, WPA. "An Introduction to the WPA Slave Narratives." n.d. *Library of Congress*. Ed. Norman R. Yetman. U.S. Library of Congress . <http://memory.loc.gov/ammem/snhtml/snhome.html>.

Yetman, Norman R. "An Introduction to the WPA Slave Narratives." n.d. *Slave Narratives*. <http://memory.loc.gov/ammem/snhtml/snbio.html>.

ZenLem. "1850 U.S. Federal Census - Slave Schedules." *1850 United States Census, Avoyelles Parish, LA*. Ancestry.com, 1850.

ZenLemBridesBook. *Brides Book of Avoyelles Parish*. Marksville, LA: Ancestry.com, 1820. <http://mv.ancestry.com/viewer/f5a27e1c-1638-42d7-8508-e8e8a718823a/1039174/-1959699574>.

ZenLemDeath. "Zenon Lemoine." *Dana's Famiy Tree*. Ancestry.Com, 6 12 2016. On-line.

ZenLemLife. "Zenon Lemoine in Dana's Family Tree." *Ancestry.com Family Trees*. Ancestry.com, n.d.

ZenLemProb. "Succession de Zenon Lemoine, dicide'." *Louisiana, Wills and Probate Records, 1756-1984 , Avoyelles Probate Sales, Vol A-B, 1847-1858*. Marksville: Avoyelles Parish Clerk of Courts, 12 December 1850. 208. Ancestry.com.

ZenLemSlaves. "Succession of Zenon Lemoine - Probate Sale." *Succession of Zenon Lemoine*. Vols. A-B. Marksville, LA: Ancestry.com, 12 December 1850. 208-220. Online. <http://interactive.ancestry.com/9067/007688576_00638?pid=834040&backurl=//search.ancestry.com//cgi-bin/sse.dll?_phsrc%3DzPJ6%26_phstart%3DsuccessSource%26usePUBJs%3Dtrue%26indiv%3D1%26db%3Dusprobatela%26gss%3Dangs-d%26new%3D1%26rank%3D1%26gsfn%3Dzenon%26g>.

ZenLemSlaves1850. "1850 U.S. Census for Avoyelles Parish, Louisiana." *1850 U.S. Census*. Washington, DC: U.S. Government, 1850.

ZenLemSuc. "Succession of Property of Zenon Lemoine." Marksville: Avoyelles Parish Clerk of Court Office, 10 December 1850.

Acknowledgements

This author wishes to acknowledge and thank the large number of contributors to this work without whose help, this would not have been done.

Considerable and enthusiastic assistance in the form of contributed material, pictures, ideas, editing, reviewing and encouragement was provided by the following people. Hopefully, I have left no one out.

- **Jacqueline Oliver Batiste**
- **Vera Blackman Batiste**
- **Paul Berzat**
- **Max Bonton**
- **Susane Lavalais Boykins**
- **Michelle Cadoree Bradley**
- **Marvin Blackman**
- **Shelia Blackman Dupas**
- **Charlene Francisco**
- **James Francisco**
- **Karen Francisco**
- **Michael Francisco**
- **Allie Jackson**
- **Vanessa P. Jackson**
- **Constance James**
- **Nita Johnson**
- **Huey L. Perry**
- **Marilyn Augustine Pierre**
- **Arnold Prevot**
- **Tammy Price**
- **Mary Bernell Augustine Prier**
- **Elaine Sampson**
- **Larry Sampson**
- **Leanna Sampson**
- **Harold Gene Taylor**
- **Hattie Oliver Turner**
- **Shirley Whitmore**

About the Author

Donald Gregory Prier was born in Mansura, Louisiana. He was one of 12 children whose parents, Oliver Prier and Beulah Walter, were born and lived during the most difficult years of the Jim Crow era.

Donald attended Our Lady of Prompt Succor and Cardinal Cushing elementary schools in Mansura. He graduated from Mary Bethune High School in Marksville and from Southern University with a BS in Chemistry and LSU with a PhD in Chemistry. He retired from the Dow Chemical Company in 2009 after 28 years of service.

Donald has been married to Mary Bernell Augustine of Mansura for 47 years. They have three children and four grandchildren.

Following his retirement, Donald has pursued his passion for history, especially where it involves African-Americans. His interests in genealogy has led him to a much more interesting area, the history of African-American families in his home town of Mansura, Louisiana.